Horsemanship

HORSEMANSHIP

The Horse in the Service of Man

Tom Coombs

The Crowood Press

First published in 1991 by
The Crowood Press Ltd
Gipsy Lane, Swindon
Wiltshire SN2 6DQ

British Library Cataloguing in Publication Data

Coombs, Tom
Horsemanship.
1. Horsemanship
I. Title
798.2

ISBN 1 85223 384 2

Picture Credits

The pictures on pages 12, 22, 33, 43, 70, 73, 79, 82, 88, 97, 99, 120,
125, 131, 143, 151, 152, 161, 169 and 206 are reproduced courtesy of
Bob Langrish. The picture on page 28 was kindly supplied by Les
Hurley; that on page 56 is reproduced courtesy of The Imperial War
Museum and *Horse & Hound*. The pictures on pages 109, 116, 185
(Mike Roberts) and 210 (Stuart Newsham) are reproduced courtesy of
Horse & Hound . The picture on page 135 was kindly supplied by The
Public Information Officer, Headquarters, London District, and that
on page 175 is reproduced courtesy of
Stuart Newsham.

Throughout this book, the pronouns 'he', 'him' and 'his' have been
used inclusively and are meant to apply to both male and female,
whether human or equine.

Photoset and printed in Great Britain by
Redwood Press Limited, Melksham, Wiltshire

Contents

1

Horsemanship in History

This book is written about 5,000 years after horses were first used in the serious service of man, and not just as meat. Archaeological research has revealed that horsemanship was probably first practised in Sumer, an ancient kingdom in Babylonia near Ur of the Chaldees at the northern end of the Persian Gulf, as long ago as 3000 BC. The animals concerned, though certainly equine, were mostly Onagars or Asiatic Wild Asses which were bigger and stronger than the diminutive 12hh. horses or ponies of those times. Onagars, like their cousins the zebras, are wild and intractable with a tendency to be savage, so the process of breaking and training them to pull two-wheeled chariots in pairs – which was what they were used for – must have required quite a high degree of practical horsemanship then as now.

Onagars, and any small pony-sized horses which may have been driven to similar chariots, were controlled by bits and reins as all horses have been ever since, but they were attached only to the poles of their chariots by straps round their necks without traces. Their harnessing would therefore have been inefficient and uncomfortable, which seems to emphasize the skill required to train and drive them.

If anyone did any riding in those days, about the time of Noah and his Ark, it will probably only have been for fun, and perhaps occasionally as a means of subduing the Onagars, because, without saddles or stirrups, it would hardly have been a practical proposition on a horse the size and build of a modern Caspian pony, and it would have been a hazardous undertaking on an Onagar, which bites as freely as it kicks.

2000 BC

The effective use of chariots spread from Babylonia and Mesopotamia through Syria into Egypt. Ordinary donkeys, which had by now become domesticated, were the normal beasts of draught and burden, but horses of pony size between 12 and 13hh. were also driven in pairs to chariots to provide fast travel for important people and furnish

1

them with stature and status on ceremonial occasions and in war, for which they started to be used.

The chariots themselves were improved, with more spokes in their wheels, but harnessing was still inefficient. The draught was from the horses' necks rather than their shoulders and this limitation remained until the middle of the first century AD when people began to ride with saddles and stirrups on rather bigger horses and no longer relied on chariots for practical mobility.

Egyptians themselves seem never to have been great natural horsemen and horsemanship was introduced into Egypt by the Hyksos – semi-nomadic warriors from Canaan who invaded part of Egypt and infiltrated the rest of it during the eighteenth Dynasty in about 1700 BC – and to a lesser extent by Nubians from the south, both of which people were innate horsemen.

1500 BC

The cost of chariots and the relative rarity of horses big enough to pull them at reasonable speed with two or sometimes three men aboard made their use socially exclusive and led to the establishment of 'chariot aristocracies' throughout the Near and Middle East, notably in the Babylonian and Egyptian Empires and, later, in the Assyrian Empire (1000 BC). Chariots were used for war, particularly by Egyptian armies, under Rameses II, and were deployed tactically to serve the same purpose as cavalry in later years.

Horses may well have been used in harness in China before 1000 BC but this seems to be conjectural, even in academic circles, although it is recognized that an ancient Chinese civilization was quite advanced enough for the necessary technicalities to have been possible.

Nomads from the steppes of Central Asia, and probably from Mongolia and Manchuria, started to ride their small, tough, pony-sized horses. Being small men in an age when all men were smaller than they are today, they could begin to travel effectively on horseback. However, they must have done this mainly in herds, without much need to attempt any precise independent control of their mounts. A natural affinity between Tatars and Mongols and their horses was established or revealed at about this period in history and they certainly learned and practised the first rule of equitation, which is 'to keep the horse between yourself and the ground'. They are said to have practically lived on their horses, of which they had plenty of reserves.

1000 BC

Chariots pulled by pairs of pony-sized horses penetrated into Europe and northern India and began to be used in Britain to a very limited extent. They were used for war and for hunting as well as for travel, and races for them were held in Greece – as described in Homer's *Iliad*.

In Assyria, horses began to grow bigger than the 12hh. which was the norm at this time: the Assyrians started to feed them specially, and probably to breed them selectively, and thus to practise proper horse-mastership, with which horsemanship is so closely associated. The mounted man, still bareback or at best sitting on a blanket without stirrups, began to achieve significance and the first cavalry was formed.

500 BC

The conquest of most of the Near and Middle East by Cyrus, Cambyses and Darius, which established the mighty Persian Empire, was significantly dependent on light-horsed cavalry with some heavy cavalry on elephants, and the extraordinarily efficient communications system with which this empire was governed for over 200 years was provided by horsemen.

When Alexander the Great defeated Darius, the resulting Greek Empire was even bigger than the Persian one and must have had even greater need of horses and horsemen, but the Greek army seems to have been short of cavalry because Pheidippides brought the news of its victory over the Persians from Marathon to Athens on his feet. However, Bucephalus, Alexander's charger in 330 BC, is the first horse personality or celebrity to be recognized in history and Xenophon (about 390 BC) is the first horseman whose ideas and methods are recorded and can be studied today.

Bucephalus means 'ox-headed' in Greek, so it seems that the man who conquered most of the known world in the fourth century BC was not elegantly mounted for the task, but his horse shares his fame in a memorable partnership, which is what horsemanship is all about.

Xenophon can lay claim to have been the first master of equitation, and really the first truly educated horseman. He ran the first proper riding school (in the sense of one which students were willing to pay to attend) and, although there are some references to the driving of horses in a few books written before 400 BC, *Hippike* by Xenophon is

3

the earliest book solely on horsemanship to have survived intact to the present day.

His pupils rode without stirrups, and generally bareback, on horses which were no bigger than about 13hh. They generally used snaffle bits, although a form of mild pelham was recognized. In contrast to the practice of the nomadic horsemen from the East, which was essentially that of the loose rein, he advocated constant contact with the horse's mouth and the maintenance of restraint and some degree of collection, resulting in arched necks – as depicted in Greek sculptures of the time. He insisted on his pupils sitting up straight and being supple in their spines and he sensibly recommended hanging on to the mane when jumping ditches.

Above all, Xenophon taught that horses should be trained with kindness, patience and sympathetic understanding of their natural tendency to take fright in unusual situations. He studied horse psychology as virtually no other horseman did for 2,000 years after him and reflected in his methods of training and schooling both horses and riders the enlightenment of the golden age of Greek civilization. Despite Xenophon, the Greeks were not notable horsemen then, as now, and the best horses and riders throughout the 1,000 years of Persian, Greek and Roman Empires (from 500 BC until AD 500) came from Parthia to the east of Arabia, which is now the area covered by Iran and the Southern Soviets of Russia.

The Parthians bred and fed some horses to be bigger than any yet known, up to 14hh., and became effective cavalry soldiers and horse archers. They maintained a loose-rein style of riding, but demonstrated a high degree of control and handiness, at least in mass formations. The 'Parthian shot', which involved their charging towards opposing armies and then wheeling away and firing arrows over their horses' tails, was one of the most effective military manoeuvres recorded in the history of the ancient world and is evidence of their agility and confident horsemanship.

200 BC–AD 300

Parthians continued to serve the Roman Empire as mounted auxiliary troops after the Parthian Empire itself had declined, but Rome itself produced few cavalry soldiers. Although chariots had virtually ceased to be used for actual fighting in battle, Roman commanders and dignitaries generally preferred to travel in them than to ride. Chariot racing was very popular in Ancient Rome, and by AD 100 had become entirely professional as an arena attraction, with much betting involved. Horses were driven four-abreast (*quadriga*) in most chariot races but, lacking proper collars, they were still not very efficiently harnessed.

Communications were highly efficient throughout the Roman Empire and they depended mainly on posting stations which were established every 10–15 miles along the excellent Roman roads throughout Europe. At these, a reliable ex-soldier would be in charge of some chariots and teams of horses or ponies, normally two driven abreast (*biga*), each with its own driver and always available to take envoys, couriers and mail onto the next staging post. By AD 100 important people and couriers with urgent mail were making the journey between London and Rome in thirteen days, given fair weather for the channel crossing. The distance, then as now, was 1,300 miles and this average of 100 miles a day stood as the record for long-distance overland travel until the route was largely covered by the railways 1,700 years later. The achievement owed more to good roads and their maintenance and administrative efficiency than to horsemanship, but good horsemastership was none the less needed to keep the horses and ponies 'on the road' and their drivers had to be very competent to maintain their times between stages. A single rider, without stirrups (they still had not been invented) would not have been able to travel half this distance in twice the time, even with regular relays of horses, but in these chariots a comparatively unathletic man, as for instance an envoy, could be transported in some discomfort but with a good sleep each night at this speed, over any distance covered by roads and staging posts.

There were chariots in Britain, owned by some chieftains, like Queen Boadicea, and pulled by small native ponies no more than 13hh.

Parthian and Scythian cavalry was the best in the Ancient World, but beginning to be matched by that of Spanish auxiliaries serving in the Roman Army who had begun to appreciate the quality of Barb and Arab horses from North Africa. The best Arab horses probably came from southern Arabia in the Yemen, and may have been bred there since the time of the Queen of Sheba (950 BC). They are highly prized to this day, and the better stallions there carry their pedigrees permanently with them in a leather purse slung around their necks.

Horses were expensive and relatively rare west of the Ural and Caucasus mountains, so that their ownership was generally confined to aristocracies and the Roman equestrian order, even in terms of military service. Further east – on the steppes of what is now Russia – and in Mongolia, Siberia and probably Manchuria, great herds of less advanced and less cherished horses were owned communally by no-madic tribes, all of whose members rode and ate them. Men from these tribes, or at least the most westerly of them, were the followers of Attila the Hun and others later formed the Khanates of Genghis Kahn and Kublai Kahn in the Far East and of the Golden Horde and of Tamerlane further west.

Stirrups were invented, or introduced into the realms of civilization by Attila the Hun in about AD 450. This rare but valuable benefaction on his part is quite well documented, with suggestions that he may have got the idea from China. (This is highly improbable because it was all of 3,000 miles away and he certainly never went there.) Modern academics who are not well disposed to the memory of Attila the Hun suggest that stirrups were invented by Mediterranean people, before this time. The latter would have got their idea from people who lived in the Indus valley of North India and who were accustomed, when riding, to stick their big toes through loops at the ends of a rope passed over their horses' withers. This also is a most unlikely theory, since recent excavations at Mohinjo-Daro and Harappa reveal that a very advanced civilization existed in this region before 2500 BC. The people who formed it would hardly have been content with such a primitive and uncomfortable aid to equitation, and a more efficient one, like proper stirrups, would not have escaped the attention of Darius and Xerxes, let alone Alexander. There is no evidence of the existence of stirrups anywhere in the world before the fifth century AD, and it is curious that almost 4,000 years should have elapsed between the invention of the bit, undoubtedly the most important achievement in horsemanship, and stirrups, which may fairly be regarded as the second most significant one.

Stirrups, attached to a shaped saddle with pommel and cantle, gave riders a more secure and comfortable seat on a horse and enabled them to rise in their stirrups and to 'post' and thus relieve the pressure on their horses' backs. Horses could thus travel farther and faster, and singly and in small groups as well as in herds or hordes, and also brace themselves against the shock and sudden deceleration resulting from charging at enemies with couched lances. Stirrups also made it poss-ible for horsemen to jump big fences, although they did not start to do this for at least another 1,000 years. Too great a dependence on stirrups, however, induced rigidity and stiffness which has dogged riders – particularly in western Europe – ever since they started using them.

AD 500

Full collars with traces properly attached to them are thought to have been introduced to Europe from China at about this time (AD 500) and these enabled horses to pull carts and wagons much more efficiently. However, invasions of mounted Barbarians from the North brought about a swift decline of the Roman Empire and, with it, the excellent Roman roads which fell into disuse and could no longer be used for fast travel by wheeled transport. Most of western Europe was covered by forests or bogs, over which only mounted travellers could journey at any speed. Wheeled vehicles, by now generally bigger but less manoeuvrable than chariots, were effectively confined to the steppes and plains of central and eastern Europe, over which sleighs could also travel quite easily in the snow of winter.

AD 1000–AD 1500

Armoured knights riding comparatively large, heavy, cold-blooded horses from the swampy forests of northern Europe formed the spearheads of invasions which established the Frankish Empire of Charlemagne in about AD 800 and the Norman conquest of Britain some 300 years later. Arab horsemen, lightly armed and riding smaller horses of more spirit and quality than those from the forests of the North invaded southern and eastern Europe and, between AD 620 and AD 950, established an Islamic Empire stretching from Spain to Persia. This was the cause of the Crusades about 200 years later, and a long-lasting conflict between the heavy cavalry of the West and the light cavalry of the East.

By AD 1200, Mongol, Tartar and Hun invaders had receded east of the Black Sea, but mounted Arab warriors had invaded north-west India 400 years earlier and the whole of northern India was under Moslem domination. A Tartar or Mongol invasion led by Tamerlane in 1400 was followed by another led by Babur into India from the North in about 1500. Babur was actually an Afghan but he was thought to be a Mongol because he looked like one and came from the North. Thus was the Moghul Empire founded, mainly by a spelling mistake. It was extended by Akbar in the sixteenth century and lasted until the nineteenth century when India became part of the British Empire. In a sub-continent whose people are not distinguished for producing good horses or riding them well, the renowned horsemanship of the Rajputs and Marathas probably owes much to the influence of foreign invaders from the steppes of central Asia.

From AD 500 until AD 1500, horsemanship in western Europe was largely a matter of endurance on long journeys – with a primary need to conserve the strength and soundness of tired horses – and slow ponderous charges over quite short distances by heavily-armoured knights – which were seldom as heroic or effective as history relates. The long, fast journeys, usually completed by large bodies of armed men, were impressive by the standards of any age as evidence of the practical application of horsemanship. King Harold II's forced march from York to London to meet the Norman invaders on the eve of the battle of Hastings stands comparison with any in history. The whole Saxon army covered the distance of 200 miles (320km) in six days, at an average speed of 33 miles (53km) per day, over going which was mostly rough, deep, and generally unpredictable. Although they did not intend to use their horses, which were for the most part quite small ponies, in battle when they arrived, they had few spares and could not afford to leave many stragglers behind.

Horsemanship for knights in armour was more a matter of skill at arms than equitation and was learned in the tilt yard rather than the riding school. The war horse or 'destrier' (a northern French word whose nearest, if irrational translation is 'right-handed') was a strong, coarse, heavy horse, nearly always a stallion, as big as his owner could afford, but contrary to popular misconceptions, hardly ever taller than 15hh. His nearest descendant both in appearance and ancestry is probably the Ardennes horse of Belgium and, at his best, he may have looked like a modern Dales Pony, though many were not much bigger than today's Fell Ponies. With his own horse-armour and an armoured knight on his back, he carried in all-up weight of about 3cwt (some 150kg) and this was a heavy load which made him slow in the charge and in battle and necessitated his being led unmounted on the march.

After the Middle Ages, in Tudor times, heavier armour and extra embellishments increased the total weight carried by 'coursers' (as destriers had generally become to be called) to nearly 4cwt (200kg). This was only used for tournaments however, since knights no longer went to war in full armour.

It seems a pity to dispel illusions nurtured by films and books by eminent directors and authors, but the concept of knights wearing their own weight of armour being hoisted by derricks onto the backs of 17hh. Shire horses which would then thunder into battle at an earth-shaking gallop (carrying a total weight of about a quarter of a ton) to dominate the wars of the Middle Ages is absurd and without foundation in fact or reasoning.

8

Knights frequently had to try to fight on foot, either for tactical reasons or because their horses got killed. They did not abandon their very expensive armour, but would have been quite immobile if it had weighed more than half their own weight, which was not likely to have exceeded 13 stone. There is enough armour for men and horses still in existence, as well as plenty of horseshoes of the period, to provide proof that medieval knights rode strong horses which were rather less than 15hh. and which carried a total weight of rather less than 24 stone (about 130kg). It is an interesting if undramatic fact that all horses used effectively in war from the early Middle Ages to the twentieth century have been an average height of 15 hands (Napoleon's favourite charger, Marengo, was only 14.1hh.) and have carried an average weight of 22 stone (140kg). The bigger soldiers of the twentieth century and the ammunition and extra equipment with which they have been accoutred has compensated for the reduction in the weight of armour.

In the Middle Ages aspiring knights ('esquire') received most of their riding instruction in armour as part of their training in skill at arms, and people who did not aspire to be knights probably received no riding instruction at all. The inflexibility of the armour and the importance placed on the pupil charging with couched lance at an opponent and withstanding the shock of the resultant collision induced rigidity in the saddle, which was at variance with the ancient precepts of Xenophon and of all the masters who taught riding in Europe several centuries later. It also put the knights at a considerable disadvantage in terms of agility, dexterity and manoeuvrability against the defter, handier, Saracen horsemen with whom they were committed to battle in the Crusades. Their Arab and Syrian adversaries, on their quick, smaller, but better-trained horses, literally rode rings around the knights from Europe, frequently firing arrows from the saddle which usually crippled the knights' horses even if they did not always penetrate their armour. Although European nobles and knights used bows and arrows fired from their horses for hunting, which was a favourite recreation of the aristocracy of the West from the eighth century onwards, European armies never included mounted archers. English, and especially Welsh archers on foot were the most effective soldiers in Europe throughout the Middle Ages. Bow-skill was widely and firmly established at least in England, but it took one or two extra men and at least four horses to keep each knight in the field so there were never enough horses to mount the bowmen as well, and they could never have been taught to ride well enough to operate as mounted troops.

9

The destriers, or war horses, of the medieval knights were trained to go forward boldly and straight, as this was essential in the charge, and the more so for single combat and in tournaments. The necessary impulsion was induced by long sharp spurs, which figure so prominently in the accoutrements of knighthood, and it was maintained by the herd instinct and the excitement of battle and controlled, up to a point, by severe curb bits. War horses managed to gallop for short distances with their heavy loads in tournaments, but their best pace in battle was probably no better than a lumbering trot which was often too slow to bring their riders to close combat with their enemies before multiple volleys of arrows had inflicted heavy casualties on them.

Destriers as well as the 'palfreys' and 'hackneys' (the word meant just a common riding horse before the well-known breed was established in the nineteenth century) which were ridden on the march and for peaceful journeys rather than war, were usually taught, or at least encouraged, to amble. This gait, which is not a truly natural one for a horse, involved a lateral sequence of footsteps, like those displayed by a pacer in harness racing, only much slower. Faster than a walk, but much smoother than a trot, it is not tiring for horse or rider and being something of a shuffle, tends to be naturally adopted by horses carrying heavy loads.

Throughout the Middle Ages horsemanship in Europe was almost entirely confined to the practical requirements of travel, combat and the pursuit of beasts. This pursuit was largely conducted in forests, so that the thrill of riding a good horse across country did not figure prominently and no one jumped fences. The semantic connection between horsemanship and chivalry must therefore seem to be tenuous and not based on any high ideals of virtue or morality acquired by association with horses. In fact, the true ideals of chivalry, which have ameliorated some of the horrors of all wars since the Crusades in the twelfth century, were originally promoted by the Saracens under their highly chivalrous leader Saladin, and not by the crusader knights, whose behaviour was often anything but edifying.

Chivalry in Europe became a complicated code of social conduct which dominated relationships between kings, nobles, knights and their ladies. It also prompted the establishment of highly intricate regulations and procedures for the conduct of tournaments, which were most important social entertainments and functions until well into the sixteenth century. It is interesting to reflect that from the chariot aristocracies of ancient Babylon and Egypt through the equestrian order of ancient Rome and the knight service of the Middle Ages, right up to the social structure of the present day, horses have seemed to confer on their owners a degree of distinction, with accompanying privileges and obligations, which can be acquired through no other possessions except large areas of land.

AD 1500

By the sixteenth century the tilt yard had begun to give way to the riding school and horsemen started to study equitation for its own sake, in its pure or limited sense of the training and management of horses by riders. The *manège* was the arena for this new art or recreation which revived the skills taught by Xenophon in Greece 2,000 years earlier.

Xenophon's first successor as a recognized riding master was Federigo Grisoni, an Italian who started the Neapolitan School in about 1550 and wrote a book about his methods called *L'Écurie de Sieur Grison*. The intellectual and technical complexities involved in teaching horses to perform intricate movements not entirely natural to them instantly appealed to the Italian men of the Renaissance, and Cesar Fiaschi of Ferrara quickly started another school to extend the teaching of his compatriot. Another Italian, Pignatelli, learned from Fiaschi and started his own school at which two Frenchmen studied: Salomon de la Broue and Antoine de Pluvinel. They returned to teach in France and founded what became known as the Versailles School of horsemanship.

De Pluvinel, who was born in 1555, ran an 'Academy for the Education of Young Gentlemen of Noble Birth' in Paris where the King of France, Louis XIII, studied riding. Like his contemporaries in Italy and France, de Pluvinel wrote a book about horsemanship. De Pluvinel's book, which was published after his death by one of his pupils, René Menou de Charniray, is something of a classic. It took the form of an imaginary dialogue between the King and his riding master, in which the royal pupil not surprisingly seemed to know all the answers. The book is excellently illustrated with engravings by a Dutchman, Crispin de Pas, who taught drawing at de Pluvinel's academy. Royal patronage gave pre-eminence in Europe to the Versailles School of equitation from 1600 until the French Revolution in 1789.

Although the famous riding hall, designed by Fischer von Erlach and adjoining the Hofburg in the centre of Vienna, was not opened until 1735, the Spanish Riding School, which has its home there to the present day, was founded in 1572 in the garden of the Hofburg, with riders and horses from Spain. The horses, owing much to Arab or Moorish blood and the ancestors of the admirable modern

11

The Quadrille of the Spanish Riding School on one of its comparatively rare tours away from Vienna. The magic of this sublime equestrian spectacle is diminished when it is performed in an arena other than Fischer Von Erlach's classical riding school at the Hofburg in Vienna, if only because the Lipizzaner horses are rather small for their present-day riders.

Andalucians and Lusitanos, became the famous Lipizzaners which were originally bred at the two Austrian Imperial studs at Kladrub (founded 1562) and Lipizza (founded 1580). They are now bred at Piber near Graz and confined to seven male and fourteen female blood lines. The original Spanish riders were soon succeeded by Austrians.

In England in the sixteenth century, several Italian instructors were engaged to teach the classical riding of the Neapolitan School to the young King Henry VIII and an Englishman, Thomas Blundeville, was entrusted with the tuition of Henry VIII's daughter, who became Queen Elizabeth I. Blundeville was ordered by the Earl of Leicester to translate Grisoni's book *L'Écurie de Sieur Grison* into English and follow its precepts in arranging the instruction of the young Queen, but he seems to have found this task beyond the scope of his rather limited intellect, and instead wrote a book of his own called *The Four Chiefest Offices of Horsemanship*. Many of the recommendations contained within this book would have got him prosecuted for cruelty in any later or more humanitarian age.

12

AD 1600

Thomas Blundeville's deplorable ideas about horsemanship were happily contradicted almost a century later by William Cavendish, first Duke of Newcastle. Cavendish was a humane and highly educated horseman who can be said to have introduced school riding into England and who considerably influenced the horsemanship of western Europe throughout the seventeenth century. Exiled as a supporter of King Charles I, this enlightened nobleman set up a riding school in Antwerp where he gained inspiration from contact with continental riding masters and began to influence their methods. While in exile, he wrote a book in 1658 in French which he translated into English and entitled *A General System of Horsemanship*. He returned to England with King Charles II at the Restoration, maintained his interest in horsemanship and wrote a second book, in English, entitled *A New Method to Dress Horses*. Today's dressage enthusiasts should note the title of this book: the verb '*dresser*' is the French for 'to train'.

The Duke of Newcastle's teaching and writings and his general influence on the European equitation of his age are of considerable significance because, unlike almost all his predecessors except Xenophon, and most of his successors until almost the twentieth century, he was not beholden to any patron or ever seeking to flatter royal or august personages in what he taught or wrote; and he practised what he preached. He was quite simply more august than anybody else who shared his interests in his day, and his views and ideas, which were admirably practical, enlightened and humane, prevailed over those of his contemporaries and are mostly still valid today.

Despite some degree of sense and sensitivity displayed in their approach to horsemanship by de la Broue and, notably, the Duke of Newcastle, school riding in the sixteenth and seventeenth centuries tended to be a rather brutal business. It involved extreme restraint, much flexion and constant collection, imposed by unrestrained application of long whips, sharp spurs and severe curb bits. The movements and evolutions induced by these methods were rather unnatural and of little practical value. They were performed to astonish spectators as much as to gratify riders, and they reached their zenith in the exercises of 'airs above the ground' which for most people typify High School.

The rather extraordinary postures, leaps and bounds which comprise these 'airs' and will be explained in a later chapter have to be taught between the 'Pillars' in a manner which was first devised by de Pluvinel and seemed originally to involve a number of dismounted assistants armed with long whips, and an unseemly use of force. They are still demonstrated at the Spanish Riding School in Vienna and the

13

French Cavalry School at Saumur and by a few of the most skilled circus riders, but they have no utilitarian value or real relevance to the study of practical equitation. The suggestion that they were of value in battle is nonsense and was condemned as such by both Blundeville and Newcastle in their times. They both point out that it is difficult enough to persuade a horse to perform any of these 'airs' in the calm of the riding school so that it would have been impossible to induce them in the heat of battle. They might have added that they would have been much more likely to unseat the rider than defeat his enemy. These 'airs' are much copied in heroic military statues and paintings and are essentially examples of the Baroque in taste and art.

During the sixteenth century the *conquistadors* brought their Spanish horses to America. Their horses and their horsemanship owed much to Moorish and originally Saracen and Arab influence, and they passed this on, through the Mexican gauchos, to the cowboys, whose western riding thus traces back to the horsemanship of the East. Some Red Indian tribes acquired horses about three centuries later and, starting from scratch with no saddles or stirrups, became remarkably agile and effective horsemen.

During the sixteenth and seventeenth centuries Poland produced the best cavalry, in terms of both horses and horsemen, and have arguably remained the best cavalrymen ever since. Hussars originated in Poland, not Hungary and together with Cossacks, formed the light cavalry units which supported armoured knights until almost the end of the sixteenth century. From about 1580 onwards fully-armoured knights with their ponderous retinues no longer went to war in Poland or anywhere else in the world, and Polish hussars became heavy cavalry, wearing some armour and supported by Cossack light cavalry. In this role they took Moscow in 1610 and for two years put a Polish tzar on the throne of Russia. The relief of the Turkish siege of Vienna by King John Sobieski's legendary Winged Hussars in 1683 remains one of the most famed forced marches and cavalry actions in the history of war in Europe.

Hungarian hussars remained light cavalry and had their distinctive uniforms copied by armies of other nations, but Polish hussars retained the splendour of their variegated uniforms and accoutrements, and throughout the seventeenth century, in most cases, their Wings. They were always designated as heavy cavalry; as the counterparts of the cuirassiers of western European armies. Cossacks, Tartars and Lithuanians formed most of the Polish light cavalry units. The uhlan, or lancer, originated in Poland and in the nineteenth century became his country's best-known cavalry soldier.

Hunting became fun and an excuse for a good gallop early in the fourteenth century when spears, arrows and nets were dispensed with and 'beasts of the chase' were pursued and caught by hounds alone in their own natural environment. The stag or 'hart' was the most favoured quarry in the forests of France as, apart from the wild boar or *sanglier* it still is today. By the fifteenth century, however, the hare was beginning to promise more sport in the open fields and commons of England than the deer, and was regarded by Edward Duke of York, 'Master of the Hart Hounds' to his cousin King Henry IV, as 'king of all venery'.

At the end of the sixteenth century the fox began to be appreciated, in England only, for his capacity to provide a good hunt in open country and ceased to be regarded purely as vermin to be attacked and killed below ground. A gentleman called Sir Thomas Cockayne is thought to have been the first master of hounds to have hunted foxes deliberately and he wrote *A Short Treatise on Hunting* in about 1580. Hunting in the sixteenth and seventeenth centuries was a slow business involving a dawn start from the quarry's overnight lair and a process of ponderous perseverance in which the fox was almost walked to death by heavy, short-legged hounds with very good noses and voices. The fox, of course, often went to ground during the course of a hunt, but his pursuers apparently did not mind the tedium of having to keep digging him out and reckoned that the fact that he went farther and straighter than the hare compensated for this. The deer was hardly ever caught in the open and probably seldom brought to bay by hounds alone. The unsporting Tudor monarchs generally hunted him in enclosed parks and waited in ambush to shoot him with crossbows, but King James I objected to this distasteful practice and repressed it.

Because the pace was relatively slow and there were no fences to be jumped, hunting before the eighteenth century did not demand a very high standard of horsemanship; only some stamina and a good eye for a bog. However, the horses involved needed plenty of staying-power and this requirement added timely support to the efforts of King Henry VIII and his daughter Queen Elizabeth I to improve the breeding of English horses in an attempt to match the substance and quality of the Spanish ones ridden by King Philip's cavalry.

The first coach with springs of a kind and a forecarriage which enabled it to be steered properly, and thus to carry passengers in comparative comfort at a reasonable pace, was built in Hungary in the fourteenth century. Its successors were rattling over the plains and *pusztas* of central Europe in fair numbers by the time Queen Elizabeth came to the throne of England, but the first one to arrive from Holland for her use in 1564 was confined to the roads in and around London, which provided the only suitable surfaces for its operation. Despite being virtually limited to use in towns, coaches quickly became popular in England and by the early 1600s efforts were being made to restrict their use by law, on the grounds that this was effeminate and liable to cause a deterioration in horsemanship, as well as traffic jams. Coaches did not become practical for fast travel in England until the middle of the eighteenth century, when good roads between towns and cities began to be made.

A vast Mongol Empire which covered most of Asia from the thirteenth to the sixteenth centuries had been established by horsemen and continued to rely on them for its government and communications. Its offshoot, the Moghul Empire of northern India, was also dominated by horsemanship. Afghan, Rajput and Maratha horsemen played polo 500 years before British army officers started to do so. Horses were greatly prized in Arabia and North Africa throughout the Middle Ages and well beyond, until European armies filled the souks of the Near East with those which they jettisoned after the wars of the nineteenth and twentieth centuries. Horsemanship was highly esteemed in Arabia, as it still is today, but the camel has always been the main beast of travel, burden and commerce throughout the Middle East so that the horse was generally restricted in practice to sultans, emirs and tribal leaders and their retinues.

A little known historical fact which deserves wider recognition, at least among horsemen, is that at the dawn of the Renaissance, Leonardo da Vinci, himself a keen horseman, wrote a treatise on *The Proportions of a Horse* and originated the system by which a horse's height is measured in hands.

AD 1700

School or *manège* riding in the eighteenth century was dominated by France and particularly by the principles established by Monsieur de la Guérinière, who taught riding in Paris up to the time of the French Revolution. The greatest *écuyer* of his time, and some would say or any other, he invented the exercise known as 'shoulder in', which is still crucial in classical equitation and the training of dressage horses. He wrote a book, *École de Cavalrie*, which has been re-published since his time under several different titles and is still studied today, and, as a highly educated horseman, took the teachings of de Pluvinel several stages further in teaching riders and schooling horses along classical lines with sympathy and understanding.

The influence of the Italian School of equitation waned before the end of the seventeenth century when Pignatelli died, but the Spanish Riding School in Vienna maintained its prestige and its tradition for teaching classical High School, including the 'airs above the ground'. The splendid carousels which it presented, mostly during the reign of the Empress Maria Theresa, were among the most magnificent equestrian spectacles of the age.

In Britain foxhunting was transformed in the middle of the eighteenth century by The Enclosure Acts which divided farmland into fields bounded by walls, ditches and bullock-proof hedges which had to be jumped by riders who wanted to keep with the hounds. It now demanded boldness and equestrian ability, as well as endurance and a knowledge of venery, and the authentic thrill of the chase was greatly enhanced so that it enticed riders away from the more staid exercises of the *manège* and a new and more exciting concept of horsemanship was born. Flat racing started in earnest in England in 1750, when the Jockey Club was formed; and very soon afterwards in France, and it introduced concepts of jockeyship which became embodied in horsemanship.

The first Derby was run at Epsom in 1780 but racing, mainly on Newmarket Heath, had been taking place for fifty years before this. Three great Arab horses, The Byerley Turk, The Darley Arabian and The Godolphin Arabian were imported into England in 1689, 1705 and 1728 respectively; the Godolphin Arabian arrived via France. They are justly credited with being the founding fathers of the English Thoroughbred, whose stud book was started in 1791, and have thus had an enormous influence on the breeding of the best horses throughout the world.

By the middle of the seventeenth century cavalry soldiers had ceased to wear armour, which afforded them no protection against firearms and artillery, and had become more mobile, if only by a reduction in the numbers of their attendants and camp followers. During the eighteenth century the cavalry of most European armies was organized into regular regiments and the concept of military equitation in terms of training for men and horses was established.

In America, British colonists and settlers from Europe along the eastern Seaboard rode horses in English or western style and some foxhunting started in Virginia. In the southern States and further west the riding style of the South American gaucho with its Spanish/Moorish/Arab influence prevailed and established the Western horsemanship of the cowboy which extended north into Canada. Some, but not all, tribes of Red Indians acquired horses and began to breed their own and to learn to ride from scratch, uninfluenced by outside sources. Their primitive horsemanship, mostly practised without stirrups or

17

saddles, was remarkably effective on buffalo hunts and in the Indian wars of the next (nineteenth) century.

AD 1800

After the French Revolution, to the surprise of people who thought that egalitarian principles would prevail to condemn an elitist interest in classical *manège* riding, the Versailles School remained pre-eminent in its teaching, which, promoted in a number of 'acadamies' in and around Paris, spread virtually unchallenged throughout Europe. The nineteenth century produced two school riders and trainers of genius, one at its beginning and one at its end. Baucher, a Frenchman who lived all his life in France and is alleged never to have ridden outside a *manège*, was the greatest riding master in Europe for the first half of the nineteenth century. James Fillis, an Englishman who was born in London in 1834, but rode and taught only in France until he went to Germany in 1891 and thence to Russia where he was appointed *Écuyer-en-Chef* at the Russian Cavalry School in 1897, was the supreme authority until the early years of the twentieth century.

Baucher was an undoubted genius. He practised what he preached because he was a rider of rare skill and ability who could impose extremes of flexion and collection on the rather common horses which he habitually rode without inducing resistances from them. Very few other riders were able to achieve this and Baucher was not good at explaining his methods, or well able to justify them. He wrote two books, which were largely incomprehensible, and in old age completely changed his ideas and expressed the opinion that: 'Whenever and wherever difficulties occur with a horse they can only be cured permanently by the use of a snaffle bridle.' That Baucher's genius was passed on in some of his teaching is due to some of his highly intelligent pupils, notably Farerot de Kerbrech, Lenoble du Teil, Raabe, Barada-Dutilh and François Caron; and the latter taught Fillis.

James Fillis became world famous and his teaching was much more widely accepted than Baucher's. Although he was a High School expert and, like Baucher, appeared regularly in the circus before spectators who paid well to wonder at the unnatural movements which he persuaded his horses to perform, he cultivated a freer style with more forward movement than most of his predecessors and rode carefully-selected Thoroughbred horses which enhanced the impression of lightness and elegance which he always sought to achieve. Being no scholar himself, Fillis sensibly persuaded Georges Clemenceau, one of his pupils and later the great French statesman, to act as ghost writer for his first and most famous book *Principes de Dressage et d' Équitation* which was translated into several languages, including eight editions in English, since its initial publication in 1890 and is still widely read and studied today.

The teachings of Baucher and Fillis had some influence on the great French Cavalry School at Saumur, which reached the height of its fame in the middle of the nineteenth century under an enlightened commandant, Le Comte d'Aure. D'Aure was a cross-country rider who insisted that horsemanship should not be confined to the *manège*, but he appreciated the need for training in the riding school and marked this by appointing a dedicated school rider, Capitaine Guérin, to succeed him.

Equitation in Germany was centred on Hanover in the nineteenth century and its great exponent was Gustave Steinbrecht, a veterinary surgeon. Steinbrecht learned his school riding from Seeger in Berlin and taught Plinzner. Plinzner in turn taught Colonel von Heydebreck, who influenced German dressage riding at the beginning of the twentieth century, as so brilliantly demonstrated by Otto Lörke. Seeger disapproved of Baucher's methods and harked back for his inspiration to de La Guérinière. It may be that dissension between the French and German Schools of classical equitation at the beginning of the nineteenth century persisted to maintain the difference between French and German dressage which is still apparent in the twentieth century.

The Spanish Riding School continued to go its own way in Vienna, with a justifiably Olympian disregard for innovations, new ideas and changing styles and fashions.

By the end of the nineteenth century school riding or classical equitation was being studied in most European countries and continental riding masters had found their way to the United States of America. Best known of these was Count Baretto de Souza who came from Portugal at the turn of the century to teach fashionable horse enthusiasts in New York. His instruction was tailored to the requirements and ability of his students, who were of social rather than equestrian eminence, but he inculcated generally sound principles and wrote several intelligent books.

In Britain the last riding master to teach classical equitation had been Richard Berenger towards the end of the eighteenth century and he, though designated 'Gentleman of the Horse to His Majesty' (George III), was more an equestrian author than a practical trainer. Interest in the training of cavalry horses and soldiers increased throughout Europe in the nineteenth century and the English soldier, J G Peters and Captain L E Nolan of Balaclava fame, wrote books in the style of cavalry training manuals. British horsemanship between 1820

19

and 1890, however, was firmly and gloriously centred on foxhunting, which was the envy of the world for the joy it created in cross-country riding. Foxhunters were following hounds and jumping fences with delight, but often in a rather unhorsemanlike and bulldozing manner, all over Great Britain and Ireland and in the eastern States of America at the dawn of the nineteenth century. During that century packs of foxhounds were established in Portugal, Spain, Italy and Hungary as well as in Canada, Australia and South Africa while, in India, fox-hounds hunted jackals and a few bold horsemen chased wild boars and killed them from the saddle with spears.

Steeplechasing started in England soon after 1800 and was established in many other European countries by 1850. The early steeple-chases were run straight across country over natural fences, with church steeples defining the course – hence the name. The first Grand National was run at Aintree in 1839 over growing hedges which form virtually the same fences today. Meanwhile, flat racing became a major spectator sport in England and soon afterwards, in countries throughout the world, which acknowledged the English Jockey Club to be its universal ruling body.

Good roads in England, made by Telford and MacAdam, enabled coaches to travel quickly and regularly between most major towns. Most of western Europe was served almost as well and was accessible to wheeled vehicles. With a lead from the Prince Regent, who became too stout and heavy to ride, driving in England became a Corinthian recreation for men of fashion, recognized as a skill rather than just a manual labour, and thereby regained some of the social status which it had had in the Ancient World.

AD 1900

At the very start of the twentieth century a significant revolution in horsemanship took place in Italy when Captain Federico Caprilli introduced his concept of 'the forward seat' for cross-country riding. His ideas, which were that horses should be allowed to balance themselves with as little interference as possible from their riders when jumping fences and descending steep slopes, were eminently sensible and not entirely unheard of because a very modified version of them had been advocated for foxhunters in England by one John Adams who, in 1805, had published a book called *An Analysis of Horse-manship*. Caprilli died tragically young in 1907, but his teaching was promoted with enthusiasm by his contemporaries and brother officers at the two Italian Cavalry Schools at Pinerolo and Tor di Quinto.

Major Piero Santini (1881–1960) in particular wrote three books about it which were all translated into English. At the invitation of their Italian opposite numbers, the chief instructors from the world's cavalry schools came to the two Italian ones to study the Caprilli system. They were led by Colonel (then Captain) Paul Rodzianko, who returned to Russia to teach it to the Imperial Cavalry School and train a Russian World Championship Show Jumping team on the strength of it, and included Generals Chamberlin and West (then Majors) from Fort Riley in the USA and Colonel Geoffrey Brooke from the British Cavalry School at Weedon. Many other soldiers came to Italy to learn *Il Sistema Caprilli*, as well as some civilian riders of repute, so that in a few years some 150 distinguished horsemen from other countries had confirmed the prominence of the new Italian School and the history of the sixteenth century was repeating itself.

Most casual horsemen thought that Caprilli's 'forward seat' was relevant only to the new competitive activity of show jumping, but it actually was, and is, the best way to sit on a horse for all cross-country riding. It may indeed even have influenced race riding because in the early 1900s, with a lead from the American Tod Sloane, jockeys shortened their stirrup leathers considerably and quite suddenly, and adopted a crouching position just behind their horses' withers. They used that position for riding over fences as well as on the flat, which proved to be permanently effective in balancing them and the weights on their backs the better to enable them to gallop faster.

Classical school riding in the *manège* virtually died out at the start of the twentieth century and High School, though still popular in the circus, was mainly confined to Vienna, Saumur, and a few specialists in Spain and Portugal.

Riding masters extended the scope of their instruction beyond the limits of their riding schools and taught their pupils to jump fences and ride across country, achieving distinction as trainers rather than just teachers. Most of them also made their teaching available to much wider audiences by publishing practical books about their methods. Prominent among the best horsemen and instructors of the first half of the twentieth century were: Geoffrey Brooke, Jack Hance and Henry Wynmalen in Britain; the latter was actually a Dutchman who settled permanently in England in his middle age; Yves Benoist-Gironiève in France; Wilhelm Viebig in Germany; Piero Santini in Italy; Harry Chamberlin in the USA and Vladimir Littauer who came to America from Russia after the Revolution and Paul Rodzianko who started in the Imperial Russian Cavalry School in St Petersburg and moved on to teach riders and train teams in Britain, Ireland and the British Army of the Rhine in Germany.

A meet of the hounds; one of England's most cherished traditions.

In 1921 the International Equestrian Federation (FEI, *Fédération Equestre Internationale*) was founded and the three competitions with which it was concerned: Show Jumping, Dressage and the Three-Day Event, were included for the future in the Olympic Games. The Three-Day Event was originally called 'The Military' in all the continental countries.

By this date, classical school riding in the *manège* with its spectacular displays by numbers of riders performing together and occasional demonstrations of individual brilliance, had largely given way to the practising of stereotyped movements and tests for dressage competitions demanding precise accuracy rather than original artistry.

The great dressage rider of the first half of the twentieth century was Otto Lörke of Germany, who set a standard for his country which, maintained by his star pupil and disciple Willi Schultheiss, has prevailed to the present day.

Show jumping and the Three-Day Event (now called Horse Trials in Britain) are sports solely of the twentieth century. Before 1950 they were, at their higher levels, almost the exclusive province of army officers.

Cavalry became obsolete for all but ceremonial occasions during the first half of the twentieth century, although a British Cavalry Brigade went to war in the Middle East in 1940, and tragically left its horses there, and a fully-horsed Turkish Cavalry Division was in operation in eastern Turkey until the end of the 1960s.

Hunting has retained its popularity throughout the twentieth century and, at least in Britain, has broadened the scope of its appeal. More than 250 packs of hounds in Britain mostly hunt foxes, some 250 hunts in France and Belgium hunt deer or less specific quarry, and, of sixty more hunts throughout the rest of the world at least half are in America.

Point-to-points and hunter trials were started by British hunts in the early 1900s to provide out-of-season sport for their members, and they have served well to satisfy the competitive aspirations of amateur horsemen of moderate ability ever since.

In 1928 British hunting people founded the Pony Club which, contrary to many misconceptions, is an international and not just a national organization. Its branches are attached where possible to hunts all over the world, but this arrangement simply provides them with an established identity. The function of the Pony Club, which in general has been admirably achieved world-wide, is to give children up to eighteen years old a firm understanding of the proper principles of all aspects of horsemanship and to help them to enjoy riding their ponies.

Western riding – as exemplified by the cowboys of America and with its links back through the vaqueros of Mexico and the gauchos of Argentina and South America to the Spanish *conquistadors* and thus to the Moors and the Saracen horsemen of Syria in the time of the crusades – became universally recognized early in the twentieth century. Glamorized and sometimes misrepresented in the cinema, it was nevertheless approved by the best classical riders as embodying the proper principles of true practical horsemanship. It appealed to many people throughout the USA and in other countries who did not have to herd cattle but wanted to ride comfortably for quite long distances over trails and open country purely for recreation. Working cowboys (ranch hands) devised the competitions for rodeo riding and by 1910 rodeos were established as annual events in many of the western States of America and Canada and have been exciting spectator attractions ever since.

Harness racing for trotters and pacers became standardized in the USA just before 1930 and American regulations were adopted by most countries in Europe and by Australia and New Zealand shortly afterwards so that international standards were able to be recorded. Fast trotters had been driven in competition against each other in many European countries, including Britain, for at least a century before this, but on a spasmodic and purely amateur basis. Trotting races were an instant success in America, where they now exceed the number of races for Thoroughbreds, and they are also big business in Russia, France, Germany and Scandinavia. They have not yet attained such popularity in Britain where their sporting administrators must always beware of the possibly disruptive influence on them of the uniquely British off-course bookmakers.

AD 1950

That year and the ones that followed saw the development of regular air travel for horses as well as riders so that, starting with racing, competitive horse sports became truly international, at least at the top of their respective leagues. From about 1975 onwards horses travelled regularly by air between continents as quickly and comfortably as human passengers and the best of them have been competing against each other world-wide. Regular world and inter-continental championships and frequent competitions between nations, as well as highly important international races, have accordingly resulted and records have been established and quickly broken while horsemanship in its various modern aspects has continued to improve among the world's best riders. However, the great expense of flying horses all over the world, and the much greater expense of providing worthy tournament sites and conditions for them to compete in, have involved very high costs, and these have inevitably escalated year by year, fuelled by national pride and a determination by organizers to do better each year. With the end of the twentieth century still not yet in sight, most forms of competitive horsemanship at anywhere near top level are beyond the financial resources of people who normally ride their own horses and their organization is usually beyond the resources of local or regional horse enthusiasts, and sometimes even those of the genuine horsemen of a whole nation. Sponsorship is nearly always needed by top class riders as by top class horse shows and racecourses, and sponsorship is usually commercial and leads to commercialism which, as some would have it, is at variance with the high ideals of equestrian endeavour.

The driving of horses in harness seemed to have no future after 1920 except in a few countries of eastern Europe and some of the more remote parts of the world where motor vehicles, and the petrol to operate them, were still not much in evidence. Its positive revival came curiously enough in a country of high petroleum technology where Britain's wish to have a fully-horsed procession for the coronation of her new Queen necessitated the enlistment of some fifty amateur coachmen who came out of retirement with their horses for the occasion and stayed out to found the British Driving Society. In 1970 the Duke of Edinburgh, patron of this society and newly-elected president of the International Equestrian Federation, added competition driving for teams of four horses, designated Driving Trials, to the Show Jumping Dressage and Three-Day Event (Horse Trials) for whose international regulation the Federation was responsible.

The Olympic Games, held every four years, was not able to cater for the new Driving Trials with all the extra horses which they involved, but these trials have their own world championships in each year of even date and take place, together with Show Jumping and Dressage, each year at the Aachen Show, which is the biggest in the world with up to thirty nations competing against one another.

Thus by the end of the twentieth century, horsemanship has become more international than ever before and, in 1990, the first World Equestrian Games in Stockholm, with Vaulting and Long Distance Riding added to Show Jumping, Dressage, Horse Trials and Driving Trials, was reckoned to have been the biggest and best assembly of horses and horsemen for peaceful purposes that the world had ever seen.

2

Horsemanship on the Racecourse

A good jockey has to be a good horseman, but a good horseman need not be a good jockey. It has been suggested that a moderate jockey who rides only on the flat need not be a very good horseman and this may well be true, but it is equally true that the best flat race jockeys are very good horsemen indeed. A National Hunt jockey who rides over fences must be a good horseman to be able to do this at all without undue risk to himself and the other jockeys against whom he rides. A jockey needs all the qualities of a horseman, some of them to a specially developed extent, and a number of extra qualities and abilities as well.

Physically, a jockey must be very light but very strong. For the flat he cannot afford to weigh more than 8 stone (50kg) and he will get more rides and more opportunities at the start of his career if he weighs not much more than 7 stone (45kg) and can take advantage of the allowance of 7lb (3kg) which he will be able to claim in most races as a beginner. For National Hunt races (steeplechases and hurdle races) a jockey's rides will be limited if he weighs more than 10 stone 7lb (67kg) and he will get many more rides and chances as a beginner if he can claim a 7lb allowance and go to scale at 9 stone 7lb (60kg). These bottom weights have been much the same for over a hundred years during which the average size and weight of people of both sexes, at least in Britain, has increased significantly. Many jockeys have to battle constantly with their own weights and some, while remaining remarkably fit and strong, keep themselves almost permanently up to 2 stone (13kg) lighter than the minimum weights recommended by doctors for people of their heights and builds. This requires continuous dieting and a daily intake of food and drink amounting to about a quarter of that enjoyed by normal people. In addition, jockeys go through frequent severe short-term extra wasting to do an especially low weight for particularly important rides, which involves taking laxatives and diuretics and deliberately inducing extreme dehydration. This sort of regime is punishing physically and depressing mentally. It can only be maintained with great willpower by really dedicated people, but up to one third of all jockeys riding regularly under either flat or National Hunt rules probably have to follow it for most of their careers.

Length of leg, so useful in most forms of horsemanship, is of no great value to a jockey whose thighs and knees do not grip his horse in any way during races. A jockey's knees are at about the level of his horse's withers, or slightly above it in the case of many flat race jockeys. Length below the knee will therefore only bring his ankles slightly lower down his horse's sides and afford an extra inch or so of grip, on which he will not be relying in any case, while extra length of thigh will only tend to push his bottom up into the air and create extra wind resistance besides providing some extra frame for extra weight.

Bruce Hobbs, who was seventeen years old and 6ft 1½in (1.87m) tall, won the Grand National in 1937 on Battleship, who was an entire slightly under 15.2h. Lester Piggott, almost certainly the greatest European flat race jockey of the second half of the twentieth century is more than a foot taller and about 3 stone (20kg) heavier than his American counterpart Willie Shoemaker who, with over 9,000 winners to his credit, is the most successful jockey the world has ever known. Thus good jockeys seem to come in all shapes and sizes and their top weight-limit is probably all that really matters.

Jockeys are invariably very strong in their backs and shoulders as well as in their arms and wrists. This strength is undoubtedly developed by holding and 'sitting against' hard-pulling horses on the gallops, but it is also transmitted through a jockey's loins to induce sustained and vigorous extension in a strong driving finish, where inches are critical. All horsemen need quick reactions and good muscular co-ordination and jockeys need quicker reactions and better co-ordination than most other riders (with the exception of show jumpers) because everything happens faster in a race. Instant reaction together with the ability to apply just the right amount of strength to achieve a desired result may win a race or save a fall. Mainly physical, partly mental and owing more than a little to experience, this capability to take the correct action immediately in emergency depends considerably on physical fitness and is difficult to develop in middle age. A good jockey must therefore start young and keep going until he finally retires and he cannot afford long holidays or lay-offs even after painful falls and slow-healing injuries.

A jockey needs mental attributes of a high order and cannot acquire all of them just by learning or being instructed. The most important of these must be courage, because without it all other qualities will be of

A match at Cheltenham in 1989 between two great champions: Willie Shoemaker in the lead, of the USA rode 9,000 winners, more than any other jockey in history, on the flat and Peter Scudamore has ridden more National Hunt winners than any other jockey.

little significance. Courage to face the risks of falls and injuries is crucial to a jockey riding under both flat and National Hunt rules.

A flat race jockey may survive several seasons without a fall or any injury, but a fall in a flat race is often worse than a fall over fences because horses are likely to be more tightly bunched with less chance of avoiding fallen riders, and the fall will invariably be totally unexpected.

A National Hunt jockey will be lucky if he averages less than one fall in every ten rides and, although modern medical checks ensure that he cannot ride again until he has recovered from the effects of concussion or internal injuries, he will undoubtedly ride in many races while still suffering some pain and discomfort from sprains, bruises and broken bones.

To falls and injuries sustained on the racecourse must be added those which a jockey may suffer while schooling and riding work on the gallops and in trainers' yards, and these are not likely to be much less than those expected by any other well organized horseman who works with young horses. A jockey's career is accordingly a high-risk one in which he must anticipate being injured from time to time and be willing to keep going despite this.

All horsemen need to have 'horse sense' and jockeys need this to a marked degree and essentially to a greater degree than most other horsemen. 'Horse sense' is difficult to define to people who are not themselves horsemen, but horsemen recognize it as an understanding of horses in respect of their physical capabilities, both actual and potential and, more critically, of their temperaments and their mental processes. To discerning horsemen with horse sense, these physical and mental qualities vary considerably between different horses and a simple employment of horse sense will, for instance, usually enable a horseman to choose the better of two.

A regularly employed jockey, who will frequently get onto a strange horse for the first time only a few minutes before riding it in a race, must make a very quick assessment of its physical and mental capabilities, together with any unusual quirks or peculiarities in its mental make up. He must do this if he is to get the best out of the horse in the race and avoid triggering any undesirable responses which may cause it to withhold its best efforts or even fall; and he may only receive sketchy and hurried advice from its trainer. If he can assess a horse's capabilities, particularly in comparison with others which he has ridden in the same class, and sum them up comprehensively and succinctly to its trainer on the strength of one race, or even just one training gallop, he will establish himself as a valuably discerning adviser. He may sometimes even be in a position to choose between two fancied horses to ride in an important race when the success of his selection may have a great effect on his career.

A jockey must be a very good judge of pace, and he needs this ability more than any other sort of rider. The crucial concept involved in judging pace is that, in races longer than 5 furlongs, virtually no modern Thoroughbred horse can maintain his best and fastest pace from start to finish and must have some of his energy reserved for a burst of speed at the end of the race in a tight finish. Sprinters get tired more quickly than stayers, but can travel faster over short distances. A jockey on a horse which is bred and trained for the distance of the race in which he is riding will therefore want to start fast so as to get a good position. He will then settle to a pace which will tire the sprinters before the end of the race, but leave him with enough speed in hand for the last one or two furlongs to catch and overtake the stayers who may have gone on well ahead of him. In his final burst of speed he will aim to reach the winning post with his horse travelling at its best pace just before it gets too tired to maintain this.

This is an over-simplified explanation of a complex set of calculations which a good jockey will make on the basis of his trainer's instructions, but largely by instinct as regards the exact pace which he must set in the middle of a race. If he gets the calculations right, he may often win races against horses which are really better and faster than his own. Other factors can confuse these calculations: a horse's exact state of fitness – which will affect its stamina – the state of the going – which will affect the speed as well as the stamina of all horses in a race, though not consistently for all of them – the weights allotted in a handicap – which are supposed to even up the capabilities of all the horses and give each of them an equal chance of winning, but which always give some of them no hope and may sometimes seem to favour a few – and unforeseen misfortunes during the race – which may create disadvantages for several horses in addition to the ones to whom they actually occur.

The horse's trainer will have weighed up all the predictable factors and will usually give his jockey fairly definite instructions about the position he should occupy in relation to the rest of the field for the first part of the race and the place on the course at which he should start his run at top speed to try to overtake the leaders. A jockey will ignore these instructions, particularly that concerning when to start 'riding his horse out' for the winning post, at his peril, but may often be told to use his own discretion and may sometimes do so with advantage when the pace during the early part of the race is much slower than the trainer anticipated. This is the occasion when judgement of pace really counts and it is not unknown for a really confident jockey on a genuine 'stayer' to go off in front of a moderate field of other horses and stay there to 'slip his field' and win the race without even being effectively challenged. This cannot happen in a big important race in which one or two fancied horses are likely to be accompanied by pace-makers from their own stables. These pace-makers will not be expected to win, but only to go off in front and ensure that a good pace is maintained in the early stages of the race.

A jockey who manages to win races by starting in front and staying there is sometimes credited by racegoers with particular cunning for having 'waited in front'. This is a rather absurd commendation because he will not have waited at all. He will only have used his sound judgement of pace to appreciate that his horse will be able to keep going at close to his best pace and still produce an extra effort to quicken if necessary at the finish, and that this will be faster and more sustained than the other jockeys think possible. It has been known for a tearaway horse to adopt these tactics himself, regardless of his jockey's efforts to restrain him but, in such cases, they are seldom successful and he usually becomes exhausted and is headed before he reaches the winning post, to the discredit of his suffering rider.

Except in important races when records may be at stake, a trainer will not want his horse to win by a great distance and attract undue attention from the handicapper. A jockey dare not ease up too much when he seems to be winning easily and risk getting caught just before the winning post by horses travelling much faster behind him, but all his horse's connections will be the better pleased if, by exercising good judgement of pace, he contrives to win by a length or two rather than a distance.

A jockey needs to have a calm placid temperament, but a lively active disposition, and the two do not usually go together. That he needs to be lively and active in his work and most of the circumstances surrounding it goes without saying, but he will encounter constant moments of extreme stress during races and longer periods of more continuous stress between race meetings (as when driving himself to them in a hurry) and he needs to be able to keep calm to cope with these. An even temperament will help him to avoid extremes of elation and depression and a touch of tact, coupled with an ability to express himself clearly, should enable him to give an accurate, but appropriately encouraging account of the performance and prospects of any of the horses which he has ridden. If he is also something of a diplomat, he will commend a horse more highly to its owner than to its trainer.

The jockey's 'seat', with very short stirrups, is more like a perch or crouch and seems to be at variance with many of the tenets of most other forms of equitation. It evolved very quickly 100 years ago from an American initiative which demonstrated immediately its practical advantages in enabling horses to gallop faster and farther at full speed, when their riders' weights were clear of their backs and loins and kept firmly over their withers, just behind the line of their front legs. This is the centre of gravity, and thus the point of balance for a rider when a horse is moving forward in extension. It moves further to the rear when the horse is collected, but racehorses are not expected to work at collected paces.

A jockey's seat bones should be clear of the saddle when his horse is cantering or galloping, and there will not be much saddle for them to rest on anyway if, for reasons of weight, he is using a saddle which weighs less than 2lb (1kg). The rather cramped crouch which he must maintain imposes considerable strain on his thigh muscles and he develops these by riding regularly at all paces with very short stirrups and, sometimes, to get fit, riding a bicycle with no saddle.

A jockey always 'bridges' his reins over his horse's neck by holding

31

the loose parts of each rein in the opposite hand so that two 6–8in (15–20cm) lengths of spare rein form the 'bridge' just in front of the horse's withers on which he can balance himself and prevent himself being jerked forward by any sudden deceleration. A racehorse usually possesses plenty of natural impulsion and willingness to go forward and, at a gallop or canter, takes a fairly strong hold of his bit. To cope with this, a jockey must 'sit against' it. He must be prepared to use the weight of his body and the strength of his back and shoulders, braced against his feet (which may be thrust well forward). In addition, he must be prepared to use the strength of his fingers and wrists, applying leverage through the 'bridge' formed by the reins over the neck, to maintain the strong contact with its mouth needed to balance, restrain and control the horse.

'Good hands' are as important to a jockey as to any other kind of horseman. A rider is said to have 'good hands' when he manages to maintain a firm even contact with his horse's mouth and to adjust this smoothly but instantly to keep his horse 'on the bit' and not resisting or evading it and to apply more or less restraint to call for changes of pace. The fact that a racehorse usually takes a stronger hold at the gallop than most other horses does not permit a jockey to be more rigid or less sympathetic in the contact which he maintains with his horse's mouth than riders engaged in other activities.

A horse which is fighting for its head against a heavy hand which is imposing undue and unsympathetic restraint is liable to become unbalanced and distracted from its work of trying to win races. If rein contact is lost even momentarily through the horse dropping its bit, or if the jockey suddenly relaxes his contact with its mouth, the horse's stride is likely to shorten with consequent reduction in its pace. One possible outcome is for the horse to get too close to a fence before taking off to jump it, and accordingly hitting it hard and falling. 'Good hands' depend on the application of physical strength, particularly where hard-pulling racehorses are concerned, but the strength must be correctly and sympathetically applied with instant precision if it is to be effective.

Ordinary racegoers seldom appreciate the minor but acute anxiety which jockeys sometimes suffer in getting their horses safely and decorously to the start. Jockeys in the USA are generally spared this because at most American race meetings, attendants mounted on steady ponies accompany the runners to each start and will actually lead by the bridle any which seem likely to become over-excited or uncontrollable.

In Britain, Europe and the rest of the world however, jockeys have to manage without the assistance provided in America and they take the risk of being run away with more often than most of them would care to admit. The prospect of being unable to stop and go on to make one, or even two, circuits of a normal circular racecourse – usually in the opposite direction to that in which the races are run – is dismaying. Moreover, the exhausted horse will be withdrawn from the race – whose start will have been delayed during this performance. The possibility of this happening at Newmarket where a horse might gallop for miles over the open heath is appalling. It seldom does happen on any racecourse – the nearest to it is when a horse canters to the start rather faster than it should, or when it is permitted to go early to the start to avoid being excited by other horses. The rarity of any major disasters is tribute to the horsemanship of jockeys and their ability to keep all kinds of headstrong, excitable horses under calm control just when their excitement and urge to gallop is at its peak, and from a position on their backs which many ordinary riders would consider to be distinctly precarious.

Most horses 'jump off' very quickly out of starting stalls, leaving their jockeys only to cope with the sudden acceleration and their need to adopt instantly a correct position to avoid being 'left behind' and thus hampering their horses' efforts to get quickly into their strides. Tapes or a start by flag are now normally only used for steeplechases

A point to point – only for sporting amateurs.

and hurdle races in which, because they are longer than most flat races, starts are less critical. The ability to get a horse quickly away at the start and into his full stride without hesitation is an essential skill for a National Hunt jockey. It enables him to take up a position in relation to the other horses consistent with the orders he has been given and the tactics which he wants to adopt prior to the closing stages of the race.

Before the introduction of starting stalls many jockeys were experts at getting good starts in flat races by ensuring that their horses were on their toes and moving slightly forward rather than standing flat-footed when the gate went up. Some experienced horses co-operated wonderfully to this effect and seemed also to watch the starter's arm to anticipate, by a fraction of a second, his action in releasing the starting gate.

Most races are won ultimately by finishing speed, so a jockey has to get his horse to the closing stages of a race close enough to the leaders and with enough strength and energy left to produce the acceleration to pass them and win, and he must also help and sometimes compel it to do just this. The ability to ride a strong finish is probably the most crucial, and the most obvious, skill for a jockey to acquire and develop; at least for flat races. However, he is hardly ever able to practise it except in close finishes in actual races because owners and trainers understandably do not want their horses to be ridden out desperately to the point of exhaustion at home on the gallops. National Hunt jockeys are usually involved in fewer close finishes than their flat race counterparts and accordingly get less chance to practise them, although when the need for them arises it is just as urgent and critical.

To produce effective finishing speed a horse must be balanced and fully extended, but must quicken its pace when it is already becoming tired. To maintain the balance and the extension, a jockey must keep contact with his horse's mouth because if the reins are slackened, the horse will usually become unbalanced and shorten its stride. There are in fact plenty of pictures of jockeys riding stormingly effective finishes on an apparently loose rein, and many of them are of the late Sir Gordon Richards who was adept at this, but timing is as vital as balance and the reins can only be slack for a very few strides before the balance is lost.

The aids to increasing pace in a tight finish are reckoned to be hands, heels and whip. When a jockey does not resort to his whip he is said to 'ride his horse out with hands and heels', or in slang to 'scrub it out'. The part that his actual hands or heels play in inducing his horse to gallop faster is doubtful, but there is no doubt that a jockey can drive a horse forward at increased pace by creating impulsion with his shoulders and back and transmitting it through his thighs and his hands, holding bridged reins over the horse's neck. Although it looks very different, the action of the lower back and pelvis is similar in essence in the case of a jockey riding a strong finish to that of a school rider wanting to set up impulsion to induce either extension or collection.

The whip has an important part to play in the riding of a finish on the racecourse. Used with artistry and discretion it is effective in winning races but, if it is wielded clumsily or with imperfect timing, it is more likely to cause a horse to swerve and/or shorten its stride and accordingly travel more slowly.

The art of using the whip in a finish lies in switching it quickly and neatly through the fingers so that it points upwards and forwards rather than downwards and backwards, or possibly drawing it through to this position in the opposite hand, and then swinging it in rhythm with the horse's stride through a 180deg arc from its nose to its quarters, keeping it always below the level of the horse's head. The swinging of the whip without any contact usually seems to encourage a horse to stretch out and increase its speed, provided that it is done properly, but it is invariably more effective if it includes one or two smacks on the quarters. These need to be delivered at the back of the swing and at every other stride, not every stride. They must be well up on the quarters and not under any circumstances land on the flank or stifle, and the stewards will want to interview any jockey who hits his horse more than eight or ten times, or in the wrong place, or so as to cause any wound or injury.

Used in this way in the appropriate hand, the whip can be a great help in keeping a horse straight if it is tending to drift or veer from a straight course – as many tend to when they start to get tired – and is threatening to interfere with other horses. The only alternative correction which a jockey can apply to keep a horse straight is to stop riding him out at full extension and pull much harder on one rein, and this inevitably reduces speed and may lose races.

The use of the whip in this way is one of the arts of horsemanship, employed only by jockeys on the racecourse and, like the riding of finishes in general, it cannot reasonably be practised at home or in any circumstances other than the finishes of actual races, so that it is not easy to acquire to the degree of perfection which its proper implementation demands. The sight of a tired but willing horse being driven to make efforts beyond its inclination by blows of a whip at the end of a race is repugnant to spectators and most racegoers. However, some racehorses are generally lazy and need some extra coercion to persuade them to give of their best and others, affected by the deep-rooted herd instinct to gallop with the leaders but not much in front of them, will only go on in front to establish a lead if they are especially encouraged to do so.

Steeplechase fences are at least 4ft 6in (1.37m) high and open ditches are at least 6ft (1.82m) from their guard rails to their frames on the landing side. The biggest of them all, the Chair, at Aintree is 5ft 2in (1.57m) high and rather more than 10ft (3m) in spread from the guard rail to the landing side of the fence, where there is a drop of 2 or 3 feet (60 or 90cm). Even hurdles are 4ft (1.20m) high. Despite the fact that fences on a racecourse are considerably bigger, although admittedly far less complicated, than any encountered in Three-Day Event Horse Trials and all but the biggest in open show-jumping competitions, racehorses are expected to jump them 'out of their stride'. They must gain distance and speed while in the air over them rather than shorten their stride to place themselves to jump carefully, thereby reducing speed and wasting time in the process. Indeed, a racehorse which jumps slowly and takes several strides to reach full speed again after landing will have little chance of winning races, however fast it may gallop between fences.

In hurdle races most jockeys sit still as for a flat race and virtually ignore the hurdles, riding at them as if they were not there. This requires a measure of nerve and the ability to inspire the horse to keep going at an extended pace if it has any tendency to dwell or hesitate. This is the right way to win hurdle races, because horses are astonishingly quick to make the extra effort required to surmount any obstacle which they can see in front of them, particularly when they are going too fast to be able to stop. The extra effort which a fit, strong racehorse needs to make to jump a 4ft (1.20m) hurdle is not extraordinary and it can easily take off up to 25ft (8m) before it; clear it adequately at the top of a fairly low trajectory; land 25ft beyond it, thereby gaining a length over less bold rivals, and even get a momentary breather in the process.

If a horse hits a hurdle on the upward half of its trajectory by taking off too close to it, the hurdle will normally fall and the horse will just lose a length or two by the interruption caused to its stride, and the deceleration is unlikely to unseat the jockey. If it stands off much too far – usually by being unsighted and 'half-lengthed' by taking off at the same time as a horse alongside but closer to the hurdle – and hits it coming down with its forefeet extended in an effort to reach to clear it, there is a risk that its front feet will go through the hurdle which will trip it up and give it a very nasty fall. Happily, this is a rare occurrence and a bold jockey will not allow the possibility of its happening to influence his race riding.

Some chasers jump their fences boldly and fluently, regardless of

36

any help or interference from their jockeys, but most of them probably appreciate at least some encouragement from the saddle. Some jockeys can 'see a stride' at racing pace and some cannot and do not reckon they would ride any better if they could. The ability of a rider to 'see a stride', which is crucial in show jumping and critical in the cross-country phase of Horse Trails (One or Three-Day Events), is certainly helpful in steeplechasing. It simply means that a rider is able to determine exactly when his horse should take three, or better still, four, good full strides to bring him to the place where he should, ideally, take off to jump the fence.

A show-jumping rider may legitimately check his horse so as to bring it precisely to the right place before driving it on for the three strides before take off, but a jockey must not do this in a race and can only take a discreet steadying pull about 50 yards (45 metres) before a fence if his horse seems badly unbalanced. He can therefore only drive his horse on for the last three strides to make sure that there are three long strides, and not three medium ones and a short one, provided that he can be sure when to start doing this. Left more to its own devices, as without a jockey after a fall, a horse will nearly always shorten its stride going into a fence and often put in a very short last stride which will bring it uncomfortably close to the fence for take-off and result in an awkward jump which loses ground. Horses which continue in races

Lester Piggott 'riding' John Francome after a memorable match between these two champion jockeys at Warwick in 1988. They both retired just after this; Lester from the flat and John from National Hunt Racing. However, Lester Piggott resumed race riding in 1990 at the age of fifty-five.

without their jockeys very seldom fall, so there must be a presumption that ill-judged interference from jockeys causes plenty of falls. However, it is always right for a jockey to 'kick on' and if he can see exactly where he should kick on from to meet a fence right, his horse's jump will be the better and the faster for his encouragement.

Not all jockeys can get this right, and not many can get it right each time. John Francome, who came to race riding after several years of success as a junior champion show jumper and was Champion National Hunt Jockey for seven years before his retirement in 1988, was the great expert at 'seeing a stride' even when it was one of several long strides taken at racing pace, and horses always jumped very well for him and fell less often than with other jockeys.

It is not sensible for a jockey to sit as still riding over fences as over hurdles. If his horse is at all hesitant before a fence, he will need to sit down and a little bit backwards to drive it on and if it hits a fence hard, he will have to sit back quickly to avoid being unseated by the sudden deceleration and the peck on landing which is likely to result from it. The need for a jockey riding over steeplechase fences to be able to sit back, sit down, and grip to some extent with his legs is crucial, because the horse cannot win without the jockey and disappointed owners and trainers, not to mention backers, are all too liable to criticize the jockey for falling off, unless he gets up from the ground before the horse does.

A jockey will often need all the agility he can muster to avoid parting company with his horse and to get right back into the saddle very quickly after a bad landing. The horse needs to have its head, neck and shoulders free to be able to recover and stay in the race and it will be seriously hampered in this respect if the jockey is clinging round its neck and hanging on by the reins.

Many jockeys hunt regularly and ride very well to hounds, though flat race jockeys who do not go abroad in the winter get much more chance to hunt than National Hunt jockeys. Professional jockeys do not have the time to take part seriously in competitive riding activities besides racing, but when they do occasionally compete for fun and charity in show-jumping competitions or over the cross-country courses of Horse Trials, they invariably give a very good account of themselves and prove their versatility by scoring few (if any) more penalties than the regular show jumpers and eventers against whom they ride. In fact, most jockeys are very good horsemen.

3

Horsemanship in the Hunting Field

Some fifty years ago a British Colonel, who was quite a distinguished horseman and the author of several books on horsemanship, wrote in a national magazine that, 'The horsemanship of England is ruined by hunting'. There are two versions of the ending of this story: one, that the editor of the magazine refused to publish this statement on the grounds that it amounted to an offensive heresy; and two, that he published it but that it marked the end of his magazine, because everyone ceased to buy it in protest.

Whether or not the Colonel's opinion was ever published in print, he disseminated it widely and was promptly and properly condemned by all the horsemen of England, most of whom thought they rode very well and many of whom did so only to hunt. In fact, he hunted regularly himself and probably made his contentious pronouncement to secure some publicity for his writings and to shock his fellow horsemen out of their undoubted complacency. He was proved largely wrong twenty-five years later when British competitors scored noteworthy successes in the Three-Day Event, mainly on the strength of their excellent cross-country performances; and partly right when most other European riders beat them hands down in dressage – a state of play which has maintained until the present day.

People only started to jump fences out hunting in the eighteenth century in England when the Enclosure Acts established hedges, ditches and walls to divide farms and fields, and the fox, which would run straight through or over them and could be found in almost any part of the country, became the favourite quarry. The riding and the horsemanship became an integral part of 'the chase', and for most people much the most exciting part of it. Happily, English horses were beginning to improve as a result of imported stallions from Spain and, during the century itself, the progeny of the three great Arab stallions which became the forefathers of the English Thoroughbred.

Although riding is nowadays a more competitive activity than ever before – and it has been internationally competitive for the past thirty or forty years – many, if not most, horsemen in Britain still ride primarily so as to be able to follow hounds across country. Provided that he has a bold, well-mannered horse and the essential ability to remain on top of it while it gallops and jumps; provided also that he can steer it and stop it to prevent it running into danger or other people, what a hunting man needs as much as any special equestrian skill is courage and 'an eye for a country'.

Courage is a vital quality required for all forms of horsemanship and for a person who wants to ride well to hounds, it is crucial and indispensable. The courage required is general, and indeed moral as well as physical, but its manifestation is particular and amounts to willingness to risk a fall, mainly in jumping fences which have not been jumped before and may prove difficult, dangerous, or even impossible. A bold rider will inspire his horse and, provided that it is reasonably brave to begin with, he will make it also bold and create a courageous combination. A timid rider will destroy his horse's confidence in itself as well as in its rider and, unless the horse runs away with him in exasperation, it will refuse to jump fences, especially any which it has not jumped before.

The proverbial boldness of English- and Irish-bred horses in jumping fences across country is due in no small measure to the environment, hereditary as well as actual, in which they have been bred and brought up. It is also often due to those horses carrying good bold riders. Extra boldness is required on the part of horse and rider in hunting, and particularly foxhunting, because it is now the only recognized equestrian activity in which a horse is constantly required to jump hedges, ditches and all sorts of other obstacles which have not been specially prepared for this purpose and may never have been jumped by any horse before. Joint boldness stems from mutual confidence, and since the ability to inspire his horse with confidence in him is one of the key hallmarks of a good horseman, any one who rides really well to hounds can claim to be a good horseman, however deficient he may be in the more technical skills of pure equitation.

'An eye for a country' is an acquired skill, not an inherited attribute. It is an essential requirement for hunting folk, soldiers in conventional mobile battles, and people who want to make journeys overland other than by roads, railways or rivers. Although many eminent horsemen possess it, and take great pride in it, it is nothing whatever to do with horsemanship, but only very much to do with hunting. A person with 'an eye for a country' will generally contrive to ride within sight and/or sound of hounds throughout a day's hunting, as indeed the huntsman must do and the master will wish to do. However, except over moorland and uncultivated country, most people other than the field master and hunt servants will usually be following other people. These 'other people' will themselves be led by the field master over fields where the hunt is not unwelcome and often over specially constructed hunt jumps. They may sometimes have to be led by roads and tracks in the general direction of the line which hounds are hunting, rather than be at risk of damaging crops, disturbing stock, or in any way causing annoyance to the farmers and land owners on whose hospitality they depend for their sport.

To be following a party of other riders, particularly over a line of specially constructed fences, is not the same as riding to hounds. This, incidentally, is the real reason why drag hunting, which necessarily consists in galloping over a pre-selected line of country, can never be as exciting, enthralling or satisfying as genuine foxhunting. It is anticipation of encountering the unknown and unexpected which gives riding to hounds its special thrill; and it is surviving such encounters which gives it its special satisfaction. There must be many regular hunting people today who have never experienced the supreme enjoyment of riding alone with hounds, or even of riding slightly behind and on the down-wind flank of a pack of hounds, hunting fast over a strongly-fenced but negotiable line of grass fields with only hunt servants in front of them. In truth it should be conceded that many regular hunting people, themselves the backbone of their particular hunts, do not really aspire to this glory. It is, however, what constitutes riding to hounds, as opposed to getting to where hounds are from time to time by an admirable but distinctly different exercise of knowledge of the country and of the principles of venery.

A good day's hunting is a critical test of a horse's stamina and endurance, and it was more so in the days before motor horse boxes, when people hacked up to 20 miles (30km) before and after their day's hunting and horses might have riders on their backs for up to 10 hours, covering as much as 70 miles (95km) and jumping as many as sixty fences in a day. Now that very few people hack more than 5 miles (8km) to meets, the maximum hours and mileage for a day's hunting are reduced to six hours under saddle and 40 miles (65km) of distance covered. There may be just as many fences to be jumped, however, and these, together with trying to gallop fast through deep going, are what really tires a horse. Hunting people also own fewer horses today than they did a hundred years ago, so the same horse is likely to have to turn out again in two or three days' time now, instead of having a week's rest like his predecessor.

The ability of a rider to nurse his horse and keep it going throughout a long fast hunt became critical during the nineteenth century, at least in terms of foxhunting in England. Costly and complicated arrangements for the provision of second horses, and even third ones, could not prevent horses becoming exhausted and their riders missing good hunts so long as the second horses, held in reserve, could not be transported to where they were wanted but had to be ridden there at their own best paces. Incidents of horses foundering or even dropping dead from exhaustion are quite commonly recorded in the annals of nineteenth century English foxhunting and, as the century progressed and the foxes and the hounds ran faster and the horses became better-bred and more high-couraged, so such incidents tended to increase. In a less humane age, they were usually attributed to misfortune rather than regarded as cruelty as they would normally be today, but either way the rider missed the end of a good hunt and probably had a long walk home.

To ease the burden of their weight on their horses' backs, English hunting men developed a modified version of the forward seat 100 years before Federico Caprilli introduced it and promoted it internationally for military and competition riding (*see* Chapter 1). The chief protagonist of this sensible seat for cross-country riding was one John Adams and, in 1805 in a book to promote it called *An Analysis of Horsemanship* he wrote:

> The hunting seat is that of riding in the stirrups to relieve yourself from that friction and heat which the bottom would receive from the strong and continued gallop if seated close down on the saddle. The stirrup must be somewhat shorter than that recommended for military or road riding and when the horseman is raised in the stirrups he must have a forward inclination from about twenty to forty-five degrees short of perpendicular, as the rider shall find most pleasant and convenient for himself. Whether the body has a great or small inclination the position otherwise must be the same as when upright; that is the breast open, the back hollow, the head firm and the hands kept low.

This advice, which was first given 200 years ago, is as sound and valid today as it was then although, then as now, only a few of the people to whom it was addressed really accepted it or tried to follow it. However, people who ride and hunt for recreation are generally conservative by nature and may be pleased to reflect that what was considered the best way for their great, great, great grandfathers to do it has stood the test of time and is still just about the best for them. The essence of this 'hunting seat' is still comfort for horse and rider at all paces, for long distances, and for jumping fences.

Stirrup leathers must be short enough to enable the rider just to clear the pommel of the saddle with his crutch when he is standing in his stirrups. For people of normal dimensions, this length, from the buckle of the stirrup leather to the tread of the stirrup iron, is the same as that from the armpit to the knuckles of a straight arm, and anyone who feels more comfortable in the saddle with it very different from this must either be an unusual shape or adopting an unnatural position on his horse.

Although the length of the stirrup leathers is critical to within an inch, it is essentially a moderate length which should suit all riders for all normal purposes and is thus appropriate for the hunting field. His stirrups will be just short enough to enable the hunting man to keep his bottom slightly above the saddle and not quite touching it when he is galloping or cantering. He will lean forward at an angle between 20 and 45 degrees from the perpendicular, in accordance with John Adams's original recommendation, to be able to keep his bottom just above the saddle without strain, but this angle will by no means stay constant and will vary and alter continuously depending on the pace, whether the horse needs urging or restraint, and the shape and fitness of the rider.

He must make a 'bridge' over his horse's neck with the spare ends of his reins, and hold this with both hands at all paces faster than a walk to prevent himself from pitching forward and losing his balance as a

A typical hunting scene. The field is moving round a covert, probably in immediate anticipation of a good fast hunt, and youth is prominantly to the fore.

result of any sudden deceleration, whether caused by a shy, swerve or jink or just landing over a fence.

This 'bridge' is a simple elementary aid to the security of a rider's seat on his horse. It provides crucial support and anchorage and greatly increases the rider's confidence without inducing any rigidity. Surprisingly, it is seldom mentioned in books and other published riding instructions. Whether this is because it is considered to be so elementary as to be obvious, or whether it is disapproved of by purist professors of equitation, its omission often leaves a gap in the learning of novice cross-country riders which has to be filled by unnecessarily painful experience.

Most hunting people in Britain would probably not care to contemplate, or even admit, that most of their day and most of their mileage is at a trot. Some of them like to echo the sentiments expressed by the more haughty of their pre-motor age predecessors that 'Gentlemen and their horses only gallop and the trot is a pace which should be confined to coachmen'. However, they no longer gallop to and from meets on covert hacks to give credence to this pronouncement and, although they have horseboxes to relieve themselves and their horses of this tedious aspect of their day's sport, they almost certainly still do more trotting than galloping between the meet and the end of the day.

Much of this trotting will be behind the pack of hounds, moving between coverts and draws along roads at a hound jog. This is a very suitable easy pace for the hounds, but a most irritating one for the horses and their riders, since it is too fast for a walk, but too slow for a steady trot. Riders need to post at this pace; i.e. rise at the trot, if they are to avoid giving their horses sore backs and themselves sore bottoms. An irregular pace with much stopping and starting due to 'concertina'ing' makes this a much rougher and more tiring procedure than it should be, even with stirrups at the right length for hunting across country, which will be equally right for trotting along roads.

Hunting people in most parts of England now spend more time than they ever did some years ago trying to keep up with hounds by riding along roads as close as possible to where they are hunting. Those who kept mainly to roads in the old days were ridiculed as 'funkers' who did not want to jump fences, but very few riders to hounds choose the roads as a soft option nowadays. They certainly do not form a soft option, because hurrying along a tarmac road on an excited horse is a high-risk and potentially lethal proceeding. Most horsemen only resort to roads when they are not allowed to ride on the land over which the fox has travelled, or would become hopelessly left behind in trying to skirt the edges of enormous fields of heavy plough.

Galloping along tarmac roads is very bad for horses' legs and feet and nearly always leads to early lameness and the tragic end of a hunter's working life just when he is beginning really to know his job. Galloping along roadside grass verges with their concealed drainage channels and accumulation of litter, including bottles and tins, is just as likely to lame a horse, only more quickly, suddenly and seriously.

Trotting very fast on a hard unyielding surface causes only slightly less concussion and jarring than galloping on it and only slightly reduces the chances of a horse slipping up. The horse, which in all other circumstances is a remarkably sure-footed animal, seems unable to detect or recognize a treacherously slippery surface and will seldom moderate his pace of his own volition or avoid turning sharply, even when he is already slipping and sliding on one. Most of the worst, and often fatal, falls which horsemen experience today in the hunting field are on slippery roads, and probably the most unnerving experience which any of them may suffer is to be run away with on a public road by a horse which has got left behind and is determined to ignore any restraint in his efforts to catch up quickly with his companions.

Being run away with generally out hunting is a traditional subject for mirth and comic relief which has inspired many good jokes and entertaining pictures. It is a common misadventure which nearly all hunting people have suffered from time to time, and any who claim to have been spared it have either done very little hunting, or done it only on very dull horses. Being run away with out hunting is always embarrassing and can be very frightening, depending on the nerve of the rider concerned and the extent and duration of his loss of control. Although it may seem only academic to a luckless rider who is trying to stop his horse from charging into the middle of a pack of hounds, there is an essential difference between a bolter and a horse which sometimes runs away and it is a crucial difference in terms of the horse's suitability as a hunter.

A horse which bolts does so in panic induced by intermittent pain, fear or mental disturbance. It generally ignores all efforts to control or restrain it and often ignores any human being, other animal, or obstacle in its path with which it may collide. A bolter is a dangerous menace in the hunting field and cannot be cured unless the root-cause of its panic can be discovered and eradicated, which is seldom possible.

A horse which sometimes runs away generally does so out of a mixture of over-excitement born of high spirits, over-anxiety to get in front of other horses and 'lead the herd' born of high courage, and impatience at having to suffer possibly clumsy and undue restraint.

Such a horse will probably become a very good hunter once the initial excitement of the chase has worn off and it has settled to a regular routine.

A bold rider with good horse sense can usually settle an impetuous horse which resists restraint early in a day's hunting. All he needs to do is find a fairly straight four furlongs of good going, preferably uphill, in the general direction in which hounds are moving on which to give him his head and let him gallop as fast as he can. The trick is to kick the horse on and make him go faster than he wants to, so that after about half a mile he will respond willingly to suggestions that he should slow down and halt. This procedure is inclined to astonish other members of the field and to enrage field masters, but it works nine times out of ten and on the tenth time it is usually possible to steer in wide circles.

Horses which have regularly carried a huntsman, whipper in or field master will not normally like to be relegated to following behind others and will often be unpleasantly strong and tiring for an ordinary member of the field to ride in a crowd. They will, however, be safe jumpers and not alarmingly scatter-brained. They will usually settle fairly happily into a new and more subordinate role if they can be introduced to it by a good horseman who is able to hunt them for three or four days in quick succession. A few ex-racehorses make very good hunters, but most of them never really become reconciled to being ridden far behind the leaders of any procession and they tend to jump too quickly and boldly to suit any but the bravest horsemen.

Prize-winning show jumpers are seldom retired from the arena in time for them to start second careers as hunters, but those of them that are well managed usually get a certain amount of recreational hunting, if only to refresh their outlooks. A show jumper which is retired prematurely after four or five years because it does not make the grade, or has even become sick of coloured fences and begun to refuse at them, can become a very good hunter indeed, though not in the hands of a complete novice for which it is likely to be too strong.

Jumping fences, or the prospect of doing so and the recollection of having done so, is the keenest interest of most of today's hunting people in Britain, although by no means all of them are willing to admit this. It is a pity that so many of them ride over fences so badly. Few of them lack courage, but many of them lack balance, agility and muscular co-ordination and some of them seem to lack judgement and even a basic instinct for self-preservation. What passes for an old-fashioned hunting seat is still much in evidence, as taught generally to the previous generation by old family grooms, whose customary advice to their charges when they were approaching a fence to jump it was 'Lean back, lean back Master Jimmy and pull very hard on the reins'.

Bold ponies carried light children over small fences well enough, despite the handicap imposed on them by this teaching, but when the light children grew into heavy adults, their horses often abandoned the attempt and either stopped or ploughed ponderously through hedges and rails in the manner of a tank. Ladies riding side-saddle usually fared rather better because, although they leaned back just as much as their menfolk, they were generally lighter and did not pull so hard on the reins.

A number of very heavyweight gentlemen were known to boast, publicly and even in print, that they never jumped fences out hunting from a pace faster than a trot. They claimed that this encouraged their horses to jump 'off their hocks' and prevented them from 'rushing their fences like steeplechasers'. Their enormous, admirable, pachydermous horses mostly remained wonderfully willing, despite the restriction imposed on them by the stately pace, but simple lack of momentum frequently caused them to land on top of fences and in the middle of hedges, and gigantic struggles generally ensued to release them and reduce or flatten the fence in the process. Numbers of lesser hunt followers invariably took advantage of the gaps so caused, and widened them considerably, and the wire used to close them as a temporary expedient was eventually replaced by rails which became a hunt jump.

Hunt jumps have been a prominent feature of hunting in Great Britain since World War II and, in the form of panels in or over wire fences, they have made riding across country possible without grave risk for longer than this in many regions of America, Canada and Australia. They provide a cheaper and easier, but less effective solution to the problem of enabling horsemen to ride across country than taking all the wire down in the winter, and in all but the very best Leicestershire hunting country the easier option now prevails, so that very little wire will ever be taken down again to facilitate riding to hounds.

Hunt jumps would serve pretty well if one could be built in every 500-yard stretch of wired fencing or hedgerow – which was originally formidable between pastures and is now unjumpable between ploughed fields. When only two or three provide entry and exit in completely enclosed fields of thirty acres or more and when 200 riders have to queue up to jump them, and hounds are not running in the direction to which they provide access anyway, hunting tends to become frustrating rather than exciting and even the keenest followers are tempted to take to the roads and wish they had a motor cycle instead of a horse.

When jumping fences out hunting, most people reckon to leave the arrangements as much as possible to the horse after selecting the place to jump, which in most cases is where someone else has just done so. They try to give the horse his head by avoiding hanging on by the reins, even when they get 'left behind', and to keep their weight off its loins and generally to interfere with it as little as possible. This is sensible and essentially horsemanlike, given a reasonably temperate, well-mannered horse which is not going to be required to jump much higher than 3ft 6in (1m); and many people out hunting very sensibly do not attempt to jump fences which are much higher than that.

A horse which approaches a hedge of this height at a strong steady canter with the intention of jumping it will clear it easily and comfortably, without having to alter or adjust its stride. It will also land far enough beyond it to clear a normal ditch or even a wire 'oxer' as well, provided that the latter is at least 1ft (30cm) lower than the hedge and not more than 4ft (1.20m) beyond it; and this may be assumed if the rider does not see it on approach.

This degree of jumping ability is all that many hunting people expect or require from their horses and it usually serves well enough to keep them generally in touch with hounds for the better part of most hunts whose pace is not too fast. However, on a good scenting day when hounds drive on hunting a bold straight fox which is not headed and makes a 7- or 8-mile point or better, horses must travel virtually as straight as hounds if they are to stay with them and not be left behind, and it is on days such as these that a good brave horseman on a well schooled, high-couraged horse comes into his own to ride truly to hounds and really experience the joys of the chase.

On fast straight hunts of this kind, there is no time to look for gaps or hunt jumps or sometimes even to open gates, and a rider who wants to stay with hounds must take on hedges well over 4ft (1.20m) high, with the sole redeeming feature that the top 3in (8cm) may be fairly yielding, and solid rails with a top bar 4ft above the ground which will certainly not be. To jump these bigger obstacles requires a significant effort, particularly from a tired horse, and when they incorporate a ditch which forms a spread of 7 or 8ft (2.10 or 2.40m), then the bigger the fence and the more tired the horse, the more precisely must the effort be applied if it is not going to end in a fall.

As well as deciding very quickly whether his horse is going to be able to jump the fence at which he is aiming, so as to exercise discretion if he thinks that it is not, the rider must help it to do so cleanly. This is achieved by presenting the horse at the fence at a balanced pace with plenty of impulsion, measuring its approach so that its last stride brings it into an effective take-off zone of limited extent, and the rider must be agile enough to sit well forward very quickly if its hind legs drop into a ditch. A reasonably powerful horse which will allow itself to be 'placed' at a fence and jump off its hocks without losing enthusiasm or impulsion can be trusted to clear 4ft (1.20m) of unbreakable timber, provided that the ground on the take-off side is not too boggy or poached, and this is enough to get it safely over most post and rail fences, many gates, and indeed most tightly-strung barbed wire fences.

Horsemen, and particularly English horsemen who go hunting, have a well founded horror of wire. Loose strands can certainly cut a horse most dreadfully but, if it is well and tightly strung between solidly planted posts and stands by itself unconcealed by any hedge, a wire fence is just as visible to a horse as to a rider and will cause much the same fall as a solid rail, unless the horse actually lands on top of it. In parts of Australia and New Zealand, where wire is the only fencing to be seen, hunt followers jump it regularly and would not see the end of many hunts if they did not.

It is asking a great deal of a horse to expect it to make its own arrangements about jumping most of the fairly small fences which it encounters but to submit to being 'placed' by its rider at a few bigger ones. This adaptability seems to demand experience, confidence in the rider, and general sophistication of an order which many horses may never possess, and the majority of riders in the hunting field cannot 'see a stride' or place their horses correctly to jump fences, and would just be interfering and liable to cause a fall if they tried to do this. Thus, only a relatively few good horsemen on very good horses ride straight to hounds today over a well fenced English hunting country, but the many who have to employ some extra circumspection and discretion to avoid over-facing their horses or themselves enjoy their hunting none the less and also display horsemanship of the most practical kind.

An afterthought which may also occur to many other hunting people is 'Whatever happened to the amble?'. The amble is a true lateral gait very like pacing, but much slower and therefore not involving any rolling motion. It is easy for the horse, comfortable for the rider, faster than a walk, but slower than a trot and thus about right to match the speed of hounds moving at an easy trot to or from the meet or between draws. The amble was the popular pace for fairly leisurely travel throughout the Middle Ages, all over Europe and in much of the rest of the world, and could well be re-introduced and developed in our modern hunters to replace the uncomfortable and irregular hound jog.

'Pig sticking' used also to be called 'hog hunting' and involves the pursuit of wild animals by mounted men, but it is not true hunting because no hounds are used. It does, however, demand a high standard of horsemanship in which skills appropriate to a number of different equestrian activities are incorporated. It grew up with the British Raj in India and reached its zenith between the two World Wars and, since it finished effectively at the outbreak of the second one, hog hunters must now be old and rare. I was privileged to know the late Brigadier Scott-Cockburn, doyen of pig stickers in the heyday of the sport and three times winner of its Blue Riband, the Kadir Cup, and know something of it at second hand from him.

The quarry was the Indian wild boar, male only; fierce, fast and a very brave and cunning adversary which would turn and charge if wounded or when tired and could inflict fearful wounds on horse or man with its long sharp tusks. 'Tent clubs' performed a similar function to that of hunts in arranging and organizing the sport, and this included selecting the area to be 'hunted' on the strength of the number of pigs expected to be found in it and providing beaters to flush them for the horsemen, who would walk up with them, as for walking up grouse or partridges.

Each boar put up would be pursued by a 'heat' consisting of two, three or four riders who would compete with each other, under strictly enforced rules, to gain 'first blood' by being the first to spear the boar, making every effort to kill it cleanly with one thrust. The 'spear' gaining 'first blood' would be the winner of the heat, unless the boar were to escape after being wounded, in which case 'first blood' and a win would go to the man who finally killed it. No crossing, 'riding off' or other interference was allowed between riders in a 'heat' and, to avoid the likelihood of pigs being wounded rather than killed cleanly, riders were expected to use their spears only on the off-side of their horses and generally not on pigs crossing in front of them. A pig spear was like a cavalry lance, but shorter, and had to be razor-sharp.

There is probably no pig sticking done today, even in India or Pakistan, and it would no doubt be condemned as cruel by the growing number of animal rights supporters. A contemplation of what it entailed should, however, be of interest to horsemen because it required a combination of several vital qualities and abilities in both horse and rider. The horse, ideally about 15.2hh., needed to be as quick and handy as a polo pony; and many of them also played polo. It needed at least some of the sagacity and courage of an American Cutting Horse to follow a boar, turn with him, and quite often face a charge from him; and cutting out and holding a bullock from a herd was a well established schooling exercise for pick-sticking horses.

It needed all, and more, of the bold sure-footedness of a good hunter and at least some measure of its jumping ability to be able to gallop confidently over very rough country – usually intersected with dry ditches or nullahs and sometimes covered with head-high grass – to follow the boar over country which the boar himself chose to try to defeat pursuers.

The human hog hunter needed the agility in the saddle of a polo player combined with the firm steady seat of a hunting man, and the ability to avoid falls and survive them. He needed the same 'eye for a country' as a foxhunter and the same skill at arms with his spear as a lancer able to win tent-pegging prizes. Above all, he needed supreme confidence in his horse and its ability to carry him at a fast gallop over very rough country without any significant help from himself. The horse needed an equal degree of confidence in its rider, and this could only be mutually developed by mount and man learning, practising and operating together from the start.

Pig sticking, with its historical links which are older than those of any other kind of hunting, embodies a true test and demonstration of practical all-round horsemanship.

4

Horsemanship in War

The last full-scale cavalry action in history took place in November 1941 when the Russian 44th Mongolian Cavalry Division charged the German 106th Infantry Division near the village of Musino during the German advance on Moscow, and was virtually annihilated by machine-gun fire with artillery support. A French Cavalry Division took the field in the Ardennes in the same year, but was not involved in any major battle and a British Cavalry Division with some 8,000 horses was in operation in Palestine in 1940, but was committed only to patrols and minor skirmishes.

The Polish army which faced the German invaders at the beginning of World War II included a high proportion of horsed cavalry regiments and the German army had horse-drawn artillery, mounted units, including at least one designated *Waffen SS*, and horse transport, throughout the last war. A Turkish Cavalry Division was fully operational though never involved in actual fighting on its country's eastern frontier until the 1960s. The British army used mules for pack transport, particularly in Hong Kong, until 1975.

War was hell for horses and the traditions of the cavalry and the glamour of the *armes blanches* can only be enhanced rather than diminished by the near certainty that they now belong firmly in the past and horses will have no place on any future battlefield. There are plenty of inspiring stories, in history as well as in fiction, about devoted partnerships between soldiers and their horses. The chargers of some famous generals are known by name to have endured long campaigns with their masters and survived to enjoy honourable retirement, but horse casualties in war were invariably much higher than human ones and few ordinary cavalrymen kept their original horses for very long or brought them home with them.

Because horses go lame for so many reasons, many of them quite trivial, and cannot keep up with their companions on the march when they are seriously lame, it is not surprising that many of them were lost other than through enemy action, particularly during retreats and strategic withdrawals. It is thus understandable that cavalry soldiers had constantly to accustom themselves to new mounts, some of which were likely to have had little or no schooling or training. Accordingly, army riding schools have always concentrated on teaching soldiers to be adaptable and to ride all sorts and conditions of horses competently enough to keep pace and station with their comrades without tiring them unduly, rather than on producing combinations of horse and rider to demonstrate classical equitation or be capable of high performance in competitive trials. This same manner and standard of riding is that to which most people who do it for pleasure and recreation aspire. Plenty of horsemen learned and still remember military methods, so that instruction in the Pony Club, riding clubs and many commercial riding schools is based quite closely, though not too imperatively, on that which was established in the army.

Cavalry regiments, and indeed cavalry brigades consisting of three or more regiments with artillery and supporting arms, were expected to travel over any normal country at an average speed of 6mph (10kph) and to be able to march 30 miles (50km) every day for an indefinite period. This may seem a modest aim to an exponent of competitive long distance or endurance riding. If you think, however, that up to 2,000 horses were involved, each carrying an average weight of 17 stone (108kg), that the pace was necessarily regulated to that of the slowest; that they had to cover 200 miles (320km) in a week, consistently enough to be relied on for strategic planning, you will realize that this attainment demanded good horsemanship as well as efficient administration and strict discipline.

On a forced march, a cavalry regiment could cover 60 miles (95km) in a day, and a battery of Horse Artillery could keep up with it but, unless committed immediately to battle or pursuit, the horses would normally have a 24-hour rest after such a march and were not expected to maintain this pace for longer periods. The proud boast of Horse Artillery to be able to keep pace with cavalry over any country which the latter could negotiate was nearly always justified, but Field Artillery, with heavier guns, was not expected to maintain a pace of more than 4mph (6kph) and horse-drawn army transport only averaged 3mph (5kph) but could speed up in an emergency. Pack mules marched at a pace of 3–4mph, which was in part dictated by that of the men on foot who led them, and they could normally be expected to travel at least 20 miles (30km) every day.

Cavalry horses on active service carried an all-up weight ranging from 15 to 20 stone (95 to 130kg) depending on the size of their riders and whether they carried their day's, or larger, rations with them. Both soldiers and horses of the Household Cavalry (The Lifeguards and The Royal Horse Guards), being at least 5ft 10in (1.76m) and 16hh. respectively in height, were bigger than average, but gained no real advantage from their extra size in action, except perhaps in a charge, and were if anything rather disadvantaged by it on active service.

Most cavalry horses were not much more than 15.2hh. and many were under 15hh., particularly those bought as remounts in foreign countries. They were all essentially of weight-carrying conformation and ideally like weight-carrying hunters, although many were more of cob type. The average weight of a cavalry horse in the British army was 9cwt (460kg) so that, with an average all-up weight of over 2cwt (100kg) on his back, he was required to carry a load equivalent to about a quarter of his own body-weight for long periods and occasionally at fast paces. He was thus more heavily laden than a well chosen hunter, which normally carries about one-sixth of his own weight, and, on active service, was under saddle for longer periods, had far fewer rest days, and was sometimes asked to display almost the same speed and activity.

The Royal Horse Artillery in the British army had horses of the same size and type as the cavalry. The six-horse gun teams, driven *à la* postillion by a rider on each near-side horse, pulled a gun and limber which together weighed at least $1^{1}/_{2}$ tons (1.4 tonnes), equivalent to half the aggregate weight of the horses in the team. All the officers and men of a horse artillery battery or regiment were mounted and none rode on the limbers as with field artillery, so that a battery or a regiment of Horse Artillery without its wheeled transport could keep pace with cavalry over almost any country. Field Artillery, with heavier guns and gunners riding on the limbers as well as driving the teams of six horses, were not expected to average more than 4mph (6kph) for a day's march but could usually cover 30 miles (50km) in a day on roads or reasonably good going.

British army transport was based on the General Service Waggon which weighed up to 3 tons (2.7 tonnes) fully loaded and was pulled by a pair of horses driven from a box seat. The horses were generally designated as Heavy Draught Horses by the army, but were of vanner type and not the size of Shires or other English Heavy Horse breeds. They pulled an all-up load which could be as much as twice their own aggregate weight and were generally confined to roads and an average speed of 3mph (5kph), which enabled them easily to keep pace with infantry.

In mountainous or thickly wooded country where tracks were too steep or narrow for wheeled vehicles, the British Army used Pack Mules but, influenced no doubt by apocryphal stories about their stubbornness and intransigence, did not recognize their value or start to use them until World War I. (The Indian Army had employed them for many years before this.)

The big, high quality mules which carried the dismantled parts of the screw guns with which batteries of Mountain Artillery were equipped were up to 15hh. and carried loads of over 3cwt (150kg). Smaller mules used for ordinary transport, which were usually between 13.3hh. and 14hh., carried loads weighing less than 2cwt (100kg). The pace of pack animals is effectively restricted to that of their pedestrian drivers, which cannot reasonably exceed 3mph, but mule drivers had no equipment to carry themselves and were sometimes virtually towed along by their charges so that they often moved rather faster than infantry.

The primary need for mobility required that army horsemen kept their horses always fit enough on active service for the equivalent of a day's hunting, often on sub-standard forage and sometimes on reduced rations, and frequently in the face of demands on their endurance and stamina far greater than those encountered in the hunting field. The men themselves had to be active agile riders with firm seats so as to be unlikely to fall off, and they had to do much of their riding with their reins held only in their left hand so as to leave their right hand free to wield their weapons or control led horses.

Ordinary cavalry soldiers had to be able to sit firmly but lightly on their horses, particularly at the rising trot, so as to avoid giving them sore backs. They had to be able to control them with all four reins in their left hand well enough to keep them in their places in the ranks, sometimes in line with others at the gallop, and to turn them instantly through 90deg to effect changes in front and formation. This, in addition to being able to use swords and sometimes lances and pistols from the saddle, to fire rifles accurately from the ground, and to perform all the duties of a competent groom.

Recruits had to learn the skills quickly to replace casualties in war, to maintain the effective strength of cavalry regiments at all times and, in the Household Cavalry and the King's Troop Royal Horse Artillery still today, to be able to perform ceremonial duties for most of the comparatively short duration of their service on mounted duties. Their basic training could never be allowed to exceed six months and was often shortened in emergency to six weeks, so that it had to be essentially practical and highly intensive. The training period, in practice, usually lasted about five months and included training in riding for about 2 hours, six days a week. The cavalry recruit was then ready to look after his own horse under fairly constant supervision and take his place in the ranks on it for any military purpose, from exercising it, leading a second horse, to charging on it against an enemy, without the risk of letting down his comrades by falling off or losing control.

He had to learn quite quickly, in less than 250 hours of practice in

A cavalry officer on the march with his horse and dog in France in 1916.

the saddle, because the horse strength of a cavalry regiment did not allow for an allocation of more than one horse each day for each recruit and much of his time was taken up with dismounted training and other duties. In effect, soldiers learned to ride more quickly than any civilians (even including lads employed in racing stables) and more comprehensively in terms of the variety of functions which they were taught to perform on horseback than any civilian professional riders, except perhaps hunt servants.

Soldiers learned to ride quickly and quite well. They were taught by good practical horsemen, according to a system which had been established for over 100 years and was constantly revised and improved by dedicated experts who studied equitation as well as the use of the horse in war. Recruits for the British cavalry were taught to ride when they joined their regiments by specialist non-commissioned officers (NCOs) whose semi-official designation was 'Roughriders'; an unfortunate appellation which did not really describe their methods but was hallowed by tradition and not resented.

'Roughriders' were remount riders who were responsible for training young horses as well as young riders. From about 1900 in the British army, most of them had served at a Divisional remount depot where they had been required to break, train and school young horses from scratch. The more senior of them had usually attended a nine-month course at the national cavalry school where, besides undergoing further instruction in higher equitation, including jumping and cross-country riding, they had been taught the most effective methods for teaching riding. They had also been responsible for three horses throughout their course, a trained horse, a half-trained horse and a completely new remount, whose standard of training was expected to be highly advanced at the end of the course as a condition of their rider's passing it.

Regimental Roughriders, or Remount Riders, were in the charge of a Roughriding Sergeant Major (Corporal Major in the case of the Household Cavalry) who instructed most of the recruit rides himself. He was ultimately answerable to the Colonel through the Equitation Officer, whose qualifications were expected to be the same as those of the remount staff, but whose designation was a more delicate one in deference to what was supposed to be his more sophisticated equestrian education. The Equitation Officer sometimes shared his responsibilities with a Riding Master (who was a commissioned Warrant Officer who had been a Roughriding Sergeant Major). He seldom did much instructing himself but was concerned with the horsemanship of the whole regiment. He was always on the lookout for horses and riders of special ability, and frequently discovered and produced combinations of high standard for army, national and even international competitions, as well as regimental teams for competitions and demonstrations of equestrian skill.

Army riding instructors have an advantage over their civilian counterparts in that their pupils are strong, agile, fit young men who cannot complain to any avail if the exercises which they are required to perform make them stiff, sore and generally uncomfortable, or even if they fear that they are likely to cause them painful injury. Civilian students of equitation are seldom so consistently strong and fit as young soldiers and because many of them do not ride every day and most of them pay, at least indirectly, for their instruction, their teachers cannot press them physically as hard as sergeant majors can press soldiers and seldom try to do so.

Army horses used for recruits' riding schools may also have the edge over those available in most commercial riding schools since they are normally worked and exercised more regularly. They are less liable to be over-fresh, except on Monday mornings, and unlikely to be tired and sluggish through being overworked during peak holiday periods. Reminiscences and biographies of cavalrymen tend to dwell on the harsh treatment and discomfort which they claim to have suffered in the riding school, but few of them suggest that the instruction which they received was not effective and, despite the absence of crash helmets or protective headgear until very recent years, very few soldiers have been permanently injured while learning to ride or have developed a distaste for the process which blights their memories of it.

Roughriding Sergeant Majors and their assistant NCOs knew just how far they could go in stretching their pupils to the limits of their physical endurance but not beyond it. The army riding school seemed to be a rough tough arena in which recruits always had to mount without using their stirrups and to remount immediately as soon as they fell off. They soon learned to vault into the saddle of a trotting or galloping horse, and eventually to vault right over it from one side to the other and back again without losing contact with it; the basis of an eventual activity rider and a skill which might one day have saved their lives in battle. They experienced the excruciating discomfort of a 'blanket ride' usually every Saturday morning, and learned to mitigate it by relaxing and keeping their backs supple; an exercise which would eventually save their own bottoms and their horses' backs from getting sore on long marches and instil the rudiments of a deep firm seat in the saddle as a basis for more advanced school riding.

Recruits were and are required to jump fences, although they did not really expect to do much jumping on the battlefield or the parade ground. The fences were never very big, but they were set at difficult distances and awkward angles and often had to be jumped without reins or stirrups. This practice encourages agility in the saddle and determination to stay on the horse and keep 'with it' rather than 'behind it' during moments of sudden acceleration. It also gives a novice rider an insight into the extra difficulties involved in riding actively and making positive demands on his mount, rather than remaining a virtually passive, if tenacious, passenger.

A wider variety of horses is available to army riding instructors than to civilian ones and the warrant officer or NCO in charge of a ride enlists the unwitting co-operation of their individual quirks and foibles to boost the self-confidence of the more timid of his pupils and to deflate that of those who seem to have become over-confident. A nice easy jump on a willing horse facing towards his companions and the riding school door will make a dispirited beginner feel that he is making great progress, but there are always several horses which can be almost guaranteed to stop at a fence, however low, when they are facing it in the other direction and not ridden strongly and kept well in hand. The misanthropic sergeant major will make good use of this probability by ordering conceited young soldiers to ride such a horse at a low fence with his arms crossed and his stirrup leathers four holes shorter than usual, and the result is usually an ignominious fall.

Falling off has always been a regular occurrence in army riding schools. Its apparent identification as an essential part of learning to ride may be responsible for the old saying, which is nowadays quoted less often than it once was, that 'You have to fall off twenty or more times before you can hope to become a horseman'. Whatever the validity of the saying, or the lack of it, the army has seemed to accept it, or at least to have made no noticeable effort to avoid the occasions which have given rise to it. Any resultant injuries, however, have been normally only to self-esteem and generally justified by the need for all soldiers to be able to withstand and survive hard knocks, physical discomfort, and the realization that being paid to ride horses is not an easy option.

The colourful invective traditionally ascribed to army riding in-structors was usually carefully studied with the intention of reducing over-confidence by ridicule and injecting humour and a touch of light-heartedness into proceedings which may have seemed depress-ingly grim to participants who did not feel that their progress was up to standard. It was seldom just coarse barrack-room language repeated boringly for lack of articulate expression, and it deserves the recording for posterity which so much of it has achieved.

The national cavalry schools, which were started in the nineteenth century by the major European countries and the USA following the example set by France at Saumur mostly still exist today, though on a more civilian establishment than was originally intended for them. They have always set very high standards of endeavour and achieve-ment in the study of equitation and horsemanship in general. Some of them have changed their locations; in Britain from Netheravon to Weedon to Melton Mowbray, which is also the Army Remount Depot, but their traditions have been maintained and they are the equivalent in some respects of equestrian universities.

Their ostensible purpose is to train the higher grade remount riders, riding instructors, and equitation officers in courses of between six and nine months' duration which involve each student in looking after and riding three horses: one trained, one half-trained, and one un-trained remount. Three rides each day, normally taken by officer instructors, provide students at such schools with many hours of very active and positive riding over a period of eight or nine months, and on a wide variety of different horses at various stages of training, so that students who pass out well at the end of a course at any recognized cavalry school are accomplished horsemen. They are ready to tackle the complexities of advanced school riding and have practical knowledge of competitive dressage. They will have ridden all sorts of horses over all sorts of fences and be competent cross-country riders with the knowledge and ability to compete in show jumping at well above novice level.

In England the officers at least will have enjoyed some of the best hunting in the world (from Melton Mowbray). They will be capable of training and schooling young horses from the unbroken state to advanced level, at least for all military purposes. They will be capable of teaching other people and will return to their regiments mainly to do this, while the best of them may remain or return to the cavalry school as instructors. The best graduates from Saumur in France can aspire to the *Cadre Noir*, the staff of the French Cavalry School whose demonstrations of advanced dressage and *haute école* are world renowned, and reciprocal arrangements make it still possible for army officers from other countries to join the courses at Saumur.

Mechanized armies make little use of horses or horsemanship, so cavalry schools now operate on a modest scale with small establishments and slender budgets, but the training which they offer is still as intensive as ever, inspired by the best cavalry traditions, and readily adapted to the requirements of present day competitive riding.

The daily routine of a cavalry regiment both in barracks and on the march affords an interesting study in horsemanship, or at least horsemastership. The system enables large numbers of horses to be kept fit and well in situations and locations which are often far from ideal for this purpose, by men who are more than adequate in number by any standards, but have many other tasks and duties to perform and are by no means all experts at the job.

The usual routine in the British army was based on three parades for 'stables' each day: the first at 6 a.m. (6.30 in winter), the second at mid-day or whenever the morning mounted work was finished, and the third at 5 p.m. At morning stables, the first parade, the bedding was removed and laid out in rows to dry and the stalls were cleaned out before the horses were quartered, or brushed over, and had their feet picked out and their noses and docks sponged and were left to eat their first feeds while the men had breakfast.

At midday stables, the horses were groomed, their bedding was replaced, and their head collars were cleaned. They were then led out into the yard to be inspected individually by troop officers or sergeants before being fed. At evening stables, each horse was whisped for about twenty minutes after being groomed and his bed was set fair before he was inspected in his stall by an officer or sergeant and given his feed.

Stable parades seldom, if ever, lasted for more than one hour although men had often to 'do' two horses to make up for comrades on leave or detached duty. Grooming was expected to be done thoroughly but quickly and constant inspections ensured that it was not skimped. One man, the stable guard, was always on duty day and night in each troop stable, where he could see and hear all the horses in his charge. He was kept busy filling and distributing hay nets, giving extra feeds and picking up droppings. It was his work which enabled his comrades to spend relatively little time attending to their horses so as to fit their other parades and duties – which included cleaning their saddlery, uniform and equipment – into a normal day's work. Special instructions for stable guards, concerning such matters as extra feeds, were written on a large blackboard in each troop stable and each horse's name was always inscribed over his stall for immediate identification.

Army horses have always lived in stalls (which are the only form of stabling in which the system can work properly and which can be fitted into a barracks of normal size). Army stables were fitted with water, piped to each stall long before this invaluable aid to stable management was common in civilian yards, and army horses learn very quickly to press the lever to fill their small bowls. Before the introduction of this refinement, horses had to be led out in pairs to drink at long troughs in the yard at the start of each stable parade. At Hyde Park Barracks in the middle of Knightsbridge, the early exercise for horses not required for other duty that day, which involves ridden and led horses on a scale of one man to two horses and which must be off the streets before the traffic fills up so that it takes place before breakfast, is still known as 'The Watering Order'.

Troop sergeants were normally responsible for feeding the horses in their troops and they doled out the appropriate quantities of crushed oats and chaff for each horse into large circular tins which were placed or stacked at the rear of each stall and could have names or special instructions chalked on them. The men tipped their horses' feeds into their mangers all at the same time at the end of stable parades, to avoid any becoming agitated through impatience or jealousy, and late feeds and any extra feeds were given by the stable guards at the times prescribed. The army has always preferred to add chaff to corn feeds because this gives them added bulk and prevents greedy horses bolting their oats. The large number of men available for fatigues makes chaff-cutting economical and means that hay nets need only be given to most horses at midday and in the evening.

In camp and on the march, cavalry horses were and still are picketed by having the head ropes from their head collars tied to a long line strung between posts at a height of about 4ft (1.20m) from the ground and one hind heel, attached to a peg in the ground behind each horse about 14ft (4m) from the picket line. Camp sites, and overnight halts where possible, were located close to rivers or clear streams at which horses could be watered directly where the banks made this possible, but a canvas water bucket and at least one nosebag for feeds formed part of the essential active service equipment for each horse.

In barracks and in camp, army horses were expected to be exercised for at least two hours each day except on Sundays, and they still are so far as their situation permits this. Unhurried marches were planned and timed so that horses would not be carrying the weight of their riders for much more than five hours and could be watered, fed and rested until the next morning after this period of work.

The march routine consisted of an early start, but well after first daylight so as to avoid preparations having to be made in the dark, a halt for 2 or 3 minutes after the first mile or so to check that all was in order, and thereafter a 5- or 10-minute halt in each hour. The army manuals recommended a longer halt every 2 or 3 hours for horses to be fed and have their saddles removed, but most regimental and squadron commanders preferred to keep going with fit horses for up to 5 hours and have a longer and more comfortable halt overnight.*

With hardened soldiers and very fit horses, cavalry and horse artillery moving in small bodies could march for up to 10 hours in a day, with a long midday halt for water and food and to avoid the worst of the heat in hot countries. This rate of travel, however, left stragglers and supply services well behind and was only justified for emergency forced marches when it could just enable mounted soldiers to move 60 miles (95km) in a day or 250 miles (400km) in a week. Cavalry units preferred to march on a broad front whenever possible and to vary their pace from the normal trot so far as the going permitted, cantering for periods of 5–10 minutes over good ground and walking with the men dismounted two or three times each day, so as to maintain an average speed of about 6mph (10kph).

British army saddles, and those of most other armies, are of a pattern which has not altered significantly for over 200 years. It is designed to achieve a practical compromise between the requirement to provide a secure and reasonably comfortable seat for the rider (which keeps him over his horse's centre of balance with most of the length of his legs in contact with its sides) and the need to keep quite

* The Royal Horse Guards (The Blues) owned a sophisticated, fast-moving, horse-drawn field kitchen which enabled them to eat more elaborately and much earlier than other troops with whom they found themselves encamped at the end of long marches. In an effort to avoid the jealousy caused by the fact that the officers of The Blues were often sitting down to a good dinner before the men of other regiments had finished drawing their rations, the same trumpet call was used for their officers' dinner as for 'cookhouse' for the soldiers; the custom is continued to this day, even in barracks.

heavy weight distributed evenly over its back between its shoulder blades and its loins, but clear of both these parts of its anatomy. Since weapons and numerous items of equipment must also be attached to an army saddle, or suspended from it, it has to be strong and generally rigid and may look rather more like a pack saddle than a hunting saddle.

The construction of an army saddle is based on two wooden side bars which lie along the horse's back, resting on the muscles each side of its spine. The bars are fixed to each other by two steel arches at front and rear which curve well over the withers and backbone and form the pommel and cantle of the saddle. The leather seat, to which the saddle flaps, girths and stirrup leathers are attached, is in effect suspended between the front and rear arches so as to be clear of the horse's back, and the side bars extend in front of and behind the seat where they are known as the 'burrs' and 'fans' respectively and carry fittings to which weapons and equipment can be secured. The side bars usually have felt panels strapped along their lengths, but army saddles must also always have a large, specially-folded blanket placed underneath them, which serves as a thick numnah and can be unfolded to double as clothing to keep the horse warm on cold picket lines.

Army saddles are made in several different sizes but are necessarily adaptable, according to how the blanket is folded, to fit any horse at a pinch. Army horses wear their own particular saddles on all occasions but, in the case of British and most foreign cavalry regiments, they are adorned with shabracks, covers and other ornate embellishments which effectively disguise their utilitarian appearance for ceremonial parades.

Service bridles and draught harness for British army horses were standardized in 1911 and all bridles now consist of a strong head collar with a bridle head secured over it to which is attached an army port-mouthed reversible bit with double reins to provide the action of a pelham bridle. The port-mouthed reversible bit, with its three separate slots to which the reins can be fixed to vary the severity of the curb action, is extraordinarily versatile and adaptable to suit most horses and it was quickly adopted for civilian use, notably with harness horses. Given the limitations of a pelham bit, it operates satisfactorily with only one pair of reins attached and is used in this way for the horses of gun teams.

Cavalry soldiers are, however, required to ride with four reins, often all held in the left hand, perhaps for extra security in case one rein breaks or is cut in battle. Officers, chargers and the horses of all ranks of the Household Cavalry wear older pattern more ornate bridles with bradoons and elegantly curved Buxton curb bits on state and ceremonial occasions. Their riders are required to maintain contact only with the bottom rein and leave the bradoon rein looped loosely over their little fingers.

Weapons which soldiers are expected to be able to use from the saddle are sword, lance and pistol. The sword, as the primary weapon of all horse soldiers and because of its associations with chivalry, has been jealously retained by all cavalry regiments, even in recent years and in circumstances in which it has been obviously ineffectual, because without it they would have become mounted infantry – a role to which Dragoons were always well, though reluctantly, accustomed although they never admitted it.

Sabres with which British other ranks were armed before 1910 were slightly curved, although officers' swords always had straight blades, and these were retained with full dress after straight service swords were introduced for all ranks, and they are still used by the Household Cavalry.

Swords and sabres used by mounted men are intended for cutting as well as thrusting and quite complicated drills for their use were devised and practised interminably – and pretty certainly forgotten in the heat of battle when increasingly rare opportunities to charge an enemy resulted in hand-to-hand fighting. The only essential manipulation, especially with a straight sword, was to thrust with a locked elbow and the wrist well turned, so that the blade entered an opponent's body straight and with the edge facing upwards so as to enable it to be withdrawn more easily from his falling body.

The lance, poetically known as 'The Queen of Weapons', has almost more association with chivalry and equestrian pageantry than the sword, but it has not been of much practical value in war for the past 300 years, even in the hands of experts in its use, most of whom have been Poles. An unwieldy weapon, it has always been cruelly effective against routed infantry soldiers fleeing on foot after defeat and has sometimes proved surprisingly intimidating against unsteady or ill-disciplined troops in the first shock of an engagement initiated by a fast charge. However, despite constant practice in drills designed to perfect its use on dummies, few Western cavalrymen ever found a second target with their lances, and many discarded them as soon as battle was joined without even blooding them. Pictures of the aftermaths of battles showing squadrons of lancers leaving the field with rows of pennons fluttering bravely in the breeze are suspect as to accuracy for this reason.

The lance was used extensively by light cavalrymen in Eastern Europe and India. It was often employed against ill-disciplined opponents, but it found relatively little favour in western armies. It was not carried in battle by any British troops after 1650, until three Light Dragoon Regiments were armed with it in 1816. They were hoping that this might help them to emulate the success of the Polish Lancers who were allies of the French in the Peninsular War, and that it would enable them to deal with their dismounted adversaries during the Sikh Wars thirty years later. (The Sikh's courageous tactics were to lie curled up on the ground and hamstring cavalry horses which galloped over them in a charge.)

At the end of the nineteenth century six of the thirty-one regular British cavalry regiments were Lancers and for a few years during this period the front rank men of Dragoon Guards and Dragoon regiments also carried lances. The last full-scale charge by a British Lancer Regiment was that of the 21st Lancers against the Madhi's forces at the Battle of Omdurman. Winston Churchill took part in this but, being an officer, and in fact detached from the 4th Hussars, he did not carry a lance and wisely did not even draw his sword, but relied on an automatic pistol. The lance was finally dispensed with in the British Army in 1927.

Early firearms for mounted soldiers were large 'horse pistols' carried in pairs on each side of the pommels of their saddles, which still form part of the state or ceremonial saddlery of cavalry regiments. Cavalry officers have always been armed with pistols as well as swords and as soon as revolvers, and later automatics, were invented they carried just one, in a holster on their belts in service dress.

Dragoons and their equivalents in most European armies were armed with muskets even early in the seventeenth century. Muskets were long-muzzle loaders and Dragoons had to dismount to load and fire them – a procedure which was considered to be contrary to cavalry tradition and has been resisted by mounted soldiers ever since.

The invention of breech-loading firearms and cartridges with percussion caps led to the development of the carbine which was much shorter than the musket and supposed to be able to be fired from the saddle. It never was, at least with any accuracy or effect, by British or Western European cavalrymen. However, Cossack soldiers, who were more agile riders with an Eastern tradition which recognized horse archers, used it quite successfully, as did American mounted troops and their opponents, who were often Red Indians.

When infantry soldiers acquired rifles with magazines and bolt actions at the end of the nineteenth century, most cavalry soldiers were also issued with them and the carbine became obsolete. Soldiers were not expected to fire their rifles from the saddle and were frequently relegated to a mounted infantry role in which one man of a section of four held all four horses, while his three companions advanced on foot to shoot. Since the turn of the century, the revolver has been the only firearm which a mounted soldier has been expected to use from his horse, and all ranks of cavalry regiments are required to be proficient with it.

The modern cavalry soldier is encouraged to demonstrate his 'skill at arms' in special competitions which form part of his training and are often arranged to provide spectator attractions at horse and agricultural shows and outdoor tournaments. The form of this competition is stereotyped and it consists of a course up to a quarter mile (400m) in length in which three spring-mounted, straw-stuffed dummies, three balloons, two 2in (50cm) diameter rings at head-height and a peg driven into the ground are set out at approximately equal distances from each other. The requirement is for the competitor to pierce each dummy through its centre with a sword (the centre is marked by a small disc). The first dummy is to the rider's right, the second to his left, and the third beside a small fence which he must jump as he engages his target. He leaves his sword stuck through the third dummy, scoring full marks only if the edge of the blade is facing upwards, and quickly draws his revolver from the holster on his belt. This is loaded with blank cartridges and he must burst the three balloons by firing it straight and close to them. The balloons are fixed, as the dummies, to right and left on the ground and the third to a small fence.

The competitor must next replace his revolver in its holster and take up a lance, on whose point he must take the two small rings which are held lightly on gallows to his right at head-height. Immediately afterwards he must pick the 2in-wide peg out of the ground on his right and carry it on the point of his lance over the finishing line. The time allowed for the course requires quite a fast gallop throughout and few competitors ever score full marks for accuracy and by finishing with both rings and the peg on their lances, so that results are seldom decided against the clock.

Cuirasses, amounting to body armour covering the chest and back, are still part of the full dress uniforms of all ranks of the British Household Cavalry except farriers and trumpeters. They were never worn in war, however, because although they are not unduly heavy, they restrict arm movement considerably and make it almost impossible for a man to mount his horse from the ground while wearing them. German and French cuirassiers, however, who were similarly attired, continued to wear cuirasses in battle until the end of the nineteenth century.

Cavalry soldiers and their horses, of all nations, amply deserve the proud tradition of equestrian splendour which history has accorded them. Their value and their victories depended more on long fast marches over very rough country during which they had to nurse tired and often underfed horses in bad weather, rather than on displays of dashing bravery in headlong charges. This, however, emphasizes the all-round horsemanship required of them without reducing the heroic reputation to which their illustrious record of service entitles them.

5

Horsemanship over Coloured Fences

Show jumping started about 100 years ago, in Paris in 1886, and rapidly became a specialized form of horsemanship in which riders aimed only to jump their horses over high, rather flimsy, fences without knocking them down, and those which jumped highest on the day usually won. By 1950 the concept altered, internationally and in Britain, and the idea that height alone should decide competitions was largely abandoned and retained only in respect of a relatively few puissance competitions in which a limited number of horses with special power and ability still compete. Show jumping at its top or international level is now a supreme test of horsemanship, as well as of the physical abilities of the horses concerned.

Any horse can jump over a fence which is 3ft 9in (1.15m) high with a 4ft (1.20m) spread, but many cannot physically manage much more than this. Because the courses built for big international competitions include fences which may be 5ft 3in (1.6m) high – 5ft 7in (1.7m) for jump offs – and others which may be 4ft 9in (1.45m) high with a spread of 7ft 3in (2.2m), early selection, and even some physical testing without a rider is a prerequisite for the training and production of a top class showjumper.

For interest and comparative consideration, the official high jump record, as certified by the International Equestrian Federation is 8ft 1¼in (2.47m). It is held by the gelding Huaso ridden by Captain Alberto Larraguibel Morales in Santiago, Chile in 1949. The unofficial uncertified record is credited to the Australian horse Golden Meade, ridden by Jack Martin, who is said to have jumped a height of 8ft 6in (2.6m) at Cairns, Queensland in 1946. Most people assume that the latter jump was achieved with the aid of a very springy take-off, perhaps even a well covered springboard, and both this jump and the one in Chile were over a special fence composed of sloping poles, which is seldom used today.

Both jumps were obviously one-off achievements which owed a lot to luck and everything coming just right at the critical moment. They were never repeated by the horses concerned and no serious attempts have been made ever since to match or surpass them, but horses do have to jump at least 7ft (2.10m) nowadays to have any chance in the puissance competitions of which there is usually one at most big shows.

In order to become a good showjumper, a horse must have good conformation, with strong loins, quarters, hocks and hind legs generally, and possess an appearance of quality and a bold willing outlook. Horses show expression on their faces rather more than most animals and this is quite an important key to an appreciation of their temperaments and whether these are likely to suit the training and the requirements of competition which they must face.

Time was when conformation and quality were not held to be of much importance for a showjumper. They were reckoned to come in all types, shapes and sizes and the adage 'Handsome is as handsome does' was quoted regularly to support this view. Some curiously shaped horses which looked as if they would have been more at home in the farm yard than the arena jumped big fences gallantly and well during the 1950s. However, during the past twenty-five years courses have become increasingly complex, with distances between fences set deliberately to demand constant alterations in the lengths of horses' strides. There is also a much higher incidence of clear rounds to be decided by jump-offs against the clock. These factors have put a premium on fairly fast horses with the natural balance and flexibility not normally found in common ugly horses to cope with these requirements, and top class showjumpers are now all horses of clear quality with a predominance, or at least a strong admixture, of Thoroughbred blood.

A few experienced show jumping riders who are also highly educated horsemen have opined that the ideal showjumper should be a slightly stupid horse. He should also show some lack of sensitivity, which will help him to put up with the repetitive tedium of jumping over interminable successions of unnatural looking obstacles, day after day, without any apparent purpose in terms of what happens when he gets to the other side of them. No animals are really clever or conversely stupid and they do not suffer from boredom in the same way that people do, but most are intelligent to some degree and, although horses do not rate highly for intelligence in general, it may well be that some lack of it, as compared with other horses, is helpful in enabling a showjumper to endure the constant nagging to which he must submit during his early training. The nagging will continue until it has its desired effect and until the horse's wonderful

Harvey Smith riding at Hickstead.

innate willingness to strive to please his rider by performing well takes over and makes him usually genuinely happy in the satisfaction that he is doing his job well.

To have good prospects for show jumping a rider must be supple, agile, fairly athletic and not too heavy (a man ought to weigh well under 12 stone (76kg) up to the age of twenty-five). Quick reactions and good muscular co-ordination are essential, and a special ability that is especially vital to a show jumping rider is that of being able to 'see a stride' (*see* Chapter 2). This jargon phrase is used to describe a rider's ability to assess the number of full strides which his horse will need to take for his hind feet to land in the middle of the take-off zone in front of a fence, from the earliest point and moment at which he is able to make this assessment. In practice, this enables the rider to allow his horse to go forward taking full strides with full impulsion from the point at which he can 'see' the strides required, with reasonable confidence that his last stride will land his hind feet in the right position for them to kick off and launch him over the fence. The greater the number of such strides that the rider can 'see', the more impulsion he can confidently impart to his horse. This impulsion will, in turn, encourage the horse to produce a powerful jump at just the right place without any hesitation or decrease of momentum, and this is important to enable him to clear big spread fences.

Some experienced riders reckon to be able to 'see' up to six strides and regularly demonstrate this ability in jumping wide water obstacles. Others seem only to be able to see two or three with certainty and plenty of people who only ride over relatively small courses where such accuracy is less significant honestly admit that they cannot 'see a stride' at all and prefer to leave these arrangements to the horse rather than try to do so themselves. There are almost certainly some people who simply do not possess the 'eye' to be able to master this skill at all and, although it can be developed quite quickly by most young riders, there is opinion and evidence to suggest that it does not continue to improve in anyone over the age of thirty-six.

Until the middle of this century in Britain, and for about twenty years after this in the case of national competitions in the USA and Canada, show jumping courses were comparatively simple. They consisted of elementary arrangements of single fences set out in stereotyped rectangular or figure-of-eight patterns with plenty of space between them. The space allowed for a separate approach to be made to each one, and no time limits were imposed to introduce any urgency to the proceedings. The sole requirement was for the horse to jump the fences without touching them and to this effect very light laths were placed on top of them. Dislodging the laths cost one penalty if it was caused by the front feet and half a penalty if it was caused by the hind feet, even if the fence itself was not knocked down for a greater number of penalties.

This procedure required very perceptive and sharp-sighted judging to determine whether laths had been dislodged by fore feet or hind feet. Most judging, unfortunately, was undertaken by local dignitaries whose seniority in the community owed more to maturity than keenness of vision. They sat in the middle of the ring on shooting sticks looking magisterial rather than vigilant, so that objections and protests to the decision of these old gentlemen were frequent, particularly when half penalties divided contestants. The obvious solution – to charge the same penalties for a touch with the hind feet as with the fore feet – was not widely resorted to and a cynical critic of the system quoted Cicero to complain in the press that 'Although justice was expected to be blind and to know nobody' judges at local horse shows, though often apparently blind, certainly knew everybody. The implication that they favoured their friends when they were in doubt was unfair, but the method of judging was unsatisfactory, not least because it led to an obsession with rapping to make horses pick their feet up higher to avoid touching fences.

Rapping was almost an integral concomitant of the training of a showjumper during the early years of the sport while the laths were in use and the slightest touch incurred faults. So much so that the late Colonel Paul Rodzianko, a world renowned rider, teacher and trainer of national teams, wrote a book in 1937 called *Modern Horsemanship* in which a chapter about the training of showjumpers started with the recommendation that a good hunter could be trained for show jumping in two weeks. The chapter then went on to devote most of its content to what Rodzianko called 'tapping' and a description of a rather complicated apparatus, involving cords and pulleys and lengths of lead gas piping, with which this could be done harmlessly and effectively. In justice to a great horseman, he did specify that the good hunter in question should have been trained and schooled from the start for the hunting field according to his own very sound methods. His own tapping apparatus was a sensible device with which a competent operator could persuade a horse to jump higher over both spread and upright fences than he would need to out hunting, and to tuck his feet up a bit to avoid any chance of a touch, without injuring or hurting him or even risking discouraging him.

When the laths and penalties for touches were finally abandoned, rapping ceased to be justified. Although experimenting continued with the weight and diameter of poles and the depth of the cups in which they were held to discover the optimum resistance to a knock which could not risk causing a fall or hurting a horse, only clumsy insensitive horses deliberately hit fences and these were unlikely to become good performers, however intense or sophisticated the training they received. Rapping was soon condemned by the International Equestrian Federation and prohibited on show grounds in Europe and Britain, and eventually, special stewards were appointed to prevent it and report offenders.

In the USA, national competitions under the old rules (with laths) continued to be held for some years in parallel with those under international ones, under which rapping was forbidden, often at the same shows. This led to a curious anomaly in the presence of the 'Poler', who was in attendance in the collecting ring, with the full approval of the authorities, during national competitions, but banned from the whole show ground during international ones. The Poler was an almost licensed or semi-official functionary who rapped people's horses over the practice jump for a fee ranging from one to five dollars just before they entered the ring to jump.

He did this very skilfully with a long light bamboo pole by giving them a rap on the front or hind legs, as requested by their riders, at the critical moment, to remind them to tuck their feet well up. He never hurt or discouraged a horse, and would have lost his job or concession if he had ever done so, and his art consisted in kidding the horse into supposing that he had hit the fence and would have to try harder to avoid doing so, and in knowing just how often he could do this in each individual case before the horse would detect his intervention and cease to be deceived. The Poler was an artist and an intelligent horseman within his own restricted sphere of operations, which could hardly have been condemned as cruel by even the most sensitive spectators. His attendance made it generally unnecessary for competitors to make other more clumsy arrangements for his function to be carried out less scrupulously behind the scenes.

Scandals concerning cruelty to showjumpers continue to hit the headlines about once in every five years. These are invariably centred on the practice of rapping, and national equestrian federations go to great and very expensive lengths to ensure that this is at least never done in public view. Most successful trainers and riders of showjumpers probably never rap their horses at all nowadays and any that do do it with great discretion and precision in exceptional cases to remind clever horses not to spare the extra effort required to jump cleanly over poles which they have discovered will roll and fall harmlessly if they do not make it.

No organization can monitor what people do in the privacy of their

David Broome in the saddle. He is sitting well forward over a big fence and giving his mount every assistance to jump it clearly.

homes however, and there is a great deal of low-level show jumping in England which involves some people who are sadly ignorant and incompetent. They try to get quick results with unsuitable horses on a part-time basis by desperate and undesirable methods. When they resort to clumsy rapping on rough ground over badly-built fences, this usually produces lame horses or habitual refusers and a general disillusionment which persuades them to try some other sport. However, more horses are probably tormented and ultimately ruined just as much by being badly ridden with inappropriate bits in their mouths by teenagers seeking a short cut to elusive equestrian stardom than by rapping.

As an arena attraction which is relatively cheap to arrange and easy to film and televise, show jumping attracts more publicity and attention from the media than any other equestrian endeavour except racing. Spectators get close to the action and gain a clear view of it, and journalists write copious magazine and newspaper articles about it, some of which are sensational rather than informative. Fans copy their idols' bad habits as well as their good ones and do not discriminate when they see them using unconventional methods or peculiar gadgetry to obtain quick results in emergency situations. They do not appreciate that these must be employed with great skill and discretion.

Some years ago a distinguished and very capable international show jumping rider rode one of his best horses in a Blair pattern bitless bridle, no doubt for valid veterinary reasons. His first few public appearances with this unusual appliance, which was incorrectly identified as a Hackamore – a Hackamore is actually an American cowboy's bridle made entirely of cord and rawhide with no metal attachments – caused unprecedented demands for similar bridles from novice riders. They thought their own horses would go better in them, and enterprising saddlers produced them, no doubt at a stiff price.

A Blair bridle is actually a very severe device which can exert great pressure on a horse's nose through the leverage imposed by its long metal cheeks. In expert hands it has great stopping power, but it obviously has limited lateral action for steering purposes and, if fitted too low which it usually is, it can almost stop a horse from breathing by squeezing his nasal passages. For some time after this unusual bridle came to the notice of aspiring show jumping riders, nervous novices who had hurried to adopt it were being run away with all over the minor show grounds of Great Britain by horses with very sore noses who had become maddened by pain, could not be steered, and would not stop until their riders became exhausted and stopped pulling on the reins, or they virtually stopped breathing on the point of suffocation.

An intelligently devised apparatus was produced and promoted in the early 1980s which was called a 'balancing rein'. It could be fitted in three different ways, or positions, which were clearly explained in a pamphlet supplied with it, and between them these managed to incorporate most of the operations and effects provided by draw reins, running reins, the Market Harborough martingale, and the two French devices, the *chambon* and the *gogue*. It could only be classified as gadgetry and was intended only as a training aid, but its ingenious inventor had managed to avoid or soften most of the ill-effects inherent in the appliances on which its construction was based. It was also approved by a number of reputable horsemen as a contrivance which competent operators could use harmlessly and effectively to take legitimate short cuts in the correction of horses with faulty head carriages.

The tentative use of this apparatus by a number of well known show jumping riders, who understood its purpose and could follow the instructions and operate it in accordance with them, quickly led to its indiscriminate mis-use by a host of inexperienced enthusiasts. These riders could not understand the principles on which it operated or the instructions which explained them, and its very proper condemnation by the Pony Club resulted in its becoming unfairly discredited in a turmoil of suspicious controversy.

To be able to compete successfully in competitions beyond grade C (British Show Jumping Association grade equivalent to the international grade L), show jumping riders need to be able to school and ride their horses on the flat to a general standard appropriate to the execution of national (British Horse Society) dressage tests of elementary standard or international tests set for Horse Trials (*Concours Complet International* or CCI).

Most regular riders bring their horses up to about this standard before they do much serious jumping. They could ride them creditably in an appropriate dressage competition if they could spare the time to divert them, and themselves, to this purpose for two or three weeks. There are probably no top class show jumping riders today who are not well able to start a young horse from scratch and give him his basic schooling, and nearly all of them do this work themselves along sound orthodox lines which provide a proper preparation for any subsequent activity, not just show jumping.

The advanced training and weekly routine of a successful showjumper must also include plenty of work on the flat in the *manège* and most riders try to give their horses about three 30-minute sessions a week of the equivalent of dressage work, in addition to their normal exercise, and this even during periods of intensive competition. Regular school work on the flat, and occasionally over *cavaletti*, is essential to enable a show jumping rider to correct incipient faults in his horses and to re-instil in them instant obedience to the aids and acceptance of control of their impulsion. Impulsion naturally tends to increase with the excitement and high spirits engendered by regular successful performances in the ring. They probably do not practise advanced movements such as passage, piaffe, and flying changes of leg at predetermined strides, but half halts, smooth instant transitions between extension and collection and balanced canter pirouettes are practical requisites of the stock in trade of a successful showjumper and his rider must know how to ask for them and induce their performance.

The value of a few days' hunting to a showjumper during a busy season is perhaps more debatable, in terms of the increased risk of injury which this involves. However, showjumpers, like all horses, need a few weeks' holiday each year and when the dictates of the competitive year destine these for the winter months, owners and riders are generally willing to take the risk. The change of scene and routine is much more refreshing for their horses and gives them an enjoyable occupation to enliven what would otherwise be a rather dull rest on reduced rations.

Riding a showjumper, no less than riding any other horse for any other purpose, must be learned from instruction and apprenticeship. The skills required can only be improved, but not established, by watching other people practise them, on film or in the flesh, or by reading books or listening to lectures. Only a few riders with great natural talent can honestly claim to be largely self-taught, and they have probably spoiled a number of good horses in the process. Sadly, the number of young riders in Britain who are very keen to go show jumping vastly exceeds the number of horsemen who are able and willing to teach them to do this to any standard above very elementary level. Moreover, the cost of learning the game in a stable qualified to teach it properly in the few years available to a teenager who contemplates it as a full-time career is generally beyond the pocket or the indulgence of most parents. Even the most successful Yuppie is unlikely to make his own fortune before he reaches the age of twenty-six and after this, it is too late to aspire to the highest levels.

Week-end showjumpers, who keep a horse at home or at the local riding school and depend on its proprietor to give them occasional tuition, can have plenty of fun at local shows under these arrangements, but this seldom satisfies them and their spasmodic efforts to upgrade themselves and their horses usually end in expensive disillusion.

The best and most certain way for a young rider to make the grade in show jumping is for him to work very hard full time at one of the regrettably few successful yards which take pupils; and to pay quite high fees for the privilege. The owner or manager, who is likely to be a successful show jumping rider nearing or just past retirement from the ring, will provide invaluable instruction, coaching and general super-vision, including at shows where he will ensure that the learner rides an appropriate range of suitable horses in novice competitions. When his protégé is ready to ride over big fences, he will find him a good honest grade A horse to buy, just past his best in terms of years, on which he will be able to gain vital experience of really testing courses designed by top class builders.

The learner will not improve his first grade A horse, and indeed will probably win few prizes on it and shake its confidence and ruin its reputation. It will be a very valuable schoolmaster, however, and worth the relatively high price which it will cost, as the most significant factor in the production of a rider of prospective star quality.

The manager or owner will quite legitimately make a good profit out of his apprentice or his parents, part of which may well be commission on the price of any horses bought for him to ride. Only an infant prodigy with very good connections can expect other people to pay for horses for him to practise on, and the guide and mentor of a keen and competent young rider will take personal pleasure in the progress of a promising pupil and provide him with introductions, opportunities and references to enable him to make the best use of such talent as he may develop and perhaps eventually earn good money.

The ideal seat for a show jumping rider is now very much like the original forward seat introduced by Captain Federico Caprilli in Italy 100 years ago, as can be seen by a study of photographs of him and his contemporaries in action. The acrobatics, sometimes verging on aero-batics, which enlivened show jumping rings during the 1930s, 1940s and early 1950s are no longer seen today. They cannot be sustained over modern courses which demand that riders keep their horses balanced and on their bits at all times so that they are fully prepared to jump the next fence the instant that they have landed over the previous one.

There may be some advantage in a rider flinging his body completely clear of his horse's back at the summit of his bascule or parabola over a very high fence – at least in terms of freeing his hindquarters of any possible weight at the point when he needs to hitch them over it. Riders still do this to a modified extent in jumping the big wall, which is the last of the three of four fences of a puissance competition.

The big wall requires riders to keep with their horses up a very steep ascent, but only really to avoid falling onto their necks or off them altogether on landing, after which they only have to cross the finishing line together. However, the weight of the rider as well as of the horse must be lifted from the ground at the point of take-off. No effort at acrobatic agility can really result in the rider effectively taking off before the horse and saving him from having to lift both weights at the same time. The practical seat for the job is therefore one in which the rider keeps the top half of his body always well forward of the verticle, with his seat bones generally just above the saddle, but ready to resume instant contact with it just before take-off and immediately after landing, and his legs in an orthodox position just behind the line of the girths.

Riders who tend, from habit or over-enthusiasm, to get too far forward up their horses' necks may often get away with this, provided that they do it after take-off and get back again immediately after landing; that the next fence is not too close and the competition is not to be decided on time. However, any tendency to be in front of the movement while the horse's feet are on the ground is liable to unbalance him and shorten his stride and this is disastrous in combinations and timed jump offs. Horses whose riders get in front of the movement between fences also seem liable to rush their fences more than others, no doubt in sub-conscious anxiety to catch up with their human partners.

Show jumping riders hold their reins in a variety of ways, some of which have been experimental and curiously unorthodox. The axiom that the line from the rider's elbow through his hand and the rein to the horse's mouth should be a straight one holds good for nearly all of them. Most riders usually bridge their reins to help them to keep their balance or regain it immediately after landing over fences, but those whose seats and confidence are strong enough to enable them to dispense with this assistance probably have more positive precise contact with their horses' mouths and may gain some advantage from this, particularly in speed competitions.

Showjumpers have a tough time for the period of their preliminary and elementary training. They have to endure strict discipline and fairly frequent testing which may bewilder them and will certainly put them under physical strain. Those which do not make the grade may have the good fortune to be passed on to go hunting, an agreeable occupation for which their schooling will have made them especially adaptable, but they will all depend very much on their owners. Those which end up in the care of incompetent ignorant people may have a rather miserable life involving long periods of semi-neglect punctuated by occasional attempts at jumping courses in public which may test them unfairly and, ultimately, almost to destruction. The primary cause of the misfortune of horses in this latter category is the very popularity of show jumping in Great Britain and its wide appeal to a great number of people, some of whom do not have the mental, physical or financial means to pursue their interest in it properly.

Horses which do make the grade (grade A in two or three years and international prospects in three or four) enjoy very happy lives, more pleasant than those of almost any other types of horses. They are the equine equivalents of tennis and golf stars, and jet setters and globe trotters of the human species. Constant travel in luxury horse boxes, and even more smoothly by air, is no more tiring for a horse standing on four legs than for a human being sitting in a padded seat. Continual changes of scene and stabling maintain interest and mental alertness in conditions which are nearly always quite comfortable. Although most people find standing about on public premises among strangers tedious and frustrating, the horse is a happily simple and very gregarious animal who genuinely enjoys the company of others of his kind in these circumstances. He will wait patiently and contentedly all day for his 2 or 3 minutes of exciting, but not too exhausting, performance before his public.

Most of all, horses clearly take pleasure in doing well what they have been trained to do, and in the applause and acclamation which

The late and much lamented Caroline Bradley riding Tigre in classical show jumping style. She died prematurely before her partnership with her other and more famous grey horse, Milton, could come to full fruition.

they receive for winning prizes. The life of a successful showjumper is therefore one of physical and mental contentment in an atmosphere of relatively carefree sophistication born of high endeavour to which few other animals can ever aspire.

The world's top show jumping riders, and there are probably about 500 people who can reasonably claim to be in this category, are all undeniably very good horsemen. They thoroughly understand and regularly practise all the basic principles and skills of equitation, horsemanship and horsemastership and could give a good account of themselves in most other horse activities besides show jumping if they could spare the time from what is now, for almost all of them, an all year round professional employment for which they are beholden to owners and sponsors as well as all the horses they ride, including their own.

6

Horsemanship in the Dressage Arena

A distinguished equestrian journalist who has been dead for some years used to regale his friends in the collecting rings and beer tents of horse shows with amusing *bons mots*. One of his favourites was that 'Dressage in Britain is old women buying fast horses and spending a long time trying to make them go slowly'. Although his pen was often caustic, he was by nature a courteous and kindly man. He admired our British 'dressage queens' and would not have dreamed of offending them, so he never published his epigram. However, none of the ladies to whom he was referring is without a sense of humour and, although the author must remain anonymous, they will surely forgive me for recording his pronouncement in this context for the benefit of posterity.

The humour on which the epigram depended did contain an element of truth. Then, dressage riding in Britain was mainly indulged in by quite mature ladies who, after doing plenty of fast riding and cross-country riding and jumping in their earlier years had learned to appreciate a more sedate form of equitation. In dressage, precision and finesse prevailed over a willingness to take risks, and they were not expected to leave the ground or suffer regular falls. Being accustomed to ride only horses of quality, they bought English Thoroughbreds for this purpose and, because they enjoyed the process of improving their own skills while they pursued the unhurried training of these horses, they took their time over this and, for the most part, evinced no urgency to enter them for competitions.

It is well known, and constantly reiterated by its adherents, that dressage is the French word for training and that its main purpose is to render horses more pleasant and more enjoyable to ride for all purposes and in almost all circumstances. In the light of this explanation, the multiplicity of dressage or training competitions which take place nowadays may seem curious. People who saw the great Granat, the World Champion Holstein dressage horse from Switzerland of a few years ago, run away with his light, but highly accomplished lady rider

81

Margit Otto-Crepin of France riding Corlandus at Goodwood. The horse looks happy and the rider is making it look very easy – an important consideration in dressage competitions.

at the trot – he did this once at the Empire Pool Wembley, admittedly only during a practice session, and got right out of the building before they could shut the doors to contain him – may be inclined to doubt the validity of the second part of it.

Dressage is of course school riding or training developed to a high level of accuracy and precision and practised today largely for its own sake as an end in itself and not necessarily as a means to an end involving any other form of equitation or horsemanship. It incorporates its own levels of proficiency for competition purposes, and these are determined by the complexity and difficulty of the movements demanded in the different graded tests and not, only, by the accuracy and precision with which they are performed.

A good dressage rider is undeniably a good horseman who must sit firmly and correctly, deep in the saddle with his seat bones firmly on it, but lightly with a straight back and his head well up, and with the whole length of his lower legs always very lightly in contact with his horse's sides. He should be able to brace his back to transmit a driving force through his seat bones to encourage his horse to go forward instantly into extension or to convert this energy into elevation in collected paces when it is restrained by his hands; this action has been likened to that required to start a swing or to tip a chair on which its occupant is sitting onto its front legs.

The position and posture required do not come naturally to a person of normal physique. They must be studied and practised, to a considerable extent in exercises without stirrups. Above all, they must result in the rider sitting elegantly and looking elegant to complement and enhance the appearance of grace which he must try to impart to his horse. Elegance is indeed the fundamental aim of the dressage rider, as it was of his predecessor the school rider. The school rider displayed his horses at their glamorous best to delight distinguished patrons in the great riding halls of Europe and thrill public audiences in the circuses of the day, before the advent of motor transport enabled him to travel between capitals and countries to compete against other riders for more substantial and enduring accolades.

Dressage is of course training, but in terms of its concept as a competitive equestrian activity, it is the end-product of training and it comprises a considerable number of graded tests. These involve series of specifically prescribed movements which are specially devised to test the state of training of the various horses of different standards which are entered for the graded competitions. To quote from the current Rules for Dressage Events of the International Equestrian Federation:

> The object of Dressage is the harmonious development of the physique and ability of the horse. As a result it makes the horse calm, supple, loose and flexible, but also confident, attentive and keen, thus achieving perfect understanding with his rider. These qualities are revealed by: 1) The freedom and regularity of the paces; 2) The harmony, lightness and ease of the movements; 3) The lightness of the forehand and the engagement of the hind quarters, originating in a lively impulsion; 4) The acceptance of the bridle, with submissiveness throughout and without any tenseness or resistance.

Most of the movements called for in most of the tests, though perhaps not quite all of them, are in themselves elegant and pleasing to watch. The great difference between the riding of a modern competitive dressage test and the impressive equestrian displays performed by single horsemen 100 years ago (and in the circus still today) is that dressage tests demand extreme accuracy and precision in the timing and duration of the movements if they are to receive good marks from the judges. Displays which are intended only to impress spectators, even quite knowledgeable ones, may incorporate many of the same movements, but not the same requirement for them to be performed at precise moments or for an exactly prescribed duration. This is not to suggest that many circus riders are not very good horsemen and at least one such rider in Great Britain has also made her name as a top class dressage rider.

A good dressage horse must be a straight, level mover, since regularity of the steps and paces is a primary requirement in almost all of the movements which he will be called upon to perform. Not all horses are naturally straight, level movers. Some lack this quality because of faults in their conformation and others have developed irregular and crooked action through careless shoeing or through being lunged and ridden badly while being broken and in their early years. A horse which takes regular even steps at the walk is generally reckoned to be likely to move evenly and regularly in all his other paces. A discriminating buyer of a horse required for dressage will often have him walked in hand along a straight stretch of sand so that his footprints can be examined and precisely measured.

The same straight and level action is also highly desirable in a racehorse, or any horse which is to be expected to gallop fast and as effortlessly as possible, and a similar critical study of his walk will often give an indication of his potential speed, while slow-motion filming has also been used effectively to determine this factor at faster paces.

A dressage horse must appear to be calm in the arena and must co-operate willingly with his rider, showing no hint of resistance or rebellion. A phlegmatic temperament, on the other hand, will not serve to produce the energy, activity and impulsion which he needs to perform most of the exercises and movements, all of which demand animation and a measure of vivacity and many of which involve considerable physical exertion. Most good dressage horses are in fact lively to the point of ebullience and would often boil over in any less capable hands than those of their own riders, so, although dressage does not involve the excitement of galloping or jumping, it is by no means a passive or lethargic form of horsemanship. It is not an easy option for riders who seek the challenge of competition without any attendant risk of strain or injury.

Thoroughbred horses tend to be more volatile than Halfbreds. There are plenty of Thoroughbreds in Britain, and British people, including dressage enthusiasts, generally prefer to ride Thoroughbreds. Dressage riders in Great Britain therefore tend to give themselves an initially harder task than their continental counterparts, because it is easier in the first instance to activate a quiet horse than to calm a high-couraged one, although a spirited horse with Thoroughbred quality may ultimately produce more inspiring performances than a Halfbred with more cold blood in his ancestry.

Dressage judges, particularly at international level, tend to look nowadays for an impression of power as well as accuracy in the execution of the movements which they must assess. This may seem to have put a premium on big strong horses, often from the Holstein or Hanover studs, to win present day dressage competitions, although it must be admitted that Swedish and Danish horses, which are often rather smaller and lighter, are also much admired, as are many of Selle Français breeding from France, whose original name was Anglo-Normand.

The famous Lipizzaners of Austria are of Spanish descent and have been specially bred for many generations for advanced training and school work – notably in the Spanish Riding School at the Hofburg in Vienna. They are really rather too small and cobby to impress present day dressage judges. Mrs Joanna Hall, Dutch-born but English by marriage and arguably the best non-Austrian rider to have studied at the Spanish Riding School since World War II, won two Hamburg Dressage Derbys and several Grand Prix competitions in the 1960s with a well known Lipizzaner, Conversano Caprice. He seems to have been an exception and his relatives are better known for their spell-binding displays in Vienna and occasional visits to other countries, where the emphasis is on advanced specialist High School movements, but the training is strictly classical and does not deviate from the principles applicable to competitive dressage.

Dressage became a competitive horse activity in the early 1900s and was established as such under the regulations of the newly formed International Equestrian Federation in 1928. In that year, a panel of distinguished school riders drew up rules for the conduct of inter-national competitions and composed some tests to be ridden at them. The original rules have generally stood the test of time, although a great many more tests have been composed since those early days and their content has changed and varied over the years.

Tests for international competitions or tournaments vary in import-ance from 'Friendly' to 'Official International', with World Cham-pionships every four years in the even year between the Olympic Games. At these, dressage is one of the competitions, as at Continental Championships which take place every two years in years of uneven date. The tests are graded from those for Prix St Georges, which are of medium standard, through Intermediate (numbers 1 and 2), which are of relatively advanced standard, up to Grand Prix and Grand Prix Special, which are of the highest standard.

Tests of lower standard, as well as some different ones of medium and advanced standard, are set by national federations for use at national competitions and there are international tests as well as national tests for Young Riders, Juniors and Ponies, as also for use in the Three-Day Event (Horse Trials) and Dressage with Jumping.

Free Style Tests (Kur) are allowed and encouraged under both national and international rules and these, which may be to music or without music, are composed by the riders who perform them. Their aims are to impress the judges with the artistry of their demonstrations as well as the excellence of their technical execution. The movements performed in Free Style Tests are usually left to the discretion of the riders concerned except that those governed by the international rules must include one piaffe of at least ten steps and a passage of at least 22yd (20m) in length may be called for. In lower grade national competitions certain elementary movements may be required to be incorporated.

Tests below medium standard, normally at national and lower level standard, are usually ridden in an arena of size 22 × 44yd (20 × 40m) but those of higher standard must be performed in a 22 × 66yd (20 × 60m) arena.

The basic gaits demonstrated in all dressage tests are the walk, the trot and the canter; canter is 'galop' in French and 'galopp' in German and it is not differentiated in those languages from the English 'gallop', sometimes also called 'the run' in America. The gallop recognizes a slight difference in the faster pace, in that the gait becomes four-time instead of three-time because the paired diagonal feet do not hit the ground at the same time, but the hind foot strikes just before the forefoot. The fast gallop is never called for in dressage.

Four separate lengths of stride, or degrees of extension, are recognized and may be demanded in dressage tests.* These are the collected walk, the medium walk, the extended walk and the free walk on a long rein.

The collected walk demonstrates collection and elevation without any loss of impulsion and the horse takes quite short steps so that his hind feet strike the ground on or just short of the imprints of his forefeet. In the medium walk and the extended walk he takes respectively longer steps so that his hind feet over-track the imprints of his forefeet and he covers more ground with his strides, while remaining always on the bit. The free walk is a pace of relaxation in which the horse continues to walk forward with quite extended strides but is allowed to lower and stretch his neck.

---

* The official descriptions of the paces and movements in the FEI rules for dressage events are much fuller and more precise than the comments offered here. They form the instructions which must be followed by competitors and judges and I have not attempted to paraphrase or précis them for readers whose interest is expected to be only academic and ephemeral just to suit the scope of this chapter. I apologize to everyone concerned if I may inadvertently have seemed to contradict or distort any official pronouncements.

The collected trot, the working trot, the medium trot and the extended trot must all preserve the same rhythm. The variation between them should be detected in the relative lengths of the strides, the degree of elevation in collection and the extent of the ground which they cover, the slight advancing of the horse's nose beyond the vertical, and a general impression of greater elongation of his whole body. There is in practice little difference between working trot and medium trot, but the latter asks for rather more active use of the horse's knees and hocks than the former. The working trot is asked for only in tests below Prix St Georges or medium standard for young horses who are not expected to remain too long in collection.

The four variations in the canter gait are effectively the same as those for the trot and are judged by similar criteria. As for the walk and trot, the rhythm must be preserved unaltered, but the strides should lengthen to cover more ground. Impulsion from the hind legs must be very noticeable in extended canter, although the three-time beat must be maintained and not allowed to become four-time as in a full gallop. In a correct or true canter the horse leads with the foreleg on the side to which he is turning or circling, which will be the inside leg as he canters in the track of a dressage arena. Some dressage movements, however, call for a false or counter-canter in which the horse is required to lead with his outside leg on a circle in order to prove his obedience to his rider's aids as a preliminary to executing flying changes of leg, without being brought back to the trot before the change, and as a demonstration of a suppling exercise.

In addition to turns, circles, half figures-of-eight, the serpentines of varying numbers of loops, five lateral movements 'on two tracks', in which the horse's hind feet do not follow exactly in the track of his forefeet, may be asked for. Shoulder in is said to have been first conceived by the French *écuyer* de la Guérinière in the early years of the eighteenth century. In this exercise, the horse is induced to move forward in the track of the arena with his head and shoulders bent slightly inwards towards its centre so that there seems to be a slight bend in his spine. His inside hind foot lands in the same horizontal plane as the print made by his outside forefoot. Shoulder in is an exercise intended to make the horse supple in his spine as a preparation for the execution of correct turns and circles in which his head and neck should be bent slightly in the direction of the turn and never outwards from it. It can be argued, however, that there can never be an actual perceptible bending of the spine, which is necessarily a rigid part of the horse's anatomy.

The progression from shoulder in is to travers. The horse's head and neck remain straight in the track, but his hindquarters are placed

Mrs Jennie Loriston Clarke (née Bullen) riding Dutch Gold in the European dressage championships in 1989. By the end of 1990 this partnership is still Britain's most successful combination in international competitive dressage. The rider reveals the intense concentration required but the horse seems to be relatively relaxed and happy.

slightly towards the centre of the arena while he continues to move forward, so that his outside hind foot covers the print made by his inside forefoot.

In renvers his head, neck and shoulders are bent slightly inwards from the track but remain parallel with it while his hindquarters remain in it, so that he moves forward with his inside hind foot covering the print of his outside forefoot but, unlike the shoulder in position, he continues to look straight ahead.

Leg-yielding is an exercise intended to prepare the horse for more advanced work on two tracks, including renvers and travers. It consists in the rider inducing the horse to move sideways as well as forwards so that his body forms an angle of 40deg with the track of the arena when he is progressing in it, or remains parallel with it when he moves forward and sideways in a diagonal direction away from it. In both cases the horse's head will be bent slightly so that he is not looking straight in the direction in which he is moving, but his neck should not be bent away from it.

These four lateral movements on two tracks, leg-yielding, shoulder in, travers and renvers, are primarily schooling exercises which are not, in themselves, elegant or impressive to watch and may seem, to uninitiated spectators, to be almost clumsy and far from fluent. They are not included in advanced tests and are only asked for occasionally in those of medium standard, but they figure quite prominently in Preliminary, Novice and Elementary tests. They serve as evidence of a horse's submission, obedience, balance and suppleness as a preliminary step to his learning to execute the half-pass, which is an elegant classical school movement essential to all advanced dressage tests and all displays of school riding, such as quadrilles.

In the half-pass the horse must move diagonally across the arena with his head and neck bent slightly in the direction of his lateral movement and his outside legs crossing in front of his inside legs. This movement may be asked for at any pace, including the canter, in which there must be a flying change of his leading leg when a change of direction to the other diagonal is demanded, but the other preliminary lateral movements already referred to are normally only executed at the walk and trot.

The rein back is asked for in most dressage tests. This is a straight walk backwards, but with the diagonal legs moving almost simultaneously so that the feet come to the ground in a beat which is virtually two-time, instead of the four-time beat of a forward walk, but without any period of suspension.

A volte is simply a circle of 20ft (6m) diameter. If it is bigger than this it is called a circle. In either case, at whatever pace required, the essential criterion is that the horse's quarters must not swing out and describe a larger circle than that called for or executed by his forehand.

A figure of eight in dressage terms is two exactly round and equal-sized circles adjoining each other and the rider must straighten his horse momentarily before changing rein for the second circle where they join.

The serpentine, starting and finishing always at the middle points of one or other of the short sides of the arena, should be ridden on a series of curves, not straight lines. These curves form, in effect, elongated half figures-of-eight across the breadth of the arena or between the prescribed markers.

A pirouette, normally executed only at the collected canter but occasionally asked for in collected walk, is in effect a turn on the haunches. The horse's hind feet remain within the small circle whose diameter is the few inches between them, while his forehand swings round them to describe a regular circle. The radius of that circle should be equal to the effective length of the horse. A pirouette at the canter is regarded as a fairly advanced movement and is only asked for at intermediate standard and above. A half-pirouette, making an arc of only 180deg, may be required in tests of Prix St Georges.

Passage and piaffe are advanced movements normally only applicable to Grand Prix or very advanced tests, although a few steps in piaffe may be asked for in an intermediate test. They are both High School (*haute école*) movements, and are both also displayed in circus routines, though with slightly different methods and standards of execution. The piaffe in particular is a preliminary exercise for the movements above the ground of classical High School.

The passage is a very collected trot which must show great elevation, with the horse's feet raised at each step to a level just below the knee or hock of the opposite leg, while the horse moves forward taking quite slow but highly cadenced paces in strict rhythm. Lateral movement, the half-pass, may also be asked for in passage.

The piaffe is a highly collected, cadenced and elevated trot on the spot in which the horse must execute the required number of paces, maintaining the same rhythm as in passage but not moving forward at all. The number of steps required for a piaffe must obviously be prescribed and limited and, in Grand Prix tests, 12–15 are normally required, but not a more precise number. It is possible for a horse to execute a pirouette in piaffe, but this would be a very advanced and difficult movement.

All dressage tests finish with a halt and most of them include an earlier halt as a preliminary to a rein back. The halts themselves are judged as part of the movements in which they occur and the horse must stand immobile for the required number of seconds (usually 5 or 15) or during the rider's salute at the end of the test. All four feet must be squarely on the ground but the horse remains on the bit and attentive and ready to move forwards or backwards as required.

During every dressage test the rider will execute a considerable number of half halts. These should be virtually imperceptible to onlookers and are not considered for purposes of judging. They are preliminaries to transitions between changes of paces or movements which catch the horse's attention and re-adjust his balance by giving him the initial aids, as for a halt, but immediately imposing those for the next pace or movement. They must never be so obvious as to interrupt forward movement or make transitions seem other than smooth, but may legitimately be just noticeable in Novice and Elementary tests.

The precise aids which riders apply to persuade their horses to perform the many movements required in dressage tests cannot be explained within the limited extent of these pages and are besides still the subject of esoteric and sometimes contentious discussion between dressage riders.

Riders are required to hold their reins in both hands, except in Free Style Tests when they may use only one hand at their own discretion during any part of a test. Double bridles with cheeks no longer than

4in (10cm) are obligatory for all competitions under international rules, but snaffles, with either cavessons or dropped nose-bands are permitted under British national rules for all tests below those of advanced standard. No whips may be carried under international rules but, curiously, are permitted under British ones in Novice and Elementary competitions. The use of the voice as an aid, and this includes hissing, whistling or tongue clicking is forbidden in all dressage tests, and this is perhaps rather sad because it is a well recognized means of communication between rider and horse, even when the former is sitting on top of the latter. Judges are expected to disapprove of tail swishing, which is often evidence of excessive or insensitive use of spurs, and to reflect their disapproval in their markings.

The marking at all international dressage competitions must be done by five judges, except for Friendly Events (Concours Dressages Amities) and competitions for Free Style Tests, where three judges are held to suffice. Most national competitions are marked by three judges, but shortage of unpaid volunteers for this work often results in local competitions in Britain of below medium standard being marked by only one judge.

Each judge awards marks on a scale of 0–10 for each movement (which may amount to up to 35) for each test, and the marks, which are added up and averaged to produce the competitor's score for the test concerned, also represent specifically worded opinions.* There is often some disparity between the marks awarded by the different judges for the same movements executed by the same competitors in the same tests, and this may give rise to criticism that the judging is inconsistent. Such criticism is usually unjustified because the judges sit around the arena and see the movements from different viewpoints and a variation between their opinions is, in any case, acceptable and even desirable to avoid their deliberations becoming monotonous and their results seeming to be stereotyped. These variations may be particularly marked in the case of the last four marks awarded by the judges for each test which are for their overall impressions of the four relevant aspects of them. Provided that there are more than two judges marking each test, any one of them whose marks are abnormally eccentric will be revealed so that a competitor need not be too elated or depressed by them and they will not affect his score too seriously.

Divergence of opinion between judges may stem in part from time-worn controversy about different 'schools of equitation' because some experts still claim to be able to discriminate between the French School

---

* Each of the separate marks from 0–10 in the scale for dressage tests represents a standard verbal assessment. 0 = Not performed, 1 = Very bad, 2 = Bad, 3 = Fairly bad, 4 = Insufficient, 5 = Sufficient, 6 = Satisfactory, 7 = Fairly good, 8 = Good, 9 = Very good, 10 = Excellent.

and the German School. It is a matter of historical record that the rigid routines with which the famous French *écuyer* Baucher dominated his horses and aimed to subdue their natural instincts and reactions in the nineteenth century were superseded, before 1900, by those of his earlier compatriot de la Guérinière whose more flexible methods involved less restraint (*see* Chapter 1).

The French School in the early twentieth century – which was established at Saumur by the Comte d' Aure and maintained by General Decarpentry until the start of World War II – was based on the original doctrines of de la Guérinière, rather than Baucher. The doctrines were generally accepted throughout Europe and supported by the classical purists of the Spanish Riding School in Vienna and those of its later counterpart in Hungary. Its teaching became indistinguishable from that of the German School, whose main centre was at Hanover, and it influenced school riding all over Europe, and the newly conceived dressage competitions, until the start of World War II.

After World War II French teaching at Saumur reverted for a period to that of Baucher and there was a divergence between the French and the German Schools, with the increasingly influential Swedish riders tending to support the current French School. Many horsemen who were not fully conversant with the teachings of both Schools gained the erroneous impression that German doctrines demanded total submission in the interests of precise accuracy while French riders allowed their horses to display their paces more freely in a spirit of light-hearted exhilaration. In fact, where any difference was discernible, the opposite was more generally the case.

By 1950 school riding had become mainly directed towards competitive dressage and absolute accuracy was essential for the recording of good scores in tests. German riders achieved the most success in international competitions, and have generally continued to lead the field ever since, and their methods, which have been copied by other competitors world-wide, can conceivably be thought of as the New German School which seems to put emphasis on power and accuracy as the key factor which has enabled them to impress judges and win competitions with their big strong Holstein and Hanoverian horses.

The gaits and paces which horses are required to demonstrate in dressage tests are all natural, except perhaps in their most collected forms and in the rein back, and can be seen being executed, at least spasmodically, by riderless loose horses even in a wild state. Indeed the passage, despite its being the most advanced movement called for in dressage tests, is natural and quite often displayed by loose horses immediately after they are turned out to grass out of sheer *joie de vivre*.

Pirouettes, very imprecisely performed, are also natural, but lateral movements and piaffes are not natural and are never executed by loose horses of their own volition. Loose horses do not make turns and circles with the slight bend which dressage judges like to see in their natural state, but invariably fall in on them with their inside shoulders and allow their quarters to swing out.

Riders who have persuaded their horses to perform an unusual movement or do a new trick often claim that it is an extension of some natural capability or has some practical use. Much debate and argument, both verbal and in writing and much of it controversial, centres on the validity of certain dressage movements and the ways in which they should correctly be executed.

The continuous discussion which this engenders is quite fun in itself and adds significantly to public interest in dressage. It also adds to the mental exertions of those people more directly connected with it. Those people are generally anxious to claim that what they do is intended to improve their horses' natural abilities and to be of value in many other fields of horsemanship.

Some of this discussion is nonsense, though perfectly harmless and quite amusing and it must be apparent to intelligent, objective observers with any knowledge of dressage that it is now a major competitive equestrian activity in its own right and not just a system of training for general usefulness. Most successful dressage riders are very good horsemen, but most of them are specialists who practise virtually no other form of equitation and indeed could hardly spare the time to do so without risking to lose their hard-won positions of eminence near the top of a fiercely competitive league.

7

Horsemanship in Three Phases

Horse Trials or the Three-Day Event

Horse Trials used to be called the Three-Day Event in Great Britain and this was a name which described it well and still would (even when it lasts for more or less than three days) if the word 'phase' were to be substituted for 'day'. Its British exponents, however, took to calling it Combined Training, thereby confusing everyone, particularly when its official name in English was finally changed to Horse Trials. Most people continued to speak of it in conversation as Eventing – any pretence of the name being descriptive of the activity concerned seemed to have been abandoned. On the continent it was originally called the Military, always and rather curiously with the English spelling, in sensible deference to the concept which inspired it, and it is still referred to by this name in conversation in all countries except Great Britain. Its official name in French is now *le Concours Complet* and in German is *Vielzeitigkeitsprüfung* and both these names fairly describe what it involves.

The Three-Day Event is a reasonably complete test of all the main capabilities which may be expected of a horse and rider. Its military origin is embodied in the concept that it tests the functions demanded of a cavalry soldier mounted on an army horse, and more specifically of an officer on his charger. The idea originated in the cavalry schools of Europe, more or less simultaneously at the turn of the last century, and the first international competition which it inspired took place during the Olympic Games at Stockholm in 1912, although the rules were not regularized into any semblance of their present form until 1936.

The three main phases of the complete combined competition are dressage, endurance, and jumping. This is the official designation. The endurance phase is sub-divided into two phases of trotting or slow cantering over roads and tracks (phases A and C), a phase of galloping over steeplechase fences (phase B), and a phase of galloping over cross-country fences (phase D). The three main phases are treated as separate contests, each of which is held on a separate day when the

Event is a three-day one, and they are judged quite separately. Their scoring in penalty points, however, is added together to produce final results.

In terms of their resemblance to a soldier and his horse, the dressage test is reckoned to make demands similar to those which he would encounter on parade: steadiness, complete control and the ability to perform set movements with well mannered precision, vitality and a degree of elegance. The two phases over roads and tracks on the second day may be likened to marches prior to battle or during a fluid engagement.

The steeplechase phase may be considered to recreate the situation which envisages the soldier having to move very quickly from one part of the battlefield to another to convey information or orders.

The cross-country phase may be held to simulate the mental and physical pressures and strain imposed on horse and rider by a charge culminating in actual engagement with the enemy. It would thus demand courage, quick thinking and highly active manoeuvrability as well as the stamina required to complete the course at top speed despite the onset of fatigue.

The jumping on the third day, over a small but moderately difficult show jumping course, is intended to test the horse's resilience and powers of recovery after the rigours of the endurance phase. It would thus assess his fitness and continued responsiveness to the demands which his rider must make of him, as well as the precisely applied skill of the rider who must also demonstrate powers of quick recovery after the strain of the previous day. The demands which it makes represent a much reduced indication of those which a cavalryman and his horse would have to meet in pursuing a beaten enemy after a battle or possibly making a hurried withdrawal after defeat.

The dressage test prescribed by the International Equestrian Federation for Official International Events (CCIO) and International Events (CCI) is standard throughout the world at any one time but for Friendly International Events (CCA) and purely national ones, a national test may be used. The tests for Three-Day Events are of elementary standard solely, so that they do not include any movements more advanced than those which a well schooled cavalry charger, or even a very well schooled hunter, might be expected to perform.

The test is judged by a ground jury of five or three judges, including its president. This jury also supervises, and effectively judges, the other two competitions of the Event. They award marks out of 10 in accordance with the usual dressage scale for movements (which may number up to 20) and the four standard collective assessments (paces, impulsion, submission, position of rider and use of aids). These are added up for each competitor, divided by the number of judges to produce an average and deducted from the maximum possible to be expressed as penalty points. Each competitor's penalty points are then multiplied by 0.6. This is intended to reduce them to a general level deemed to be relatively appropriate to their influence on the whole Event. Any penalties for errors of course, which are cumulative from 2 to 4 and then 8 with elimination for a fourth error, are then added.

A further multiplying factor is then introduced to adjust the influence of the dressage in relation to the endurance phase, and specifically the cross-country. This involves multiplying the final dressage penalties, including those for any errors of course, for each competitor by a number that will be between 0.5 and 1.5. This is done by either halving or multiplying them by 1.5, according to the severity of the endurance test and the extent to which its cross-country obstacles seem likely to exact penalties. The multiplying factor, which in practice is invariably 0.5, 0.75, 1.0 (which means in effect that it is not used), 1.25 or 1.5, is decided by the Technical Delegate only just before the first competitor performs his dressage test on the first day. It is done at the last moment before the whole Trial may be deemed actually to have begun, so that the latest conditions of the going and weather may be taken into consideration.

The Technical Delegate is an unpaid amateur official. He is appointed by the International Equestrian Federation in the case of International Events, to inspect the courses and the arrangements for running the Event in advance and see that they are all fair and in compliance with the rules. He has no judicial function other than to make this adjustment at his sole discretion.

An arithmetical alteration of this kind may seem to be a clumsy and complicated device for ensuring that a Horse Trial or Three-Day Event tests its contestants fairly, in accordance with the aims set out in its own rules. The aims are, in effect, to test the skill of the rider and the ability and training of his horse completely in all competitions, allowing for them to exert a relative influence of: dressage 3, endurance 12 and jumping 1. It has aroused controversy in the past and it still places a heavy burden of responsibility on just one man, the Technical Delegate, who must put up with much prejudiced advice and can never hope to satisfy all the competitors whose interests he aims to serve. However, the arrangement has stood the test of time and is now generally accepted as the only practical one to have been devised to date. It does take into account the last-minute effects of weather as well as inevitable variations in the severity of obstacles so that these may be equated to accord with uniform standards.

The second competition, the test of endurance, comprises four phases: A, B, C and D. Phase A is over roads and tracks for a distance of between 3 and 5km (longer for championships and shorter for Events for ponies and junior riders) which must be ridden at a speed of 220m per minute – 200m per minute for ponies. This average speed of about 13km per hour calls for a steady working trot, but competitors may canter over stretches of good going and dismount to run leading their horses, thereby relieving them of the obligatory minimum weight of 75kg, except through the start and finish, although few riders nowadays actually do this. They incur one penalty for each second over the optimum time taken to complete the section, but gain no advantage by finishing early since all the phases are separately timed.

The second phase, the steeplechase, is run over a course which must be between 2.64 and 3.45km in distance with an average of three fences for every 1km. Fences must be built in the same form as those on the racecourses but must not exceed 1.4m in total height or 2.8m in spread at ground level. The speed required to complete the steeplechase course without penalties, which are calculated at the rate of 0.8 of a penalty point for each second over the optimum time, varies from 640m per minute to 690m per minute according to the grading of the Event which, rather as in show jumping, determines the grading of the horses allowed to enter for it. There is no steeplechase phase in

Mrs 'Ginny' Leng (née Holgate) on Master Craftsman in the cross-country phase of the 1988 Seoul Olympics. An almost perfect seat on a good horse over a fence of this kind which a steeplechase jockey could safely adopt on a very good jumper.

Events for ponies. Horses start on the steeplechase immediately after finishing the first roads and tracks section (Phase A) and, on completing it, go straight on to the second roads and tracks section (Phase C) which is about twice the length of Phase A and usually covers a distance of some 8km. The rules and timing arrangements for Phase C are exactly the same as those for Phase A.

Phase D, the cross-country section of the endurance competition, which is the crucial part of it and the one in which competitors are most likely to incur penalties affecting total results, starts after a 10-minute obligatory halt at the end of Phase C during which a brief veterinary examination is conducted to ensure that horses are fit to continue and tackle the most rigorous test of the whole Event. This is over the cross-country course whose distance must be between 5 and 8km (2–3km for ponies and 3–5km for junior riders) with an average of four obstacles for every kilometre and which must be ridden at an average speed which is varied between 520 and 570m per minute (400–500m per minute for ponies) according to the grading and category of the Event.

Each obstacle must include at least one part which can be jumped, at a height of not more than 1.20m and a spread of not more than 3m. Obstacles involving only spread with no height, like water ditches, must not incorporate a spread of more than 4m. Water to be jumped into or out of must not be deeper than 50cm and the crossing involved must be at least 6m wide from entry to exit. No drop fence may demand a drop of more than 2m from the top of the fence to the normal point of landing.

Refusals at cross-country fences cost 20 penalties for the first, 40 penalties for the second, and elimination for the third at any one fence. A fall within the penalty zone, which extends 10m before the fence and 20m after it, costs 60 penalties. After three falls on the whole cross-country course, or two falls during the steeplechase or show jumping, a competitor must retire and will be eliminated if he does not do so. This regulation avoids cruelty to horses, or their being pressed beyond their capacity after they are clearly out of the running.

The jumping test on the last day is over a simple show jumping course of 10–12 fences, including one double and/or one treble combination, which must not exceed 1.20m in height or 3m in total spread. Each knock down costs 5 penalties, a first refusal costs 10 penalties, a second refusal 20 penalties and a third refusal over the whole course incurs elimination. Exceeding the time allowed, which is calculated for a speed of between 350 and 400m per minute over a course whose length must be between 600 and 900m according to the grading of the Event, costs a quarter of a penalty for each excess second.

The jumping test is relatively undemanding by show jumping standards and intended only to establish that horses have retained their suppleness, energy and obedience after the previous day's test of endurance. Clear rounds are anticipated and competitors obviously cannot improve their existing scores by performing well on the last day, but may only improve their placings as a result of faults incurred by their rivals. There is an inevitable air of anti-climax on the last day of a Three-Day Event, but also some considerable tension affecting the competitors who are still in contention. The final demonstrations of their horsemanship may well be influenced by this.

Almost as much excitement is generated by the final veterinary inspection before the jumping test as by the show jumping itself, since firm hopes of a win have sometimes been dashed when horses have been 'spun' at this for lameness and not allowed to compete on the last day and finish the Event. This final inspection has become something of a social highlight as well as a critical juncture in the programme of a Three-Day Event. It is customarily attended by a select but growing number of well informed and generally knowledgeable spectators who

Ian Stark is riding Sir Wattie in the Three-Day Event at the 1988 Seoul Olympics. The need to be able to cope with a sudden deceleration on landing over a drop fence of this kind dictates a less forward seat than that adopted in show jumping.

99

do not hesitate to criticize the decisions of the jury. The jury's decisions are guided by the advice of the veterinary delegate and decreed by its president on a majority vote.

The essential consideration must clearly be to order the retirement of any horse which is in pain or likely to suffer pain if it is ridden over fences within the next few hours. The distinction between this condition and a degree of stiffness with even some irregularity of gait, short of discernible lameness, is a critical one. The treatment and general cosseting of a horse during the period between the last two tests of a Three-Day Event is a matter of skilful horsemastership; and strict laboratory testing ensures that this does not involve the use of excessive pain-killing drugs or other forbidden substances.

The Three-Day Event, which often actually extends over a period of four or five days because all the dressage tests cannot be judged by the same jury in one day, is the most comprehensive Trial held under the foregoing international rules, which are only indicated in rather simplistic outline. There are in addition national Two-Day Events and One-Day Events for which the format, particularly as to the order in which the three tests are arranged, is rather different. These shorter Trials are generally of lower grading, demanding a less advanced standard of training and performance. They provide essential preliminary experience for novice riders, and One-Day Events in particular can be tackled by horses which lack the speed and intrinsic quality demanded by the endurance test of a full Three-Day Event.

In both Two- and One-Day Events the show jumping test takes place after the dressage on the same day. The endurance test follows the jumping test on the same day for a One-Day Event, but consists only of a cross-country course of between 1.5 and 4km including up to twenty fences. In a Two-Day Event the endurance test takes place on the second day and includes all four phases: two sections of roads and tracks, a steeplechase course and a cross-country course – although they are usually shorter than those at a full Three-Day Event. The grades or classes at a One-Day Event are designated as Novice, Intermediate and Advanced, and cross-country fences for novices must not exceed a height of 1.05m.

There are probably more Horse Trials in Great Britain each year than in any other country and they amount to some 8 full Three-Day Events (including Badminton which is the most prestigious of them all, and two or three others of championship status), 8 or 9 Two-Day Events, and about 140 One-Day Trials; a total of well over 200 days of competition catering for at least 5,000 horses.

Viewed objectively and separately the components of even a Three-Day Horse Trial may not seem to be very demanding. It involves an elementary dressage test which, though strictly judged, includes only straightforward paces and simple movements; two brisk trots interspersed with slow cantering such as any hunting man might contemplate in hurrying to a meet or even as part of a vigorous exercise routine; a short, sharp gallop over a dozen or so inviting brush fences at a speed which would not be fast enough to win a race; a very strong gallop over up to 5 miles (8km) of good sound turf and up to twenty difficult but fairly low and quite natural looking fences such as a keen hunting man might dream of jumping in the course of a great hunt, but would seldom meet or ride at in reality; and, after a good night's sleep, a small course of show jumps requiring only precision and accuracy to be jumped clear.

The tests must, however, be considered in conjunction and relationships with each other for their value as demonstrations of horsemanship to be properly appreciated. Thus, a horse must be calmly obedient and attentive only to the aids which he receives from his rider to perform a good dressage test. This may be difficult to reconcile with the need for him to be tuned up to a high pitch of fitness so that he will be full of the energy and accompanying excitement which will make him keen to go forward at his best speed and tackle the obstacles on the next day without the encouragement of other horses galloping with him.

The separate phases of the endurance test pose in themselves different requirements which may be at variance with each other in that a horse needs to settle calmly to an economical stride and pace for the two sections over roads and tracks so as not to tire himself or his rider unnecessarily, but to perk up and display great impulsion for the steeplechase and cross-country courses. There is a divergence between the demands of the steeplechase and the cross country. The horse must jump the steeplechase fences at racing pace without dwelling over them or shortening his stride unduly to achieve the speed required to complete this phase without time penalties. On the other hand, he must be prepared to shorten his stride constantly and instantly to be able to negotiate the often tricky cross-country obstacles without the risk of falls or refusals.

The show jumping test does not require any extreme physical effort or ability from the horse, provided that it is still sound, supple, obedient and reasonably keen after the rigours of the endurance test. It does require, however, accuracy and precise control on the part of the rider if he is to jump a clear round and retain his placing.

Success in Horse Trials is dependent on the rider rather than the horse to a greater extent than is apparent in many other equestrian

101

endeavours. A good horseman can often win a One-Day Event on a horse of nondescript breeding and limited speed and physical ability and British Three-Day Event Championships have been won on two or three occasions by distinguished and very determined competitors whose mounts, though supremely willing and courageous, were little more than ponies.

One-Day Events can be won by horses of lesser quality than those which are suitable for Three- or even Two-Day Events, because – apart from the shorter and generally less exacting dressage tests which they incorporate and the fact that their cross-country courses are smaller, shorter, and rather less difficult – the absence of the steeple-chase and the two phases of roads and tracks reduces their demand on stamina and staying power. Horses which possess a high proportion of Thoroughbred blood generally have the high courage which inclines them to keep going at their best paces even when they are tired and, in most cases, also the scope which provides for easy, fluent action and the ability to gallop faster with less effort than horses of more common, less selective breeding.

Absolute speed is seldom the essence of a Horse Trial and a com-paratively slow horse, such as a heavy man might choose for hunting, can gallop fast enough to complete the cross-country phase of a One-Day Event without time penalties, but he will be making more effort and using more energy to do this than his lighter-framed, more Thoroughbred rivals. Horses of heavier build and those with a high proportion of pony blood may have admirable conformation and intelligent, willing temperaments so that, provided they are bold jumpers, they will be at no real disadvantage against Thoroughbreds in a One-Day Event, but only use an insignificant amount of extra energy in the cross-country phase.

In Two- and Three-Day Events, however, they will have to exert themselves more to be in time over the steeplechase course. They may even use up slightly more energy on the roads and tracks, so that fatigue is likely to affect them earlier in the cross-country phase than it does those which are naturally faster gallopers, and fatigue brings with it a reduction in agility. This may be critical in the negotiation of difficult combination fences and those which incorporate drops, slopes and water splashes; and it also brings an inevitable and in-creasing reluctance to tackle spread fences even in the boldest and most willing horses, quite apart from a physical ability to maintain top speed.

Horse Trials are obviously excellent performance tests for horses and ponies of many different types and breeds. Standards are now so high in Three-Day Events that a number of competitors score no penalties other than those by which they fail to be awarded full marks for dressage, even in international championships, so that only Thoroughbred or near Thoroughbred horses of the make and shape of potential Hunter Chasers are generally regarded as good prospects for them. A preponderance of One-Day Events, however, provides ample opportunities for half-bred horses to prove their ultimate ability in Advanced and Intermediate classes as well as for all novice horses, and their riders, to gain experience.

A successful Three-Day Event rider must undeniably be a very good all-round horseman. Practically all the riders who have attained any distinction in this most comprehensive form of equitation have trained, schooled and conditioned their own horses. The international rules do indeed forbid this to be done by anyone other than a member of the same team or a competing fellow national throughout a whole Event and for three days before it. So, the close co-operation and mutual confidence which a rider must establish between himself and his horse cannot exist effectively unless their relationship has been a long one and they train and practise regularly together.

This means, in effect, that a winning Horse Trials rider must be a good nagsman capable of starting a young horse from its first introduction to a saddle and rider and carrying out all its subsequent training. He must also be a good school rider with a practical understanding of dressage in its purest sense and the ability to teach it to his horse as well as to be able to ride a good test himself. He may never need to perform in dressage in public at a level higher than Elementary standard but the relatively simple movements which he and his horse will be required to demonstrate will be judged very critically and his scores will often be crucial in their effect on his results and records of success.

He must understand and be able to practise the principles involved in long distance riding since, although the distances over roads and tracks which he will have to cover in the course of a Trial will always be far less than those for an actual long distance ride, he has an equally important need to conserve his horse's energy over them.

He needs some of the skills of a jockey to be able to get the best from his horse over the steeplechase course; more particularly the balanced seat to enable him to 'sit against him' with strong rein contact and encourage him to gallop fast and jump the fences out of his stride, coupled with the agility and quick reactions to sit back instantly and save a fall if he over-jumps or stands back too far and hits a fence. This latter ability is also likely to be very important to him over the cross-country course since a fall for 60 penalties will certainly put him out of the running in any present day Event and a firm seat by itself, though essential, may not always save the situation in extremes.

The Event rider needs multiple skills and abilities to be able to cope competently with the cross-country fences which he will encounter in any modern Horse Trial since they will be formidable in outline, if not in actual size, and, by design, difficult often to the point of being distinctly 'trappy'. He needs straightforward strength, physical fitness and good muscular co-ordination as indispensable attributes without which he and his horse will get tired quickly, lose cohesion and balance, and be at variance with each other in the exercise of their joint efforts. He needs balance as much as grip since, although the latter may keep him firmly stuck to his horse and give them both confidence in each other and an inspiring feeling of togetherness, the former will be more helpful in keeping the horse on his feet during pecks and stumbles and may save a situation in which they may seem almost certain to part company.

To jump cross-country fences in Horse Trials with confidence, a rider must be able to 'see a stride' as well as any show jumper. This is all the more essential since he will face combinations set at more difficult distances, including those which require a 'bounce' – i.e. a second take-off immediately following a first one with no non-jumping stride in between – and those whose approaches are further complicated by slopes and gradients, as well as water.

The reconnaissance of a Horse Trials cross-country course is very important and riders who arrange to carry this out unhurriedly and with intelligent judgement based on their own experience or that of an older and more knowledgeable adviser will greatly increase their chances of negotiating it without trouble. The art of the cross-country course builder has now become a life-long study for a number of very intelligent and well educated horsemen, many of whom have competed in the sport themselves at high level. It consists fundamentally in making quite small fences seem larger and more imposing than they really are and in creating difficulties in conjunction with them which will prevent horses jumping them too quickly and easily without subjecting them to undue risk of dangerous falls.

One of the main ploys of course builders is to establish alternative fences, or alternative approaches to them, which will be easier, but more time-consuming than the shortest and most direct routes over them or through combination obstacles. This provides problems and quandaries for riders and advantageous opportunities for those with especially bold and clever horses. The process of solving the problems and identifying the opportunities therefore becomes something of a battle of wits between course builders and competitors which is accepted as an important aspect of a Horse Trial and a stimulating mental challenge for some of the people who take part in it. The judgement and discretion which a rider must exercise in planning his route and tactics for the cross-country phase of an Event play a vital part in securing such success as he may enjoy in Horse Trials and are important components of his stock in trade as a horseman.

The hunting field provides experience for Event riders and their horses in Britain which cannot be obtained so readily or in quite the same form anywhere else in the world and this is universally acknowledged to be of inestimable value, particularly as regards the cross-country phase. Very few British Horse Trials competitors have not hunted as regularly as they have been able to since childhood. Most of them continue to get a number of days of hunting, if only for the benefit and enjoyment of their horses, during a winter season from November to March which is free of actual Events but seems to be getting shorter each year.

Riding to hounds, with all its excitement, risks, uncertainties and hazards, although some of these are likely to be far from pleasant, offers wonderfully comprehensive opportunities for schooling young horses. It provides a much more enjoyable procedure for maintaining the fitness of experienced horses and their riders than a dreary routine of steady exercise interspersed with training sessions at home and relieved only by a few weeks of inactivity in a loose box or paddock, usually during nasty weather. The risks involved in hunting a horse whose performance record has made him very valuable and whose keenness and impulsion may have made him distinctly impetuous may create some headaches for his rider and reduce his enjoyment of 'the thrills of the chase'. However, statistics seem to show that horses suffer as many mishaps when they are turned out in fields as when they are being ridden sensibly out hunting, and the extra experience and enjoyment which both horse and rider will get from a few days with hounds may be reckoned to be worth the added risk of injury. A person who rides well across country to hounds must be a good horseman and anyone who does this in the style and with the accuracy and precision which can enable him to win a Horse Trial must be a very good horseman.

A successful Horse Trial rider may have a trainer or experienced adviser to plan his progress and programmes, and even to select his horses for him and supervise their schooling. He may also have a highly competent groom to feed his horses expertly and keep them in tip-top condition. He must, however, be a good horsemaster himself, if only to be able to gauge the degree of stress to which he may safely subject his horses in training. Horsemastership is an intrinsic component of horsemanship and a successful competitor in Horse Trials must study and practise it more assiduously than those who make less strenuous use of their horses.

People whose knowledge of horse sports is gained mainly from reports in newspapers may hold the impression that Horse Trials are still a pleasantly amateur recreation whose participants compete against each other amicably and infrequently in a friendly social atmosphere and only take their riding seriously every four years for the Olympic Games. This is a misconception born of media interest which tends to be spasmodic and centred too much on social rather than sporting issues. It has failed to appreciate that the number of Events each year in many European countries, and especially in Britain, increased enormously in the 1970s so that they now occupy competitors who are seriously concerned with them for the better part of all but three or four winter months in actual competitions, and most of the rest of the time in training and preparing new horses for Events in the future. Standards at these Events have risen to heights which preclude their being contested by part-time amateurs who cannot spend most of their time training for them, such as the army officers who originally won them so often.

Evidence of the rise in the importance and popularity of Horse Trials is revealed by the attendance of spectators at Badminton, Britain's premier Event, which was about 200 when it was first held in 1949 but is now reckoned to be about 200,000 forty years later.

Apart from a few exceptions whose naming would be invidious, Event riders have not seemed to have achieved prominence in any other horse sports. This is not because they have been unable to master other equestrian skills, but because they have been unable to spare the time to pursue any other competitive activities seriously. They have clearly become highly proficient in at least six different aspects of horsemanship and they have to practise them constantly at high levels to maintain their ratings in the one all-embracing test of them to which they have dedicated their equestrian careers.

8

Horsemanship and the Herdsman

One of the earliest purposes for which man used the horse was to help him to herd other animals, including other horses. The process of hunting and killing animals for food and that of surrounding and containing them in open country to use eventually for their meat or their milk or any other domestic purpose – including draught and transport – has always been similar. In both these endeavours man has made great use of dogs and horses and made them his best friends and oldest partners. Without their help and co-operation most of his prey would have escaped and most of his herds would have scattered. He has needed horses and horsemanship to achieve the mobility and speed to enable him to keep pace with cattle and feral horses so as to protect cattle from predators and prevent them from stampeding and scattering and running right away from him.

Both the herdsman and the primitive type of huntsman, who pursues his quarry to fill his larder rather than to show sport to his companions, are essentially practical horsemen. They ride their horses on a loose rein relying on them to balance themselves, adjust to the extra weight they must carry, and change gaits and paces to suit the terrain and the speed demanded of them. Their general style of riding owes little to modern principles of equitation and nothing to the meticulous precision of the *manège* or riding school. It often exemplifies natural horsemanship at its best, however, and more sophisticated riders, including those whose aims are mainly competitive, can still learn something from a study of their practices and methods.

Herdsmen, cowboys and riders in this category seldom try to jump fences because there are no fences on the plains, steppes, and open ranges over which they operate. They do often cross rivers on their horses, frequently scramble over or through ditches, and generally ride over country which is sometimes rougher than that which any foxhunter, or even pigsticker, would contemplate.

In general they sit loosely in the saddle, in a relaxed manner which does not involve close contact with their horses or the exercise of grip, except in emergency. They give indications rather than direct aids to require changes of direction and pace and, because they must move about in the saddle constantly and quite vigorously to wield lariats or stock whips, their horses must respond only to the indications which they are trained to recognize and operate without continuous guidance and control.

The relationship between a herdsman and his horse is more a matter of co-operation between the two than obedience of the animal to the man to a greater extent than that between almost any other rider and his mount.

This co-operation is seen at its most effective when the American cowboy on his best horse wants to remove a steer or calf from a herd, and rope, throw and tie it so as to be able to brand it or examine it closely. His horse possesses a natural instinct akin to that of a sheep dog and, with this developed by training, he will turn and move more quickly than his rider can even anticipate to cut out the animal from the herd and keep it separated from its fellows, once it has been indicated to him, without relying on any aids or indications from his rider. As soon as his rider has lassoed the selected animal and jumped off to throw and tie it, the horse will automatically position himself so as to remain always facing it and move backwards of his own volition just enough to keep the lariat (which is wound round the horn on his saddle) taut and acting effectively until the job is done.

Co-operation of a different kind is demonstrated by the Cossack's horse when he continues to gallop forward at a steady pace on a dead-straight line, while his rider swings right down from the saddle to one side and virtually underneath him to perform the trick of picking up a handkerchief from the ground, sometimes in his teeth. This trick has eminently practical origins and the horse is expected to play his part in it in any circumstances and on any occasion, not just in the controlled environment of an arena.

There are some half dozen distinguishable groups of people in the world whose distinctive styles of horsemanship are recognized and generally admired as being fundamental constituents of their cultures or callings. Most of these are identifiable by their ethnic origins, but two at least owe their reputations to their professions and lifestyles rather than to any racial characteristics. The practical use of horses is no longer essential to the ways of life of many, if not most, of these people, but their skills and traditional ways of handling and riding horses have been preserved and they form an interesting study for present day conventional horsemen.

The Cossacks, who are remotely descended from the Mongol and Tartar hordes of Genghis Khan and Tamerlane, are not all Russians or even Slavs. They have, however, exercised a considerable influence in Russia and Poland since the thirteenth century, mainly as mounted warriors and irregular light cavalrymen, often as dissident or rebellious tribesmen, but frequently as mercenaries or soldiers in the service of the tsar. Their style of riding has always been more like that of nomadic herdsmen than mounted soldiers and their small, very tough horses, little bigger than ponies, are reckoned to be able to walk at 5mph (8kph) and cover 50 miles (80km) a day for days in succession, remaining always ready to carry out swift silent raids. (Cossacks almost captured Napoleon himself in 1812.) They lived largely on loot during the many wars in which they were engaged up to the end of the nineteenth century, and very much 'off the country', while taking part, often on both sides, in those of the twentieth century up to 1945.

Cossacks use single-reined bridles, usually with snaffle bits, and ride on a generally loose rein sitting high above their horses with short stirrup leathers on large-framed saddles with blankets and miscellaneous clothing underneath them. By tradition, and because of the

A two or three year old Australian 'Brumby' or wild horse feels restraint·for the first time. Many thousands of these horses, some possessing Thoroughbred blood, run wild in Australia and although many are now slaughtered, some are still broken in by stockmen in the outback for their own use.

position of their heels in relation to their horses' sides, they do not wear spurs but usually carry a short whip called a *nagaika* attached to their wrists.

Cossack communities, though never really static, tended to settle near the rivers of southern Russia, the Ukraine, Poland and Turkey and their many tribes and sub-tribes under their *Hetmans* generally took their names from these rivers; the biggest and best known of them being the Cossacks of the Don. They extended far south and, until very recent years, some Circassian Cossacks were recruited into the Arab Legion and dressed in uniforms based on Cossack dress to form a royal bodyguard for the King of Jordan.

The trick riding or *dzhigitovka* with which some Cossacks who escaped from the Russian Revolution astonished western European spectators between the two World Wars was originally a specialty of the Circassian Cossacks and was developed and practised by a few especially bold horsemen in most other tribes. Apart from the vaulting and general activity riding for which Cossacks are renowned (but which is by no means unique to them), their two most impressive tricks are those in which they pick up handkerchiefs or pieces of paper from the ground and stand on top of their saddles at a full gallop, and both these demonstrations are functional in origin.

By contriving to touch the ground without reducing their horses' pace they were able to collect loot from battlefields surreptitiously and, working in pairs, they could recover wounded comrades, while standing on their saddles increased their view over distant horizons. Plenty of trick riders stand on the comparatively broad rumps of galloping horses and, in the circus ring, centrifugal force helps them to do this, but Cossacks stand, unusually, on their saddles and they acquire the ability to do this by progressively shortening their already short stirrup leathers until their feet, though still in the stirrup irons, are effectively level with their horses' backs.

There are only a few regular Cossack horsemen left in the world today and very few of them still pursue a war-like or a pastoral way of life. Even the few nomadic tribes in Mongolia who still live as all Cossack people once did are dwindling. Cossack horsemanship has, however, made its mark on history and is still quite fresh in living memory as an unusual way of life in which tough little men rode hard and lived hard with tough little horses and achieved a remarkable affinity with them and the ability to travel on them farther and faster and more effectively than most other horsemen have ever envisaged.

The Csikos, the famous horse herdsmen of Hungary, are true Magyars like most of their fellow countrymen and not a separate race or tribe of any sort. They are distinguished by the work they do and,

although there is an element of hereditary vocation in this employment, they are paid as normal wage earners by the state studs to which
they belong.

There are three separate *pusztas* or prairies on the Great Plain of
Hungary: the Hortobagy, the biggest of the three, the Bugac and the
Mezohegyes. The Csikos who live on them, in semi-permanent camps
for much of the year although their families live in the houses of the
stud farms, can be distinguished by differences in their clothes and
styles of riding. They all wear rather well cut black knee-length boots
made of soft leather, very baggy lightweight breeches, or trousers like
women's divided skirts which hang to mid-calf length; loose-fitting
long sleeved shirts and sleeveless waistcoats, with large thick sheep-
skin coats for winter. The colours of their clothes and the shapes of
their hats differ between the three *pusztas*.

The Csikos of the Hortobagy wear dark blue shirts, black trousers
and waistcoats, and flat black hats with upturned brims adorned with
long black cranes' feathers. The Bugac Csikos wear white shirts and
trousers with red waistcoats, and black conical-shaped hats decorated
with white egrets' plumes as do those of the Mezohegyes except that
the waistcoats of the latter are black. The Hortobagy Csikos sit on
very small numnahs made of felt and leather without trees which have
stirrups attached to them but no girths. These unique rudimentary
saddles are called *patraches* which their users place on their horses'
backs. The Csikos mount by putting their left foot in the stirrup, while
holding down the off-side stirrup leather with their left elbow over the
horse's neck, in one easy movement which looks impossible but never
fails. The traditional reason for this arrangement is to enable them to
move off instantly from rest to stop a stampede and it is for the same
declared reason that Csikos of the Bugac use no saddles at all but
always ride bareback – although those of the Mezohegyes sit on
ordinary saddles.

All Csikos use snaffle bridles and never ride at the trot. They all
carry whips which have short wooden handles, less than 18in (46cm)
long, to which heavy leather thongs, 7 or 8ft (2 or 2.5m) long, are
attached by horn or metal rings incorporating spindle joints to avoid
them getting twisted. These whips, which are called *Karikas*, are
embellished with coloured leather tassels on their sticks and, although
they serve the same purpose as Australian stock whips, they are unique
to Hungary.

The Csikos crack their whips very loudly and incessantly during
displays for tourists. Their constant whip-cracking, which is a Hungarian tradition, is ignored by their own horses and only serves to
engage the attention of the horses, the sheep and long-horned cattle

which they herd, so that it may be partly responsible for the usually calm temperaments of most Hungarian horses.

During long days on the *puszta* with nothing to do except watch their herds grazing, the Csikos have taught their horses a number of amusing tricks and accomplishments which are mostly functional in origin but have been developed into entertaining displays for spectators. The horses will lie down on command to provide couches for their riders to recline against and remain supine while the latter stand on top of them cracking their long whips to signal to their stock or drive off marauders. They are taught to adopt a more unusual posture, which is unnatural for horses, in sitting up like a dog so as to enable their riders to shelter between their forelegs, as in a sentry box, from the frequent heavy rain storms which sweep across the Hungarian Plain. Most Csikos can stand on their horses' rumps, holding the ends of their reins and cracking their whips, while their horses canter steadily forward and on straight lines on open ground, not just on an exact circle as in a circus ring where centrifugal force helps them to keep their balance.

The most spectacular trick demonstrated by one or two specially skilled Csikos on each of the three *pusztas* involves the performer standing on the rumps of two horses, with one foot on each, while driving up to a dozen others in front of him on long reins appropriately coupled together, all the while cracking his whip. There is no practical value in this latter trick and, although it is called 'Hungarian Post', it is not unique to Hungary and has a very long international history in the circus, where it is known as 'Roman Ride'. The rider gets useful support by being able to lean back against the tension of the reins and makes sure that more horses are coupled abreast in the front rank than in any succeeding one so as to avoid the risk of getting stuck in gateways and to increase the lateral stability of the whole team. He may be dislodged with dire consequences if any of his horses shy or jink or refuse to go straight forward and, for this feat to be performed in large arenas, in an atmosphere of great excitement and with the need to steer around obstructions at a fast gallop requires great mutual confidence between the man and his horses and amounts to a notable achievement.

Although their clothes, their curious saddlery – or lack of it – and their whip-cracking and demonstrations of balance and agility are now recognized to be a tourist attraction and a lucrative export for display in other countries, Csikos are genuine herdsmen and highly competent horsemen who have inherited a great tradition and maintain it fully today. Evidence of their equestrian ability can be found in the fact that one of them, Joe Turi, came to Great Britain in the 1970s

112

and, without any financial resources or reputation except as a trick rider, soon became one of Britain's best show jumpers and has been for some years a member of the top British national team.

A more general tradition of wild, free but eminently practical horsemanship exists among the Rajput people of Northern India and Pakistan, who are often very good polo players, and in Afghanistan, the Pathans have a well deserved reputation as very tough horsemen and herdsmen as well as warriors. On days of national importance in Afghanistan they play an extraordinary game called *Buz-kashi* in which indefinite numbers of mounted players form two teams, usually based on two tribes, and struggle for possession of the headless, sand-filled body of a goat which they must carry between their respective 'goal posts'. (The latter may be up to 2 miles (3km) apart.) This recreation, which is effectively a cavalry battle without weapons, results in many injuries to riders but surprisingly few to their very hardy ponies. It dwarfs the Pony Club Mounted Games into insignificance.

A curious fact of some possible historical interest is that Nubians, who were horsemen of renown in the Ancient World but have had little contact with horses for the past 2,000 years, often seem to develop a remarkable and almost instant affinity with any of them to which they may be introduced today.*

The mounted herdsmen of the West are of more recent origin than their counterparts in the East because there were no horses, in their present form, on the continent of America until Cortez brought some with him to Mexico at the beginning of the sixteenth century. Their riding styles are different from those of their counterparts in eastern Europe and Asia in that they ride with long stirrup leathers and quite straight legs, sitting well down in their saddles instead of crouching on them, and they use curb bits rather than snaffles.

The gauchos of the Argentine and the vaqueros of Mexico share common roots with the cowboys of the American West in that they are all fundamentally ranchers or herdsmen. Their horsemanship is of

---

* The author lived for some four years in southern Arabia, on the borders of the Yemen, ostensibly in the military service of local rulers. During this time he was provided by one of his 'employers' with the services of a large coal black Nubian 'slave' called Nasser Islam. The word slave is a commonly misconceived bad translation of the arabic *Askar Sultan* which means 'sultan's soldier'. Nasser Islam – whose lighter-skinned comrades called him Sambo and thereby occasioned no offence in a country where racism is unknown – was the pure-bred descendant of great-grandparents originally imported by purchase by the Alowi Sheikh, in whose great grandson's household he still remained. His social status was effectively equivalent to that of the *Kabil* or tribesmen. Like them, he was never without his rifle and did no manual work.

Although he had no practical experience of horses, Nasser Islam undertook to lead a large, bad-tempered, nappy pony for me from Aden to Lodar, a journey of some 150 miles over mountainous country partly inhabited by dissident tribesmen who would have captured him if they had had the chance. He was equipped for this expedition only with his rifle, a water-bottle and a snaffle bridle and wore only sandals, a shirt and his customary lightweight kilt or *footah* without underpants. Six days after he started he rode into the camp at Lodar sitting proudly on the happy, well-conditioned pony which never afterwards displayed any signs of ill-temper or recalcitrance. Whether the success with which he completed this daunting mission was due in some measure to a remote hereditary horse-sense or just to the spirit of resource and enterprise with which he was endowed by his country of originally enforced adoption remains a mystery.

Spanish origin with its links back through the Moors to the Saracens of Crusader times. The stock riders of Australia, who have a much more recent history, copied the American cowboys quite closely in their use of horses for their work and taught the same form of riding to their aboriginal helpers who had no previous experience of horses.

Gauchos are generally all good, hard, practical horsemen and many of them have the versatility to alter their methods from the breaking and use of cow ponies to the training and schooling of polo ponies, at which they are known to be particularly adept.

Vaqueros were originally Spanish colonists and ranch owners and their descendants still ride very much in Andalucian style with a tendency to make an impressive display of their horsemanship which retains many of the customs and traditions of the fiestas and bull rings of their country of origin.

Their schooling methods and their style of riding have had much influence on those of the Western pleasure riders of California which are more showy and less purely practical than the more workmanlike procedures which prevail in the other states of America and which are generally known as 'Texas style'. In 'California style' horses are very collected and often over-bent by classical European standards, partly to ease the weight of their very heavy curb bits on the bars of their mouths. They are ridden on a single loose rein generally behind their severe curb bits, which are applied only with delicacy, at appropriately processional paces.

In Texas style horses are rather 'poke-nosed' by contrast and elongated in outline. They balance themselves and rely only on occasional indications from a single loose rein attached to a much lighter curb bit whose shanks are swept back to permit some grazing while it is still in the horse's mouth. Cow ponies trained in Texas style normally move at three paces: a well extended ground-covering walk; a jog, which is a slow untiring trot in which the rider does not normally post and which is reckoned to be the best and most economical speed for herding cattle; and the lope, which is in effect a canter but can be increased to produce short bursts of high speed. Texas style is fundamentally for work, not show, and is intended to enable horse and rider to endure long days together covering considerable distances.

Both styles of Western riding rely on indirect neck reining, with the reins held in one hand, to call for turns and changes of direction. Well trained horses respond instantly to this and will turn through 180deg with startling rapidity. Halts are called for by short sharp pulls on the otherwise loose reins and these indications also evoke an instant response in which, from any fast pace, a horse may perform a dramatic 'slide stop', as seen on the cinema. This will involve his head being raised and his hind feet sliding forward under his body – sometimes almost to meet his front feet – and his hocks almost touching the ground.

The instant speed with which sharp turns and halts are executed by working cow hands on their horses are frequently necessary in herding other animals which jink very quickly if they become alarmed or unsettled. However, they place great strain on horses' legs and may cause injuries, so that students of classical equitation are liable to regard them as rough and unseemly and to deplore a trend for them to be introduced into gymkhana-like competitions for purely recreational riders who do not work with stock or aspire to the two or three rodeo events in which such quickness is essential.

Western saddles are heavy, including all their customary attachments, and they weigh between 30 and 40lb (14 and 18kg), or sometimes rather more in the case of those used for steer roping. However, with a thick pad underneath them, which is essential, they spread the rider's weight comfortably along the horse's back and keep him firmly seated in the correct position, unless they are built up too much in front and tend to shift him backwards, which is a fault not unknown in 'dude' saddles. Many western saddles are fitted with a second flank cinch or girth to the rear of the one in the usual position to provide extra security and stability and they are used extensively for trail riding and by some people for endurance and long distance riding.

There are not many ranches left in America on which the hands do all their work mounted, and virtually none on which they select their horses from a half-wild herd and break them in themselves, instantly and rather roughly, in the manner of the Old West. This process was hurried – of necessity – and often rather violent, but it involved a kindly practical understanding of horse psychology and never any deliberate cruelty. It usually resulted in a firm basis of interdependence between horse and rider which quickly developed into willing co-operation. Many sensible cowboys backed horses for the first time in flank-deep water to reduce the effects of their initial resistance and substitute the risk of a ducking for that of injury to either of the prospective partners.

Of a few remaining ranches which still depend very largely on horse power, the 6666 or 'Four Sixes' ranch which consists of 350 square miles (900sq km) of prairie west of Dallas, Texas and is owned by Miss Anne Burnett and managed by the legendary J J Gibson is a fine example. Its 20,000 head of Hereford cattle living on the open range are looked after by twenty-odd hands who are all genuine working cowboys, all now well into middle age. These cowboys do virtually all their work on horseback and their only concessions to modernity are

Australian stockmen rounding up cattle with dogs and using long
Australian stock whips.

to be found in their pay, the nice houses in which they live with their families and the veterinary treatment and remedies which they apply to their stock.

The Four Sixes is certainly no dude ranch and its methods are obviously commercially viable and clearly demonstrated as such at the round-ups. About 500 cattle at a time are rounded up twice a year and a team of five or six men working together cut out, rope and tie each calf and then brand, de-horn, inoculate and castrate it all in a time of about 3 minutes, without any machinery except for a portable gas-fired heating furnace.

The cowboy's horse *par excellence* is the American Quarter Horse, whose number exceeds that of any other breed in the USA. Stocky, short-coupled and under 16hh with very powerful quarters, he is not named for this attribute but for his great speed over a quarter of a mile. This, together with an innate instinct for turning quickly to face and head off other animals, similar to the instinct possessed by good sheep dogs, makes him an ideal herdsman's horse. Quarter horses are true all-purpose mounts and seem to be the first choice of most American citizens for every kind of recreational riding. They also compete in well regulated races, for large stakes and a considerable volume of *pari*

116

mutuel betting money, at more than 100 tracks all over the USA over distances from 1 furlong to ¹/₂ mile, and are now exported to many other countries.

Despite difficulties imposed by quarantine regulations, American Quarter Horses have been exported to Australia via England during the past twenty years where they have proved their value to Australian and New Zealand stock riders. Australian stockmen herd sheep as much as cattle and, although they can hardly have had any chance of learning their skills or their horsemanship from their American counterparts who have been in practice for rather longer than they have, they have evolved them along very similar lines without any discernible Spanish influence and using saddlery of more conventional English pattern. They have also taught a number of aboriginal Australians to ride and work with them and these people, whose immediate ancestors cannot even have seen a horse because there were none in their country until well into the nineteenth century, have taken to practical horsemanship with remarkable facility.

A study of horsemanship, even if only academic, cannot be complete without a mention of that demonstrated by the American (Red) Indians in the three short centuries which elapsed between the time when they first encountered horses and the date when they virtually gave up using them.

Some of the descendants of the horses which the *conquistadors* brought with them escaped from their Spanish colonist owners and spread northwards in wild herds through Mexico into the lands of the Plains Indians quite early in the seventeenth century. The Indians caught them and, having never seen such animals before, treated them initially like large dogs. Such treatment seems to have led to an agreeable relationship because very soon they were riding them, bareback and with only rawhide halters for control, and hunting buffaloes with them instead of pursuing their previously mainly pastoral way of life.

The entirely self-taught skill which they displayed in this enterprise must count as truly astonishing because to kill a buffalo, the great American bison, requires a well aimed shot straight to the heart, even from a modern rifle; the animal's head is too heavily boned for a brain shot to be normally effective. The Indian hunters had to deliver this shot, just below the hump, from a short bow aimed from the bare backs of their galloping ponies. Their mounts had to carry them close up against their quarry, which was usually one of a herd stampeding and galloping as fast as the horses. With the speed and mobility provided by their new-found mounts, the Plains Indians became notable buffalo hunters, following the herds as true nomads and with their tribal wealth invested in their large herds of horses and the skill and courage of their braves.

The tribes which acquired horses and adapted to an impressive standard of horsemanship between 1650 and 1800 were: Kiowa, Cheyenne, Crow, Comanche, Arapaho, Blackfoot, Assiniboin, Cree, Nez Percés, Sioux and Apache and their various related sects and sub-tribes, and no doubt others less well documented. The Comanches are generally reckoned to have been the best horsemen of them all.

Indians took to riding with bits by the beginning of the nineteenth century but they never really bothered with saddles. Despite this disadvantage and that of having far less modern weapons than their adversaries, they proved themselves to be first class irregular soldiers in the Indian Wars – which engaged many of them during the middle years of the nineteenth century – and more than a match for General Custer's 7th US Cavalry at the battle of Little Bighorn in 1876. Without any outside help or instruction, the Plains Indians reached a standard of wild untutored practical horsemanship and rapport with their horses which was arguably more effective than that which most other races or nations had taken five times as many centuries to perfect, even with access to advice and equipment from all the horse-owning countries in the world.

Few American Indians maintained any great interest in horses after the beginning of the twentieth century, although the Nez Percés are justly credited with having established and developed the Appaloosa breed which is now one of the five most popular in the USA, and the secret of their equestrian success may never now be discovered. However, a clue may lie in their forefathers' undeniably wild and savage natures, which so terrified the early European settlers in their country, and in the remarkable sense of balance with which so many of them still seem to be born and which makes some of them such highly competent steeplejacks.

Equestrian endeavour covers a wide range of attitudes and interests and if the meticulous precision of the dressage rider, inherited from the classical traditions of the *manège*, may be considered to represent one end of its spectrum, the wild instinctive riding of the herdsman, hunter and warrior, whose horse is essential to his living and way of life, must be held to be at the opposite one. There is a common denominator which covers the whole spectrum, including both its ends, and it is the way of a man with a horse or horsemanship.

9

Horsemanship in the Circus

In the Ancient World the circus was a large oblong or oval arena about three times as long as its width but of no specific size, with a barrier dividing it lengthwise so as to leave a track round its perimeter for chariot racing. There is no direct historical connection between the circuses of ancient Rome and those of relatively modern times, of which the first was that presented by Philip Astley, ex-sergeant major of the 15th Dragoons and a very effective horseman, at Lambeth in London in 1768. He used a circular ring 42ft (17m) in diameter to present a number of acts (generally involving horses) and spectacular trick-riding but without any gladiatorial or competitive content, to paying spectators who sat round it on tiered seats.

There is no very special reason for the circus ring having a diameter of 42ft and other sizes have been tried, but horses in particular get used to it, it seems to impart just the right degree of centrifugal force to help the balance of riders who stand on their backs, and it is a tradition which is so well established that many artistes will not attempt to perform in an arena of different size.

Astley and his partner Hughes, who fell out with him and started up on his own, travelled their circuses all over the northern hemisphere and by the end of the eighteenth century circuses were being seen in Russia and America. Although there are no more than twenty circuses in Great Britain today, and only two or three big ones in the tradition of Mills and Chipperfield, there are probably still some 400 in the whole world and the biggest and most numerous are in Russia where they probably number about 100.

The modern circus started with horses and still depends fundamentally and traditionally on them, and on three different kinds of acts in which they are primarily concerned: voltige, liberty acts and High School. Voltige is the oldest of all the circus acts and variations on it were Philip Astley's speciality. In its original and purest form it involves a single horse cantering round the ring wearing a surcingle incorporating two handgrips. One or more riders use this surcingle to vault onto and over the horse, performing a number of feats of agility and balance such as are performed regularly, if less spectacularly, by

The Swiss vaulting team competing in the World Equestrian Games in Stockholm in 1990. 'Voltige' is the oldest and most traditional of circus acts, but is now recognized by the International Equestrian Federation as a competitive sport in which many children on the continent of Europe who do not own their own ponies can learn the elements of horsemanship.

children in Germany. Since 1980, children and young people in many other countries of the world practise the exercises concerned as a competitive activity regulated by the International Equestrian Federation.

There are several variations on the theme of voltige: one of the earliest, known as 'voltige *à la* Richard', involved a horse wearing no bridle or saddle or harness of any kind on which a rider performed very energetic vaults of several kinds at inevitably quite high speed. This was named after its originator, an American called Davis Richard, who killed himself while performing in St Petersburg in 1865. The immediate successor to Richard's act was called 'voltige infernale' and for this the horse wore a surcingle and bridle, but circled the ring at high speed about ten times while the rider used momentum, centrifugal force and the handgrips on the surcingle to perform very high leaps and vaults alongside and over his speeding horse.

Simple variations on this theme are voltige Tcherkesse, which copies the trick riding of Cossacks and requires the rider to hang upside down from his cantering horse with one foot hooked into the surcingle, and voltige *à la* cowboy, in which lariats are used to elaborate the gymnastic content of the act. This latter form gave rise to the extravaganzas incorporating coaches as well as cowboys and Indians which were originally presented by 'Buffalo Bill' Cody and which spread beyond the circus ring into much bigger arenas. The famous chuck wagon race at the annual Calgary Stampede in Canada has an obvious affinity with spectacles of this kind though, being competitive, is more akin to a rodeo event.

Voltige requires strength and agility, but also a fair measure of horsemanship in terms of balance and confidence. Its value in giving children a good start in some of the fundamental principles of equitation is well recognized in an environment quite removed from the circus, where they are taught to perform some of the simpler exercises on a horse working on a lunge rein, mainly in countries where small ponies are scarce.

In certain circus acts, the performers spend most of their time balanced on top of usually bareback horses while they circle the ring at a steady canter. These acts are related to voltige and they are known generally, in circus parlance, as 'Jockey acts' or sometimes as 'rosinback acts'. This latter name originated in America. It is derived from the resin which is rubbed into the horses' coats to provide better grip for the feet of the performers who stand on them and the horses themselves are known as 'rosinbacks'. Jockey or rosinback acts were developed as an early variation of voltige and are those which are primarily associated with the circus in most people's minds. The essential balance on which they depend is made possible largely by the centrifugal force which the standard 42ft diameter circle of the ring imparts, provided that the horse remains always in the track and maintains a steady speed. Horses concerned need to be strong and fit to play their part effectively.

Performers in Jockey or Rosinback acts demonstrate several of the abilities possessed by circus artistes who do not normally perform with horses, and these are not necessarily related to horsemanship but they would invariably fail in the execution of them if the horses concerned did not perform impeccably. The acts themselves may involve one, two or three horses and up to three, or occasionally more, artistes. The basis of the act is that the performers run and jump onto the rumps of the cantering horses landing on them upright and on their feet. Only a clumsy performer will use his hands or grab any part of the horse and an avoidance of this is a matter of pride for the artistes concerned. Performers then stand on each other's shoulders to form pyramids on two or three horses. The most difficult of these balances is that in which performers stand on each other's shoulders on a single horse.

The most difficult trick in all bareback riding is that in which the single performer throws a backward somersault from a standing position on the first horse of three and lands on his feet on the third horse. This trick was first performed by the Italian artiste Lucio Cristiani in the 1950s. It depends on perfect timing and the three horses keeping well closed up with heads and necks overlapping quarters, and an absolutely steady pace.

The Roman ride, in which the performer stands with a foot on the rumps of each of two horses and drives others in front of him on long reins, is the speciality of the Hungarian Czikos (see Chapter 8) and does not fit well into the confines of the circus ring. In the courier ride, the performer stands legs apart, one foot on the back of two horses, while others gallop forward between his legs in succession so that he can pick up the long reins attached to them and end up driving them in single file ahead of him. The courier ride is a traditional and impressive circus act.

A few unusual acts have involved lions or tigers jumping onto the backs of cantering horses, necessarily protected by thick pads, and balancing there. The lions and tigers have invariably taken to this performance more readily than the horses and the ultimate development of this act seems to have been a lion and a tiger sitting up side by side on the back of an elephant.

Like all true circus acts, bareback or jockey riding involves no deception and depends on balance, strength, agility, timing and considerable nerve. It becomes more comprehensible to the spectator if he appreciates that for almost 150 years it has been taught with the aid of a so-called 'riding machine', which is a derrick or crane arm, projecting from the tent pole in the centre of the ring and swivelling round it, to which a rope is attached through a pulley. The rope is attached to the belt of the learner and the trainer holds the other end of it and can save his pupil from hitting the ground when he falls by acting promptly in taking the strain. This apparatus has been used with hilarious effect by clowns, and even by bold members of the audience invited to try their skill at bareback riding, but it cannot be used effectively to teach voltige because of the entanglement which occurs.

Liberty acts, being those performed by horses without any riders or any direct control by presenters, are in the true traditions both of the circus and of horsemanship. They are considered to be of two kinds: those in which a group of horses perform concerted evolutions, apparently dictated by the whip cracks of their presenter or even by changes in the music which accompanies their act, and those in which individual horses seem to obey verbal commands and to answer questions and do simple sums by giving indications with apparently human intelligence.

In both cases the horses concerned react to signals or cues given to them by their presenter which, in the first case, are largely concealed to the audience in an apparently general flurry of the flourishing and cracking of a whip and, in the second case, are given unobtrusively so as to remain mainly unnoticed by spectators. The whip is essential as an extension of the trainer's arm and, although the loud cracks which he makes with it serve partly to create a traditional circus atmosphere, they also attract the attention of the horses to the next cue which the trainer will give them. Some of the signals made with the whip in Liberty acts are standard and traditional, as those made by a conductor to his orchestra, but others amount to private signals from a trainer to his horses.

The basis of the act is the process known to many horsemen well beyond the confines of the circus as 'whip breaking'. This involves a trainer chivvying a single horse round the perimeter of a fairly small enclosed *manège* until the horse gets fed up with being apparently chased away from him and will come into the centre to make direct contact with him as soon as the whip is held up vertically to indicate to him that he may do so. The horse is made much of as soon as he responds in this way and thereafter he can be directed by signals made with the whip to circle in the track on either rein, turn in it or across the centre and perform movements of increasing complexity at varying paces.

The procedure becomes more difficult when several horses must be worked together to form a liberty act and the trainer needs plenty of time and great patience to be able to work up an act involving up to twenty-four horses, which is about the maximum possible to fit into the ring. The basic routine must be fairly simple and unvaried and horses must always keep their same places in it. This requirement makes occasional lameness a serious problem and de-nerving sometimes a regrettable but practically unavoidable expedient.

Once the troupe is assembled and trained, the horses which comprise it always remember their basic routine and never seem to sicken of it and extra individual tricks can be added. These can involve small ponies or, exceptionally, other animals intermingling with the horses to perform a simple routine of their own, and horses standing on their hind legs – this latter being an old circus tradition known as *da capos* which can be taught fairly easily by judicious preliminary use of the pillar reins.

Tricks performed by so-called 'educated' horses usually involve their seeming to be counting and doing simple sums by pawing the ground an appropriate number of times. They are taught to start pawing by a discreet stimulus which acts as a cue and which persists until the required number of pawings are completed. The cue used to be given in most cases by a tickle with the end of a whip, but a small concealed vibrator activated by a radio transmitter has been used in recent years with more mystifying effect.

Tricks which involve horses fetching articles of clothing, etc, and bringing them to their trainers in their teeth or selecting particular articles such as national flags from a pile, apparently on command, are initiated quite simply by concealing a tempting morsel of appropriate food in the article concerned. Horses can be easily persuaded to remove rugs or bandages from their own bodies or legs by the same expedient or by the bandage incorporating an irritant. All tricks of this kind, as well as those which involve horses standing on pedestals or balancing on see-saws must be taught by the exercise of great patience and edible reward for successful achievement.

The understanding required is that of animal psychology in general and the mentality of horses in particular. Horses, like most of the higher mammals, are intelligent to a degree but can never be clever in the human sense. They have no powers of imagination or reasoning but highly developed senses which react instantly to any stimulation, excellent memories, and acute awareness of atmosphere in general and of having pleased their human associates in particular.

The trainer must trigger the reaction which he wants by applying an appropriate stimulus and immediately reward this so that the horse realizes that it has pleased him and will react in the same way to the same stimulus. A cue or aid, which can often be by voice, can usually be substituted for the original stimulus through a simple process of the one being associated with the other. The horse's good memory, together with his almost invariable desire to create or maintain a pleasant atmosphere by reacting in a way which he has learned will please his trainer will complete the procedure and enable it to be repeated as often as it may be called for.

Reward in an edible form plays an important part in the initial stages of the teaching of tricks of this kind but, unlike many other animals, horses will recognize their virtue as being its own reward as soon as they understand what is expected of them so that a constant supply of titbits is not required and may even cause distraction. Punishment has no part to play in these proceedings because a horse cannot associate any pain or deprivation inflicted on him with any failure on his part to react in any way, or to please his trainer, unless it is inflicted at the precise instant of any rebellion (and even then it is more likely to distract him and disrupt the progress of his learning).

As any old-time farm worker can affirm, horses can recognize and distinguish a fair number of different words, provided these are addressed clearly and directly to them. The vocabulary of an intelligent horse can comprise at least twenty separate words, and some would say up to fifty, including, always, the horse's own name. The intonation and accentuation of the words uttered is far more significant than the pronunciation of the actual syllables and this seems to enable horses to learn similar words in foreign languages very quickly; a useful facility in the international environment of the circus.

High School is the highest art of the circus, at least as regards acts involving horses, and also the most traditional in that its skills are inherited from the classical schools of Austria and France, which flourished in the seventeenth and eighteenth centuries. Through these schools, skills were inherited from equestrian demonstrations which enriched the *manèges* of Spain and Italy during the renaissance, with their tenuous links back to the tilt yards of the Middle Ages.

High School in the circus, though less precisely ordered than in specialist riding schools, is a genuinely expert demonstration of the highest principles and practices of advanced equitation – and short of this it cannot be worthy of the name. Francois Baucher and James Fillis, who were arguably two of the greatest *écuyers*, school riders or riding masters, of all time performed frequently and regularly in the circus ring during the nineteenth century. Their High School acts and

Jasmine Smart of circus fame, displaying her liberty horses at the Horse of The Year Show at Wembley. The connection between horsemanship and the circus is well established.

those of most of their successors have been based firmly on the movements and exercises taught and practised in the great riding academies of the world, of which the senior is the Spanish Riding School in Vienna.

The circus rider must aim to astonish his largely uninformed audience to earn his living, rather than to produce perfectly schooled horses for the edification of fellow horsemen and the maintenance of the highest principles of classical equitation. Accordingly, he will be likely to hurry the preliminary dressage training, and in some cases largely to ignore it, and he will undoubtedly take short-cuts to teach his horse exaggerated movements and 'airs above the ground' in which regularity, precision and correct bends and flexions may be sacrificed to extravagance in paces and actions. He may also perform some very artificial movements which will amaze spectators but have no place in the repertoire of a classical school rider.

The famous James Fillis was adept at increasing the range of his act in this way and his most notorious trick, which was absurdly artificial but required extreme obedience and balance and very precise and delicate aids was to induce his horse to canter backwards on three legs. However absurd or artificial, or even inexact, the movement produced may be, the undeniable fact remains that it can only be taught, and eventually induced by a rider sitting on the horse, by intelligent and finely adjusted application of the conventional aids to a horse which is in balance and on the bit and therefore able and willing to respond to them. The art of the school rider lies in establishing this situation, whether for an elementary dressage test or a complicated High School movement, and horsemanship in a high degree is an essential prerequisite for the achievement of this aim.

One minor harmless deception is practised in conjunction with High School acts in the circus on such members of the audience as may be entirely ignorant of animal mentality. The pretence that horses are dancing to the music which accompanies their acts is encouraged for those who wish to believe it, although it is never true because horses do not possess the particular sense of rhythm or the ability to coordinate their movements in response to such stimulation to make this possible. The circus band, in fact, follows the movements of the horses rather than vice versa and this arrangement, which puts a premium on an experienced conductor and can be imitated, but only to a very limited extent, by a competent operator of a tape deck, adds considerably to the traditional glamour of the act.

A little-known spectacular demonstration of horsemanship of ancient origin and rare artistry is that presented by the few remaining

126

rejoneadors of Spain who display their skill and the remarkable training of their horses occasionally in the much bigger arenas of the bull ring, generally to much bigger and more enthusiastic audiences than are to be found at any circus. The mounted *rejoneador*, who is traditionally an amateur and never a professional, 'plays' the bull and eventually kills it with a single thrust from his lance with far less assistance from picadors, *banderilleros* and other subordinate performers than his dismounted counterpart, the matador, relies on.

The function of the *rejoneador* must not be confused with that of the picador, whose role involves little or no horsemanship. The picador aims to persuade the bull to lower his head to receive the thrust of the matador's sword. This is achieved by weakening the bull's neck muscles with the infliction of a series of minor wounds from a clumsy pole-like spear incorporating a head of restricted length. The picador mounts a padded and blindfolded horse which plays no part in the action except to serve as an unwilling, fairly mobile, and always painfully vulnerable platform for the operator who is seated upon him. By contrast, the *rejoneador*'s horse is a very agile, highly trained, spirited horse of notable quality which must respond instantly to his rider's urgent aids. It must co-operate completely with his rider in avoiding the bull's charges and must ultimately place him in a position from which he can deliver a clean lethal lance thrust to terminate the performance decisively and as humanely as possible.

It is shameful evidence of his rider's failure for a *rejoneador*'s horse to be even slightly injured by the bull, and this lays them both open to the risk of more serious injury. The manoeuvring to avoid this contingency involves a demonstration of free and very active High School movements, often on a loose rein, in which canter pirouettes preponderate and cantering smartly to the rear (backwards) are a frequent and essential requirement.

In contrast to the way of working of the Western Cutting Horse, which reacts directly to the movements of the steers or calves with which it is concerned, the mount of the *rejoneador* must obey only the aids given to him by his rider and not his own instincts (since otherwise great confusion would result, frequently with disastrous consequences). The performance of the *rejoneador* and his horse obviously cannot be planned in advance or dictated by any sort of standard routine. It amounts to a most impressive demonstration of free style High School riding, always executed with immediate and urgent intent, and spectators who may have had the increasingly rare good fortune to witness it should have been able to appreciate a unique display of high class horsemanship in the highest traditions of equestrianism. There have been two opportunities during the past twenty-five years for spectators in Britain to see and study the art of the *rejoneador*, but without the bull.

Very few human beings had any direct contact with wild animals or those of an exotic or non-domestic species until a vogue for training and presenting them as a circus attraction was established in about the middle of the nineteenth century. It may not be too fanciful or far-fetched to suggest that the best of the old-time big cat and wild animal trainers must have learned many of the fundamental principles of their craft from a study of the methods employed by people who had been training horses, and to a lesser extent dogs, with success for many hundreds of years.

Horses and big cats are of course very different from each other in psychology and mental characteristics, and indeed the temperament of a lion is not identical to that of a tiger. At least two basic consider-ations, however, must prevail in any relationship between a human being and any animal whose co-operation he may be seeking to enlist. A good horseman depends on these and can apply them to the training of any other large animal.

An animal which is bigger, stronger and better armed by nature than a man can easily defeat him, usually disastrously, in any situation involving open conflict. Such conflict must therefore always be avoided, so that the animal remains unaware of its physical superiority and never thinks to try to use it to overcome the mental domination which its trainer exercises.

No animal can be induced to react to fear or the infliction of pain other than by flight, evasion or counter-attack, so that animals can only be taught to perform tricks or to act in any way which is not entirely natural to them by methods which create pleasure in achieve-ment. Pleasure can, of course, be created by relief from quite mild temporary discomfort, and this is a contrivance which all animal trainers employ quite readily, but edible reward is the simplest and most usual expedient used, especially in the case of animals with which the trainer cannot maintain close bodily contact. Once the animal has become used to performing the trick or action concerned, it will normally derive some enjoyment from displaying it and pleasing its trainer, so that the edible reward will only need to be offered occasion-ally to help in maintaining a state of harmony.

These two well-established principles amply refute the charges made all too often, particularly against circuses, that the training of animals, whether wild or domestic, to give performances which will attract public audiences must necessarily involve cruelty. Since cru-elty, being the opposite of kindness, is a comparative assessment and not an absolute evil, no circus artiste or worker can honestly protest that he has never been cruel to animals to the extent of being always kind to them. However, deliberate cruelty to animals on whose co-operation the living or reputation of their human partners depends is self-defeating and counter-productive. Experienced horsemen appreciate this and the consideration that it applies to all other animals, whether equine or feline.

The last words on the subject should be left to the late Mr Bertram Mills, horseman of distinction and circus proprietor *par excellence**: 'Training secrets? – There are none. Patience, understanding and carrots are the eternal triumvirate. There is no other way and never was.'

* In the 1960s the author enjoyed the fascinating experience of spending six days at a big circus in the company of a famous trainer and presenter of big cats. This kindly man was happy to explain his methods which were based on the principles outlined above. He was able to point to two practical demonstrations of their validity. A tiger cub which had been rejected by its mother lived very happily with a half-grown male Alsatian puppy as a prospective member of this troupe. The two animals played happily and endlessly together and shared much the same feeding arrangements. The trainer explained that, sadly, their companionship could only last another two or three months because, although they were currently well matched in strength and aggressive spirit and, lacking any means of determining their own appearance, each regarding the other as being of the same species, the tiger would soon grow bigger and stronger than the dog and after injuring it inadvertently in play, probably with its claws, would appreciate its own physical superiority and soon kill it and start to make a meal of it in accordance with its carnivorous instincts to prey on weaker creatures.

The second demonstration concerned a black panther, about the size of a large labrador dog, which had been taught by the trainer to jump from a 4ft high pedestal over a distance of about 10ft and land in his outstretched arms without touching the ground. The panther performed this trick twice nightly to order, but it was virtually unnoticed by most members of the audiences who regarded the performance as unimpressive. The trainer pointed out that this was the most difficult, and potentially the most dangerous, trick that he had ever performed with any of his animals and that it had taken much longer to perfect than any other. The panther had to have complete confidence in him and be pleased to jump into his arms of its own volition and to land in them quite passively. He questioned whether any owner of a domestic cat, however cherished and apparently biddable it might be, could ever induce his pet to perform this trick, even over a much shorter distance, and so far as I know nobody ever has.

10

Horsemanship on State Occasions

The rulers or heads of state of some eight nations still travel in horsed carriages with cavalry escorts on ceremonial occasions. In Britain, Spain, Denmark, Sweden and Portugal the carriages are turned out and driven by full-time professionals and the mounted escorts are provided by regular soldiers. The President of France rides in a car rather than a carriage, but is escorted by mounted members of the Garde Républicaine who are permanent employees of the state. The Emperor of Japan rides in a carriage, but without a military escort. The Queen of the Netherlands keeps a range of carriages and carriage horses in her Royal Mews, but relies on part-time volunteers with their own horses to provide her mounted escorts.

Both the carriage and the escort for the Governor General of Canada are provided by amateur volunteers who have the status of yeomanry, though the escort is sometimes provided by the Royal Canadian Mounted Police. Other countries, notably India, Pakistan and Egypt and some South American republics, have produced carriage processions on special occasions and the Shah of Iran had a carriage and a mounted escort available to him before the revolution.

The composition, equipment, uniforms, turnout and procedures of carriage processions and mounted escorts vary considerably between different countries, but those in Britain are held to be of very high standard and in accordance with the best traditions, so that they may indeed provide an example of these arrangements at their most impressive.

The establishment of the Queen's carriage horses and coachmen and grooms has been reduced recently in the interests of economy, but the staff of the royal mews at Buckingham Palace, working under the Crown Equerry who is responsible to the Master of the Horse, can still turn out seven carriages for any state procession or drive, and all but two of them can be pulled by four horses. There are always at least ten grey horses, which are traditionally used only for carriages in which the sovereign travels, because eight of them are needed to pull the Gold Coach which is used for coronations and jubilees, and there are normally more than twenty bay horses which are used regularly for carriages conveying ambassadors.

There are more than fifteen coaches and carriages suitable for state occasions in the royal mews, apart from the Gold Coach which can only travel at a walk, so the limitation on the size of a royal carriage procession is in terms of manpower rather than horsepower or the number of carriages available. This is not surprising in view of the high standard of coachmanship and general horsemanship required to convey The Queen and other very important people through the streets of the capital when they are *en fête* and liable to be packed with cheering crowds and other alarming distractions.

To drive a pair of horses pulling a heavy state coach or carriage in such conditions requires skill and confidence, as well as strong steady horses, and the three postillions who must manage the six horses which normally pull The Queen's coach or carriage on such occasions

The Royal Canadian Mounted Police performing their musical ride at the Royal Windsor show. They breed their own black horses at their own stud farm and produce them to perfection in show rings all over the world, as well as for peace-keeping duties in their own country.

need to demonstrate special ability which must incorporate close coordination of their actions.

The most demanding task which any ceremonial procession involves is that of driving four horses from the box seat of a state coach. The coachman sits alone, with no one to help him in emergency since the footmen are on the back of the vehicle and cannot get down and run forward in time to be of any immediate assistance. In today's royal processions footmen are, in any case, almost invariably indoor servants or security officials with no great experience of horses.

There can be no grooms on foot with processions which proceed at the trot, and attempts by bystanders to restrain frightened horses are almost always disastrous. The Queen's head coachman commits himself to the most nerve-racking ordeal in all modern coachmanship when he steers his four-in-hand, drawing his sovereign in the Irish State Coach through the narrow gateway of Horse Guards at the trot twice a year on his way to and from the State Opening of Parliament. For some thirty years during the middle of this century this particular feat was never performed because no royal coachman had the confidence to attempt it and the carriage in which The Queen travelled was postillion driven.

The Queen's carriage horses are now mostly home-bred at the Royal Stud at Hampton Court and any which are bought are young, so that they are all broken and schooled mainly in London, with a few useful visits to the Royal Mews at Windsor Castle where the Great Park provides more scope for their training. The ages of the horses in the Royal Mews range from about six to about twenty and, as with the staff – many of whom also have proud family connections in royal service – there is a constant need for youth to succeed old age to maintain an establishment which must always be at full strength and ready for a full-scale state carriage procession.

There is much to be said for horses and their handlers growing up together, learning their work together and establishing complete dependence on each other without reliance on outside experts or special training facilities. However, for this to be achieved in the centre of London by a staff of coachmen and grooms whose size is limited by the dictates of the civil list and whose state and ceremonial duties already occupy much of their time requires long hours of dedicated work and the exercise of high standards of horsemanship and horsemastership.

The big indoor riding schools at Buckingham Palace and Windsor Castle are very valuable for starting young horses for work in harness, as under saddle. Outdoor work and training and daily exercise in London, where the staff and horses spend most of their time, is effectively confined to the row in Hyde Park and must be done in the early hours of the morning before the traffic builds up and makes the journey to and from it hazardous and in itself an obstruction. The one rather curious advantage which young horses gain from learning their work in the busy streets of any big city is that there is so much for them to shy at that shying is pointless and they very soon stop doing it. They also quickly gain confidence from working in pair-harness beside an older, more experienced horse.

Learning to work in harness in the streets of London and in crowds of varying sizes and density is an ongoing process not governed by a specific period of time. The Crown Equerry and The Queen's head coachman must therefore exercise constant careful judgement in deciding the extent to which the younger horses in their care, and the younger members of their human staff, can be safely committed to the processional routes which are likely to be more crowded and noisy than others and generally more difficult to negotiate safely. Rehearsals, which have to be strictly limited in number, take place very early in the morning, mainly to determine timing, and cannot simulate the crowd conditions which will be encountered to any significant extent.

If the people concerned, at all levels, felt anxious about their responsibilities royal processions would no doubt be dominated by extreme nervous tension. However, an air of quiet determined confidence born of long experience always prevails and this undoubtedly communicates itself to the horses, so that they can all be relied upon to play their parts on impressive ceremonial occasions in which mishaps are minor, infrequent and almost invariably unnoticed by even the most critical spectators.

Horse sense is not over-ruled by the dictates of protocol or even tradition and, although their absence has never aroused comment from any member of the public, one of The Queen's bay carriage horses which regularly takes part in the most important processions always does so wearing a bridle without blinkers.*

The biggest state carriage procession to have taken place anywhere in the world during the second half of the twentieth century was undoubtedly that for the coronation of The Queen of England in 1952. This stretched the resources of the Royal Mews to their limit and required them to be augmented by volunteer coachmen with their own horses who were not in royal service and were nearly all

---

* It is a misconception that blinkers are needed to prevent horses becoming frightened by the carriages' wheels turning behind them. A horse so unintelligent as to be affected in this way after a sensible introduction to his work would be a menace in harness. Blinkers focus a horse's attention and prevent him being distracted by the movements of the people on the carriage behind him. A very few extra-sophisticated horses can concentrate on their work without this aid and resent the limitation to their arc of vision which they impose.

amateurs, though very capable ones. Thirty-four coaches and carriages were turned out to take part in the ceremonies of this great day. All were drawn by pairs of horses except for The Queen's Gold Coach with its eight greys, which was the final focus of the whole procession, and the coach of the Lord Mayor of London which was pulled, as is customary, by six grey horses from Whitbread's brewery from the Mansion House to Westminster Abbey.

The Royal Mews itself provided the postillions and horses for the Gold Coach and for three state coaches: the Irish Coach, the Glass Coach and Queen Alexandra's Coach, and five state landaus; twenty-four horses, eight postillions and eight coachmen in all, which conveyed The Queen, the royal family and members of their suites.

Ten royal Clarences were horsed and driven by amateur members of the Coaching Club to convey the Prime Ministers of the Commonwealth. Five of these closed carriages, originally sold out of royal service, were lent by the film company which had bought them and hastily re-painted. These carriages and horses were housed in the Royal Mews and turned out from there during the period of rather less than two months which was allowed for the organizing and mounting of the whole operation.

Nine Landaus, which carried the Dominion rulers and Service Chiefs were provided and horsed by two of Britain's last remaining job masters, Messrs Dave Jacobs and George Mossman, but driven effectively by amateurs.

The Lord Mayor's coach and that of the speaker of the House of Commons, which is the oldest coach in the world still in use, drove only to Westminster Abbey and did not take part in the return procession to Buckingham Palace. Four peers: the Duke of Devonshire, the Duke of Wellington, the Marquess of Bath and Earl Spencer had the enterprise to turn out their family coaches for the occasion and drive in them in convoy from Apsley House to the Abbey; only Earl Spencer failed to arrive in his.

In addition to the seventy-six carriage horses involved and a full turn-out by the Household Cavalry, including a mounted band, and The King's Troop Royal Horse Artillery, all but one of the Dominion Prime Ministers were accompanied by a mounted escort of four soldiers from their own countries and some thirty very senior officers of the British armed forces processed mounted. These latter did so somewhat insecurely for the most part, since they were reluctant to accept the instruction and practice arranged for them in the Hyde Park camp set up by the Household Cavalry and Royal Army Veterinary Corps for the hastily conscripted horses which they were to ride. The officers were over-confident in their own written assessments of their weights and riding ability which were the crucial factors affecting the finding of horses to suit them.

History must in truth relate that the coronation procession did not go off without a hitch. Apart from the incessant rain which dampened the enthusiasm of almost everyone except the Queen of Tonga, who made history and maintained the best traditions by resolutely refusing to have the hood of her landau put up and was accordingly the only dignitary to complete the course in an open carriage, the whole procession telescoped badly and finished the last stretch up the Mall double banked.

Critics suggested subsequently that a failure in timing and communication had been responsible for this confusion, but it is more rationally explained by an appreciation of the order of the procession which was led by numerous contingents of marching men, and some women, and completed by nearly 400 horses immediately preceding The Queen in her Gold Coach, who traditionally brought up the rear. The whole procession moved at walking pace, but horses walk faster than people, even when the latter are stepping out to the best of their ability, and must be liable to overtake them unless they are given a very long start or there is a halt to allow them to get ahead from time to

Part of the Household Cavalry Regiment on parade for the annual inspection of the Major General Commanding the Household Division in Hyde Park.

time. In short, the pace of the procession was deliberately and traditionally dictated by The Queen's coach and maintained by the carriages and mounted men in front of it, but the marching troops in front of them could not match or maintain it and were inevitably overtaken. The coronation procession was, however, a brave and glorious enterprise which would have been far less impressive if the Earl Marshall, the Duke of Norfolk, had not decreed that it should be a wholly horsed one. It made its mark on history and the horses made it memorable, whilst horsemanship in the widest sense, demonstrated as much by amateurs as professionals, made it possible.

The Household Cavalry Regiment at Hyde Park Barracks, Knightsbridge consists of a squadron from the Life Guards and a squadron from the Royal Horse Guards (The Blues and Royals). Each squadron has about 130 horses, some of which are with the armoured squadrons of their regiments, either at Windsor or the overseas station to which the alternative regiment is posted, to provide training for recruits or to be trained themselves. Each mounted squadron consists of rather more than 150 officers and men, including the musicians of each regiment's bands. The two mounted squadrons take turns on alternate days to provide The Queen's Life Guard, which mounts at Horse Guards and provides the two mounted sentries at the gate onto Whitehall. This is the front gate of the old royal palace of Whitehall and, by implication, that of the original royal palace of Westminster.

The two squadrons combine to provide sovereign's escorts and separately provide the smaller escorts, Captain's escorts, Prince of Wales's escorts and travelling escorts, as required. They also provide a number of dismounted guards and parties inside royal palaces where, by tradition, they are the only serving soldiers permitted to be armed.

The state or full dress uniforms of the two regiments of Household Cavalry are well known to the public, as generally is the fact that the Life Guards wear red tunics with white helmet plumes and sit on white sheep skins fitted over their saddles, whereas The Blues and Royals wear blue tunics with red helmet plumes and sit on black sheep skins. All ranks of both regiments of the Household Cavalry ride black horses, which must be 16.2hh. or bigger, except for trumpeters who ride grey horses which are allowed to be slightly smaller.

A sovereign's escort with two standards, one from each regiment, is usually provided when there are two carriages to be escorted and this consists of nine officers and 112 other ranks, including two corporal majors, who carry the two standards, and two trumpeters. With one standard, when there is only one carriage, this strength is reduced only by two officers, one corporal major, one trumpeter and one NCO who is the 'coverer' for the second standard; i.e. the party which directly accompanies the second carriage. The formation of all escorts is based on two troopers riding as 'Advance Points' well in front of the whole cortège and two troopers riding an equal distance behind as 'Rear Points'. Their original task was to clear the road and give warning of any threat of trouble through the two NCOs who link them with the actual divisions of the escort.

A sovereign's escort comprises two divisions, each of one officer and twenty-four men in front of the carriage, and two behind it. The rear divisions are now drawn from the regiment whose standard is carried behind the first carriage in which The Queen travels. This regiment is deemed to provide the escort and would have done so in its entirety before both regiments were largely mechanized and left with only one horsed squadron each. The smaller escorts are drawn entirely from one or other regiment. The squadron leader, normally a major, of the squadron whose regiment is deemed to be providing a sovereign's escort rides on the right of The Queen's carriage and is responsible for her immediate protection. He is, rather confusingly, known as the Field Officer of the Escort and his second in command, usually a captain, rides on the left of the carriage and is known as the Escort Commander.

The counterparts of these two officers from the squadron of the other regiment ride on the right and left of the second carriage. The corporal majors (there are no sergeants in the Household Cavalry since the ancient meaning of the word is held to denote a servitor rather than a commander) carry the standards of the two regiments immediately behind the carriages flanked by a trumpeter on their right and an NCO to 'cover' or protect the standard on their left.

A subaltern officer commands each division and rides on the left of the front section in an equivalent position to the Escort Commander. The Serrefile Captain, who rides on the left of the rear section of the division immediately in front of The Queen's carriage, has a curious designation and an unusual and demanding task. He must gauge the pace of The Queen's carriage, which dictates the pace of the escort, by constantly looking behind him at it, and signal necessary alterations in speed to the leading division for verbal transmission to the Advance Points. Onlookers who see the officers concerned apparently not looking steadfastly to their front and condemn this as unsoldierly are unaware of the particular responsibility which they have.

Four farriers carrying ceremonial axes form an extra final section immediately behind the last division of the escort. They parade only with a Sovereign's Escort, but a single farrier rides behind the second division of a Captain's Escort.

A Sovereign's Escort is provided only for The Queen, who may however, have a smaller escort on appropriate occasions. Smaller escorts, with or without standards, may be provided for senior members of the royal family or rulers or presidents of foreign nations. All escorts, except those for the Gold Coach, which is only used for coronations and jubilees, and for funerals and The Queen's Birthday Parade, customarily travel at the trot.

To ride at a good round trot in state or full dress uniform is an uncomfortable and unsettling experience for those who are not accustomed to it, even if they ride well with ordinary clothes and saddlery. Sheep skins to sit on provide some slight cushioning effect and are less slippery than uncovered saddles, but the rest of the clothing, equipment and accoutrements involved tends to create an initial feeling of insecurity and encumbrance which requires getting used to. An army saddle with a folded blanket underneath it and a sheep skin on top of it, plus a shabrack for an officer, amounts to considerable bulk between the rider's thighs and his horse's back and sides so that he is unable to sit close to his horse or to use weight aids effectively or any precise aids with his lower legs.

Obligatorily tight leather breeches and stiff thick jackboots (which reach to mid-thigh and are designed to resist sword cuts) further restrict a household cavalryman's use of his legs to control his horse. He must not rise at the trot while wearing state dress and is required to ride with long stirrup leathers so that his swan neck spurs are usually his only effective points of contact with his horse's flanks. Cuirasses, worn on chest and back by all ranks except trumpeters, musicians and farriers, are not heavy but do restrict the forward reach of their wearer's arms, so that it is virtually impossible to mount from the ground wearing them. Coupled with the extra height of the pommels of saddles, which is imposed by now empty pistol holsters attached over them, cuirasses severely limit a rider's range of movement in the saddle, and particularly his ability to lean forward.

The helmets worn by soldiers of the Household Cavalry are not heavy and can be adjusted to fit well by the tapes which the skull caps inside them incorporate, but their plumes make them top-heavy and liable to slip backwards or even sideways, when they become uncomfortable and look ridiculous. When they are correctly positioned, their peaks are just in contact with their wearers' nose and this restricts their range of vision slightly. It is not permissible, or possible, to wear spectacles with helmets of this pattern, so short-sighted riders are at an additional disadvantage and must either cope with not seeing too well or resort to contact lenses or, in theory, a monocle.

Regulations prescribe that, on all ceremonial parades, horses must be ridden on the bit or curb rein with the bridoon or snaffle rein hanging loose; the latter is simply looped over the rider's little finger and hangs down to its farthest extent. Horses cannot be expected to accept strong or constant contact from the severe curb action of their long-cheeked Buxton bits, to which the reins are attached at their extremity, so they must be in effect behind their bits and operate generally on a loose rein responding to neck reining and rather spasmodic rein aids as indications for changes of pace and direction. The fingers of the large, thick, leather gauntlets which form part of full dress uniform must be kept spotlessly white with blanco or pipeclay and this process does not induce precise or delicate rein handling.

With full dress uniform, swords are slung from a belt worn under the tunic so that when the wearer is mounted the scabbard hangs down to about the level of the horse's hocks and swings freely. Horses get used to the quite light bangs and raps on their legs which this arrangement occasions, but it causes some additional irritation. It is difficult for a soldier in full dress to return his sword to its scabbard when mounted, so that the drill for this is only carried out in barracks or during guard mounting at Horse Guards. Accordingly, all ranks of the Household Cavalry have their right hands fully engaged in holding either a sword or a standard, a trumpet or a farrier's axe from the time they leave barracks for a ceremonial parade until the time they return after its completion.

For the duration of an escort its members must ride 'at attention' with their swords 'at the carry', which means vertically upright instead of 'sloped' to rest on their shoulders. The strictly vertical position is maintained by the rider keeping his little finger behind the hilt of the sword to steady it and jamming it hard up against the sheepskin-covered pistol holster. In either position, he cannot free his right hand for any other purpose except in dire emergency when it is possible for him to transfer his sword temporarily to his left hand over his reins with his thumb securing the blade. The requirement to ride for several hours with only the left hand to hold the reins and control the horse is a limitation imposed on few, if any other, horseman.

The longest journey to which a sovereign's escort is normally, and quite regularly, committed nowadays is that from Buckingham Palace to the Guildhall. The whole trip is covered at a fairly sharp trot and to maintain a sitting trot for this distance is quite testing for the average rider – and for the horse if the rider is stiff and heavy. The rider needs to be supple in his spine and able to relax the relevant muscles within the confines of his uniform without seeming to slouch in the saddle or to allow his head to nod unduly. He hopes to ride a horse with smooth easy action; known to the soldiers as 'a good sit-down', but the pace is invariably too fast to amount to a shuffle or an easy hound jog.

Household Cavalry horses are expected to be as nearly as possible in show condition and to seem to be keen, bright and active in their work. It is often difficult to reconcile this requirement with that for them to be calm and steady on parade, particularly as some of them are always liable to be rather short of exercise. The thirty-two horses which will have furnished the two Queen's Life Guards on the two days immediately before a procession involving a sovereign's escort will only have walked to and fro between their stables and Horse Guards on these two days and will have had no time for further exercise before parading for the escort.

An atmosphere of excitement and jubilation communicates itself to the horses so directly involved in it, and it is not unknown for *joie de vivre* to overcome discipline and training and result in a light-hearted buck. It speaks well for the tenacity and riding ability of the soldiers concerned that incidents of their becoming separated from their horses are very few and far between and nearly always the consequence of a horse slipping up and falling. Remounting, if this happens, is unofficially regarded as impracticable and the man is expected to make his best way back to barracks, avoiding the attentions of the press, while the horse will usually try to regain his place in the ranks and become an extra hazard to his comrades. Contrary to popular belief the soldier who suffers this painful ignominy is more likely to receive sympathy than punishment.

The idea that the protection of their sovereign from possible assassination should be entrusted to some men on horses armed only with swords would not commend itself to today's security experts. Other protective precautions are of course in force and Her Majesty is also guarded by an armed policeman acting as a footman or carriage groom, but a close cordon of partly-armoured men on large horses formed instantly around her provides a very effective mobile screen against small bombs or bullets, so that the essential function of a sovereign's escort remains as practical as it ever has been.

The uniform, saddlery and 'horse furniture' of the Household Cavalry is not designed for combat or for equitation but to add splendour and magnificence to state occasions. It imposes limitations on the rider's control of his horse, calls for esoteric expedients to overcome them, and generally makes riding more difficult,* but it is superbly spectacular and enshrines most of the best traditions of chivalry and pageantry.

Horsemanship in 'The Kit', as it is colloquially called, may be seen in its most active possible form in the musical rides which the Household

---

* The Life Guards officer who undertook to attend a meet of the Quorn Hounds in full dress and jump one fence for a bet won it but declined to repeat the performance.

Cavalry Regiment manages to present at shows and tournaments during most summers, despite its prior commitment to regular state duties. A full musical ride involves from thirty-two to forty horses and the men who perform it customarily carry lances instead of swords. This does not free their right hands to any significant extent and they are encumbered with all the other elements of full dress uniform and accoutrements. However, they still manage to perform intricate manoeuvres at all paces, including the gallop, with the essential precision required by the often complicated choreographic designs prescribed by the officer who produces their display. A musical ride lasting 20 minutes makes considerable demands on the stamina of the horses who must perform it – they are carrying a total weight each of between 14 and 18 stone (89 and 114kg) – and the many rehearsals needed for it to be thoroughly learned, as well as the time spent on engagements and travelling between them, account for practically all the free time which the soldiers concerned normally have between their regular duties.

The musicians and trumpeters who form the bands of the Life Guards and the Blues and Royals are all full-time members of their respective regiments and their normal full dress uniform is of regimental pattern except that they never wear cuirasses and the trumpeters of the Life Guards have red plumes instead of white ones on their helmets. Both bands spend part of each year with their parent regiments at home, in Windsor, or abroad but they are also state musicians and must be available in London or occasionally other locations in the United Kingdom for ceremonial royal parades and engagements. When The Queen is present on such occasions, and on a few others with Her Majesty's consent, they wear the old early Georgian state dress of gold coats and velvet 'jockey' caps over their usual white breeches and jackboots and this is identical for both regiments, so that they can combine to form one band of appropriately impressive size when occasion demands.

Prior to 1960 the two bands seldom combined fully for dismounted playing and never did so on horses, but in the early 1960s the Director of Music of the Life Guards prevailed on his opposite number of the Royal Horse Guards to give his initiative a trial and the result, which increased the size of the biggest possible mounted band from thirty to up to sixty players with two drum horses leading a frontage of eight, was a more appropriately majestic muster of musicians who produced a much more resonant sound.* A large, effectively double-sized,

---

* The original suggestion came from the author and it was approved by Colonel The Hon. Julian Berry, who was Silver Stick at the time, and enthusiastically implemented by Colonel, then Major, Jackson who was the Life Guards Director of Music but had started his career in the Blues.

mounted band is provided for The Queen's Birthday Parade and for other ceremonies on Horse Guards Parade, such as Beating Retreat, where the sound produced by just one of the two regiment's bands would lack sonority and compare unfavourably with that of the massed bands of the five regiments of foot guards. It is possible in theory for the Household Cavalry to parade a mounted band of seventy-two players with three drum horses. This has not yet been done but still may be on some particularly worthy occasion.

Although all musicians and trumpeters of the Household Cavalry undergo a course in the riding school and ride regularly enough to keep in practice, they are primarily accomplished and versatile musicians who can ride horses, rather than skilled horsemen who can play musical instruments. Unlike their counterparts in other countries, notably France and Portugal, who trot and even gallop about blowing simple valveless horns and trumpets, Britain's mounted bandsmen are not expected to play or even carry their more complicated instruments at paces faster than a walk. Even so, they have extra difficulties when mounted if their horses jog or even toss their heads. Players of brass instruments only risk losing their front teeth but if the Director's choice of music includes a part for the bassoon, which is not unheard of, its player finds himself in a potentially lethal situation.

A drum horse, traditionally piebald or skewbald, with the silver kettledrums of either regiment on him will be carrying nearly twice the weight borne by most of the other horses. He will be disinclined to jog, with the extra weight over his withers, but must certainly not do so since this would be liable to loosen the drums on their fastenings and likely to put the drummer off his beat. The drummer must keep playing at all costs since his beat dictates the tempo to the rest of the band and the rolls and other elaborations which are called for when the music is scored for two-tuned timpani or kettledrums would be sadly missed if they ceased even temporarily. Unlike most of his fellow players he cannot spare a hand for the reins, which are hung loosely from a hook on the front of his tunic, in the case of the bit or curb reins, and attached to the tops of his stirrups in the case of the bridoon or snaffle reins. He can steer his horse to a certain extent with these latter foot reins and may often have to do so since the drum horse always 'marches' by himself in front of the band with only the Director of Music in front of him.

Although the drum horse does often seem to step in time to the beat of his drums, the other horses in the band or the rest of a procession do not do this and obviously have no sense of rhythm to this extent, although they seem to quite enjoy the noise which their band makes. This seems to prove that horses cannot perform to music or keep time with it in the way that humans can and it establishes the need for the music to suit the pace of the horse or horses rather than the other way about.

Horses selected for a mounted band must be suited to the instrument which they will carry as well as to its player. A horse which has become accustomed to the dulcet tones of a flute sounding two feet behind its right ear may be seriously startled if these are replaced without warning by a blast from a trombone only six inches from it. Some elements of horsemanship are incorporated in ability to play a musical instrument while sitting on the back of a horse, but chief of them are probably boldness and willingness to take risks.

The King's Troop Royal Horse Artillery was given this title by King George VI and retains it even when a queen is on the throne. It is the saluting battery of the Household Division, The Queen's Household Troops, and as such its primary duty is to fire salutes in London on days of royal and national celebration or commemoration and in honour of foreign rulers who arrive on state visits. It is now unique in being probably the only horsed artillery unit left in the world and it maintains an establishment of six 13-pounder guns, each pulled by a team of six horses.

The King's Troop Royal Horse Artillery performing their world-famous musical drive at the gallop at the Royal Windsor Horse Show.

The horses for each gun are harnessed, as for a postillion-driven carriage, with long traces and no swingle trees to a two-wheeled limber from which the pole projects and behind which the two-wheeled gun is towed. The horse drivers, so-called, who are serving soldiers and full members of the Troop, ride the near-side horses of each team. They also lead and control the off-side horses with a single pair of reins, in each case attached to an army port-mouthed reversible service bit. The drivers are not armed but the sergeant who commands the subsection – which is the total crew responsible for each gun – who rides on the left of the lead horses, and the remaining three men who ride behind it carry swords. Two subsections, with their two guns, form a section, commanded by a subaltern officer. The three sections, with their total complement of six guns, comprise the Troop, which is established as a battery and is commanded by a major with two captains and at least two warrant officers to help him in running a self-contained army unit which fills its permanent barracks in St John's Wood with a total of about 115 horses and 175 soldiers.

As well as firing a dozen or so salutes each year – of forty-one guns from the saluting base in Hyde Park but of only twenty-one guns from other locations – the King's Troop parades on certain ceremonial occasions, including The Queen's Birthday Parade, takes over The Queen's Life Guard at Horse Guards from the Household Cavalry for two weeks in the summer while the mounted squadrons of the Life Guards and the Blues and Royals are out of London in camp, and is required to perform its famous musical drive for a number of regular engagements each year, including the Royal Tournament, and as many more extra ones as can be fitted in and afforded by the big agricultural shows which seek to engage it.

The remarkable, and possibly unique, characteristic of the King's Troop's drills and operations is that many of them, including their moving into position to fire salutes, are performed at a fast gallop. This is in keeping with the role of horse artillery batteries in war, which required them to keep pace with cavalry and bring their guns into action at high speed. By way of simulating this high-speed action, the Troop with its six guns rides to the north-east corner of Hyde Park. It passes through the centre of Marble Arch because it is the only traffic allowed to do so, and then gallops fast to the south-east corner near Stanhope Gate where the guns are detached and swivelled round to fire the salute dead on time. Meanwhile, the teams and limbers and the ridden horses are led back, still at the gallop, to the north-east corner of the park, where the waggon lines with the reserve ammunition are deemed to have been established. The horses return to the guns at the gallop, again, as soon as the salute is completed and are hooked up

144

once more for the troop to return to barracks. The same high-speed drill is carried out for salutes in all other locations and incorporated in the displays which the King's Troop gives at shows.

Much of the standard musical drive is performed at a flat-out gallop and it is this which makes it especially thrilling to watch, particularly in the 'scissors' movement in which the 60ft (1.80m) long gun teams gallop from the corners of the specially marked arena – only 100 × 35yd (90 × 30m) – and cross over with each other in the centre with only about 3ft (90cm) of clearance between the lead horses of one team and the gun muzzle of another. The guns and limbers, which date from 1904 and which were in constant action in the 1914–1918 war, weigh 1½ tons (1.3 tonnes) so that their six horses can pull them forward fast and easily. They have no brakes, however, and no men sitting on the limbers to operate any brakes which they might have, so that the pair of wheel horses, harnessed to the pole, must provide any braking which may be needed.

Because stopping or slowing a gun can never be an instant process, precise timing and accurate control are essential if the movements of the drive are to flow freely and accidents are to be avoided. Collisions are not unknown and they are usually dramatic in their impact on the audience, but always very quickly sorted out and, happily, seldom serious in their consequences. There is a thin dividing line between drill movements of a fundamentally ceremonial nature carried out at very high speeds to display panache and absolute speed (such as may be required to win races and competitions) which is always liable to verge on reckless riding. All ranks of the King's Troop recognize this demarcation and are careful to preserve it, but to do so, they must demonstrate horsemanship of a high order.

The lead drivers of the gun teams, who are normally junior NCOs, are generally the best riders in the Troop and they must be critical judges of pace with the strength and ability to control two hard-pulling horses at fast paces with fine accuracy. The wheel drivers have the next most demanding task in their responsibility for stopping and steering the actual limbers and guns. The centre drivers are the comparative novices whose main concern is to avoid their horses getting a leg over a trace and who graduate in due course through wheel to lead.

In order to perfect the skills required of them and teach them to new recruits, other ranks of the King's Troop serve for longer periods of mounted duty than their counterparts in the Household Cavalry; sometimes for almost all of a twenty-two-year term of service. The King's Troop officers, however, serve for only two to four years before returning to more modern soldiering. All ranks, and virtually all members, of a self-contained unit which contains only about fifty per cent more men than horses and can look to little outside aid in keeping them fit and well for constant hard work must be good horsemen and all ranks of The King's Troop Royal Horse Artillery are good horsemen and prove this by their prowess in almost every sort of competitive horse sport, as much as by their incomparably spectacular displays of their ceremonial function.

Horses undoubtedly add an extra element to pageantry which cannot be provided by foot soldiers, however magnificent, or replaced by machines or motor vehicles, however impressive. However, they also add an element of risk to the good order and precise protocol with which state occasions and ceremonial processions must essentially be invested. To train and operate horses to enhance the dignity as well as the splendour of occasions of public ceremony requires practical application of fundamental horsemanship. Even if the horses concerned are only to be required to walk and stand still, their training and preparation must be in accordance with conventional principles of equitation and there can be no short-cuts if their performance is to be confidently relied upon.

It is pleasant to reflect that several nations still provide cavalry escorts for their heads of state and preserve the traditions of chivalry by employing horses to add lustre to public celebrations, and let us hope that this tradition is maintained.

11

Horsemanship Over a Long Distance

People who say that there is no point in riding long distances on a horse in an age in which motor vehicles can travel over almost any type of country and in which planes and helicopters can land almost anywhere on the surface of the globe have a valid argument. Horses are now much slower, less comfortable, and generally more expensive than other forms of transport, and riding them should surely be regarded as a pleasure in itself, whose intensity must depend on the degree of co-operation achieved between horse and rider. This engenders physical satisfaction and may procure competitive success, and it is enhanced by beautiful scenery and fine weather, but it is only remotely related to distance and duration.

The concept of riding for relatively long distances to precisely timed schedules originated at the United States of America's Cavalry School at Fort Riley, Kansas, early in the twentieth century, where horses were ridden over a distance of 300 miles (480km) in five days to test their suitability for military service. The idea of setting standards related to time and distance and the condition of horses checked by veterinary examination commended itself to civilian trail riders in America. The latter were already riding, usually in Western style, for long distances purely for recreation and enjoyment and without any consideration for the clock.

Competitive trail riding, in which excessive speed was discouraged and competitors were required to complete sections of courses within specified time limits and were penalized for finishing too early as well as too late, soon gave rise to more critically competitive endurance riding. This was in effect long distance racing, in which the first to finish was the winner but veterinary checks at the ends of sections of the course still determined horses' fitness to continue. Both competitions have been popular in the USA ever since they started, with competitive trail riding being generally regarded as a more light-hearted and informal variation on endurance riding. By the 1950s they spread to Australia and South Africa and soon afterwards to Great Britain and the rest of Western Europe.

In 1985 endurance riding was recognized by the International Equestrian Federation as an official competitive horse activity or horse sport, and rules for its conduct were drawn up and standardized on an international basis. Competitive trail riding and endurance riding are often confused in the minds of people. The essential difference between the two is that in endurance riding the first past the post wins, provided that his horse is confirmed to be 'fit to continue', whereas the winner in trail riding competitions will be the competitor who has kept most exactly to the prescribed times over the designated sections of the course and whose horse has seemed to be in the best condition at the veterinary checks during the course and at the end of it.

The existence of straightforward long distance races and ride and tie races adds further confusion to an understanding of competitive distance riding. Long distance races are rare but may take place occasionally and, since they incorporate no veterinary checks and horses are not required to be 'fit to continue' at the finish, they need to be strictly confined to well qualified humane riders who can be trusted not to abuse their horses. Ride and tie races are for two people using one horse who must run and ride alternately over each section of the course, the rider tying the horse to a post where it must wait unattended for the runner to catch up. The ride and tie competition, which also originated in America, is subject to the same veterinary checks as endurance riding.

In Britain today the whole concept of this form of equestrian activity is further confused by the existence of two separate associations which seek to organize it and claim to regulate it on a national basis. The Long Distance Riding Association was the first of the two to seek affiliation to the British Horse Society so that it has now become the Long Distance Riding Group of the British Horse Society and its committee is one of the executive committees of the British Horse Society. In this capacity, and because of its acceptance of the jurisdiction of the British Horse Society, The Long Distance Riding Association or Group is held to be responsible to the British Equestrian Federation for the interests of competitors in endurance riding at national level and the selection of teams and individuals who enter for endurance riding in other countries under the jurisdiction of the International Equestrian Federation. The Endurance Horse and Pony Society of Great Britain organizes the same range of competitions as the Long Distance Riding Group, and has been doing so for about the same length of time, but cannot be recognized officially by the International Equestrian Federation for its interest in the activity which forms part of its title. Equestrian politics can be just as troublesome as national and international politics and are sometimes managed even more clumsily.

Long distance riding is a good name to cover all four types of competition and any further variations which may be invented, but it is not used or officially recognized outside Great Britain, whereas endurance riding, which is the official designation of the only form of competitive long distance riding that is recognized internationally, is organized in Britain by a society which does not have official international recognition. Efforts to combine the two associations concerned to the obvious benefit of the members of both of them are still being made, at the time of writing, and may one day be successful.*

Competitive trail rides, known as long distance rides in Britain, take place over distances of from 15 to 100 miles (24 to 160km) with sections timed for speeds of from 5–9mph (8–14kph) – in Britain 6.5–7.5mph (10–12kph) depending on terrain. To win or qualify in these competitions competitors must finish each section in the prescribed time, being penalized for arriving too early as well as too late, and may score high marks for an extra evaluation over each section. In the USA the extra evaluation covers soundness (40 per cent), condition (40 per cent), manners (15 per cent) and way of going (5 per cent), and judges assess these considerations at various points along the route as at the ends of sections.

In Britain the extra evaluation is a veterinary one only, assessed at the end of each section. It includes checks of pulse rates and dehydration as well as soundness, condition and freedom from wounds or injuries and is intended to produce results in order of merit. Both forms of evaluation are inevitably inexact and the British, purely veterinary one, sometimes results in a tie which must be decided by a run-off over an extra section.

The results of endurance riding competitions do not depend on veterinary or other evaluations but only on ultimate speed, in terms of the time taken to complete the whole course, and the veterinary checks at prescribed points on the course are intended only to decide whether horses are fit to continue. The final one at the finish may be critical in this respect. The veterinary checks are thorough and include clinical tests of pulse rates and sometimes of temperature and the need for these to be completed for varying numbers of horses which must all spend an equal, and not too prolonged, period of time at rest at the end

---

* Since this was written, Britain's endurance riding team won the World Endurance Riding Championships at the World Equestrian Games in Stockholm in August 1990.

of each section makes precise time-keeping essential. It also requires meticulous organization, which may be expensive in terms of the veterinary cover which is likely to be needed.

Ride and tie races are regulated generally in the same way as endurance riding competitions. The need in them for the man on foot to catch up with the ridden horse at the end of each section automatically limits the speed of the rider. Veterinary checks can be carried out while horses are tied so that precise time-keeping is hardly needed and the finishing order is normally that of each runner at the end of the final section.

Long distance races are rare nowadays and probably in general undesirable. They have been organized, notably for Arab horses, over distances of about 25 miles (40km) and their main attraction is that the first past the post is the winner. Vigilant stewarding is needed to monitor obligatory walk sections, which are often included, and to detect and stop any horses in distress. The minimum weight to be carried, usually 11 stone (73kg) is critical.

The most famous and longest established modern endurance ride is the Western States Trail Ride, formerly known as the Tevis Ride, which was founded in 1955 and covers 100 miles (160km) of a route once ridden by the Pony Express riders in the USA from Tahoe City, Nevada, to Auburn, California. The course runs over the Sierra Nevada Mountains and involves extremes of temperature up to 100°F (38°C) and the winner nowadays normally completes it in about 11 hours. The counterpart of the Western States Ride in the Eastern States of the USA is the Old Dominion Ride in Virginia whose course runs through the foothills of the Blue Ridge Mountains, where similarly testing climbs and temperatures may be encountered and winners also record a time of about 11 hours.

The Quilty 100-mile ride in Australia, which involves less hilly country than the two big American rides, is usually won in a time of under 10 hours. Australia also stages a famous 250-mile (400km) Endurance Race in Queensland in which horses must travel 200 miles (320km) on the first day and 50 miles (80km) on the second day.

The South African National Endurance Ride covers 131 miles in three days; 50 miles (80km) on each of the first two days and 31 miles (50km) on the third day to amount to a total of 131 miles or 210km. The total riding time taken for this distance is about 9 hours because horses travel significantly faster over the three shorter distances which they must cover each day.

The Arab Horse Society Marathon Race, run in Britain over a course of 26$\frac{1}{4}$ miles (42km) is normally won in a time of about 1$\frac{1}{2}$ hours, by horses which carry a minimum weight of 11 stone (73kg), despite compulsory walk sections totalling one mile.

The premier British endurance ride, the Golden Horseshoe Ride of 100 miles over Exmoor is now being won in a time of about 9 hours 50 minutes.

The well-regulated achievements of today's long distance riders are not astonishing in terms of speed and distance as compared with many records of the past, and indeed with the unrecorded distances covered by many horses during a good day's hunting when they will also have jumped many fences. The Arab horse champion Crabbet is recorded as having covered a distance of 300 miles (480km) in 52 hours 33 minutes carrying 17.5 stone (111kg) in 1920, and many a hunting man can justifiably claim to have ridden well over 50 miles, and jumped over fifty fences, on one horse in the 6 or 7 hours of a good day's hunting without a second horse.

The justification for modern endurance riding lies in its insistence on the horse being trained, prepared and ridden to a standard which will enable it to cover the prescribed course at potentially winning speed without suffering exhaustion or any distress, and finishing fit to continue. Long distance or competitive trail riding puts no emphasis on

A steep climb during the 100 miles endurance ride at the World Equestrian Games in Stockholm in 1990. This was won by the British team and the individual gold medallist, Becky Hart of the USA recorded an average speed of 9.5mph (15.2kph).

151

Riders on a long distance ride in Hungary cooling their horses in the river Danube. These rides are undertaken only for pleasure and they cover 25–30 miles (40–50km) each day for periods of up to ten days.

speed, but rather more on sound fit condition so it tests general horsemanship and horsemastership without demanding fast paces or any unusual physical capability on the part of horse or rider.

Accordingly, long distance riding in one or more of its various forms suits horse owners whose particular equestrian skills may be limited either by reduced aptitude or want of experience and the time to acquire it at the right age. By the same token it suits horses of modest intrinsic value, which do not need to gallop fast or jump well but can give a good account of themselves, provided that they are straight movers with reasonable stamina and courage.

Arabs, whose inheritance of courage and stamina is legendary, have been pre-eminently successful in all long distance competitions in every country and have, incidentally, proved the truth of the old adage 'Blood to carry weight' by achieving this success in partnership with plenty of riders who have seemed to be disproportionately large for them. Fell Ponies and Haflingers have demonstrated the value of their calm, willing temperaments and economical action by matching the performances of bigger, longer-striding horses in British competitions, carrying riders weighing up to 11 stone (70kg), and mules have quite often been well placed in America and regained their well deserved reputation as comfortable efficient mounts for travel, which has been largely unrecognized in Europe for the past 200 years. Horses and ponies of many of the lesser-known world breeds have surprised Thoroughbred fans by excelling at this activity and only those of Russian origin, which are undoubtedly very good at it, have not yet made their mark in endurance rides in the Western hemisphere.

Long distance riding in Britain, and probably in the USA as well, is inevitably now liable to become over-administered and threatened by bureaucracy. It is also becoming increasingly influenced by pseudo-scientific theories of a gimmicky nature, some of which seem to be commercially inspired. Its central administration becomes more expensive as the number of competitive rides and the complexity of the regulations which govern them increases and the organization of the rides themselves is an increasingly costly undertaking, mainly because of the number of vets required to check the horses at the several points on the course. This must increase in relation to the number of competitors taking part, so that they are not held up at the check points for undue or unequal periods of time. Practising veterinary surgeons cannot always be expected to give their services free to enterprises of this kind, however sporting and amateur in spirit, and, although sensible people with horse knowledge but no academic qualifications could obviously be trusted to carry out certain standard tests, in the age of the expert only letters after a person's name invest him with the authority to make unfavourable decisions. Commercial sponsorship, which is so eagerly sought for almost all equestrian activities today, cannot be easily attracted to long distance riding, which is not an exciting spectator attraction, and it will be a pity if the very people for whom the sport is so ideally suited, being riders of modest means and generally modest attainments are prevented from taking part in it by rising costs.

There can really be no mystique about the training and preparation of horses for long distance riding. They need quite simply to be as fit as possible, carrying less flesh than the average show horse but being less finely tuned than a racehorse on the eve of a big race. They need to be well and very regularly exercised, much in accordance with routines appropriate for hunters at the start of the season, and the extra work which they may need in preparation for a long endurance ride will be added almost automatically in conjunction with sensible preparations for shorter preliminary competitions.

Good hay and good oats are still the best basis for feeds for horses which do not have any unusual digestive or respiratory problems and ponies as well as horses need concentrated food in the form of oats or nuts or cubes if they are to be expected to carry their riders even for only 20 miles in 3 hours. It is unreasonable to expect them to do this off grass and bad for them to try to do it with their bellies full of lush spring grass. A few of a vast range of additives and mineral supplements may benefit horses as much as their sale benefits their manufacturers, but a salt lick is always highly desirable.

Electrolyte in one or other of its proprietary forms is one of the relatively few specially-formulated synthetic compounds of real value to horses which face the prospect of becoming dehydrated on long hot rides during which they are likely to sweat copiously. This replaces salts which are lost through sweating and helps the body tissue to retain some moisture.

The addition of glucose by the manufacturers to the formula recommended for use during competitions accelerates the process and may produce some extra fairly instant energy, but the kind without glucose should be given during training to condition the horse to cope with dehydration without the risk of too much glycogen being stored in his muscles. Electrolyte should not be given to horses which have already become dehydrated, as its effect will be reversed and adverse in that it may cause water to be drained from the already too thick blood.

Respiration rates used to be checked as well as pulse rates to determine horses' fitness and their fitness to continue in long distance competitions, until it was discovered that they sometimes pant like dogs if they are very hot and thereby produce a misleading result. The respiration rate, particularly in relation to the pulse rate, does however give a good indication of a horse's general fitness. In a sound horse in good health, it should be about one third as fast as the pulse rate at rest and not much more than half as fast after vigorous exercise and, although both rates will obviously quicken considerably with fast work, they should return to the resting rate in 10–15 minutes if the horse is fit but may take up to 40 minutes to do so if it is not.

Blood testing, which is now quite commonly carried out on racehorses, provides a valuable check on a horse's general state of health, and freedom from incipient disease and the effects of any undue strain. It is worth its cost, if only in terms of reassurance, as a check before final preparations for a long endurance ride.

Saddles and bridles should obviously be as light as possible, consistent with their being completely comfortable for the horse. Ordinary Western saddles spread the weight well but are usually much heavier than they need to be and often restrict a rider's ability to ease his weight off his horse's back and sit up forward over his withers at the canter and gallop. Australian stockmen's saddles of light construction are a good compromise between East and West.

Horseshoes should be the lightest that will stand the wear because weight on a horse's feet tires him more quickly than that carried on his body.

Over long distances the horse endures the exertion and strain. The rider only endures discomfort and some muscle fatigue leading to stiffness if he is not fully fit for the ride. However, an unfit rider flopping about in the saddle will hinder and tire a horse disastrously and may even give him a sore back. Thus the rider must train with the horse so as to be able to help him by sitting 'lightly' and always in the right place with his weight moved forward just clear of the saddle and balanced steadily in the stirrups over the withers at the canter and gallop. He must obviously post or rise smoothly at the trot and should change the diagonal by bumping the saddle just once quite frequently. In competitions which permit it, an athletic rider can dismount for steep descents and climbs and may legitimately hang on to his horse's tail to get a tow up steep hills; an extra string from the bridle is advisable when this ploy is used.

The pace selected over different stretches of the course must depend firstly on the going, secondly on the proclivity of the horse, and thirdly on a sensible appreciation of the need to vary the gait so as to ease the strain on the forelegs, one or other of which must bear the whole weight of the horse momentarily in the canter and gallop, as well as to provide periods of comparative relaxation at a slower pace. Present day long distance riders seem to do a great deal of fast trotting, which may well be the best pace over rough or stony ground, but the record breakers of the past generally preferred the canter or hand gallop to which Arabs and Thoroughbreds are more naturally inclined.

In competitions in which the fastest time decides the winner, riders must obviously gallop or canter their horses at a speed well within their volition over ground which permits this without risk of injury. They must also maintain a good balanced trot over other stretches of the course. It is sound policy to ease the pace for a mile or so before the check points to allow pulse rates to reduce. Experienced competitors have found that the greater speeds demanded for 50-mile rides give rise to more risk of injury and tend to cause greater fatigue than the longer distances which necessarily involve slower speeds.

Long distance riders must be very fit – for riding but not necessarily for running or other athletic endeavours. The best and only really effective way to achieve this fitness is by riding actively, regularly, and as often as possible for long periods at a time. Fortunately for the amateur spirit of the sport, the most obviously convenient way for a prospective competitor to get himself fit is for him to train and prepare his own horse, although regular vigorous hunting will have much the same effect. If he can complete a 30-mile (48km) ride and get onto a horse again the next day to ride for 2 or 3 hours without feeling any pain or discomfort, the rider will be fit to tackle any distance and need only exercise his own horse regularly and thoroughly to preserve this state of fitness. Anyone, however, who is foolish or sporting enough to attempt a timed competition without being fit from regular riding will suffer agonies of back ache and stiffness, as well as embarrassment from the sorry spectacle he will present, at the end of only 25 miles.

When a modern craze for all recreational activities to be ultimately competitive resulted in the provision of rules for the conduct of long distance riding, the people who drew up the rules were at pains to ensure that they protected horses from undue pressure or abuse. Any tendency to equate these activities with racing, as by describing their procedures or reporting their results in terms more appropriate to the turf, may diminish the purpose and effect of the regulations by which they are controlled and, in particular, encourage the organizers of minor competitions to ignore them to the detriment of the sport and the horses concerned in it.

The endurance records of the past, both legendary and historical, were established in a less humane age when horses provided the fastest means of overland travel and they involved high-couraged horses being ridden to exhaustion and sometimes to death. It would be wrong to try to set up new records today – and pointless now in terms of absolute speed – and any ideas about creating excitement for commercial sponsors by staging thrilling finishes or trying to break records will be bad ones.

Long distance riding in all its forms involves horsemanship and horsemastership. It does not demand expertise or the exercise of special equestrian skills but anyone who can finish a 50-mile endurance ride on his own horse within 20 minutes of the winning time can call himself a horseman.

12

Horsemanship in the Rodeo

The word rodeo is of Spanish derivation but the sport or entertainment which it describes is all-American and Canadian and exclusively so. Attempts to reproduce it in other countries have never been successful and have usually resulted in complaints about cruelty to animals, especially horses, and, in Britain in particular, accusations of irresponsible disregard for human safety.

Rodeo is a rough tough sport in respect of all but one of the eight standard competitions which comprise it, but its origin, in the work and recreation of the American cowboy, is based firmly on the practical use of the horse in the service of man. It incorporates no wanton violence or gratuitous cruelty to appeal to sadistic spectators, but it provides an arena in which the strength and agility of horses and riders are tested spectacularly to their fullest extent, both in competition against each other and in co-operation with each other.

Hard-won prize money available to professional rodeo riders is not munificent by the standards of most other sports and games with such notable spectator appeal but, during the twentieth century, the equestrian skills developed by the cattle herdsman of North America have progressed from practice of their craft at work and play, through exhibitions of it on festive occasions, to regular, well-regulated contests involving crucial elements of horsemanship which now constitute a competitive sport in its own right.

The eight recognized rodeo events are: saddle bronc riding, bareback riding, bull riding, calf roping, steer roping, team roping, steer wrestling and cloverleaf barrel racing. Cutting contests and reining contests are not regular rodeo competitions but incorporate accomplishments which cowboys and their horses must possess. The Chuck Wagon Race at the Calgary Stampede is staged just once each year under its own special rules, although it is sometimes copied – less spectacularly – at shows and exhibitions at other venues.

Saddle bronc riding is one of the original classic rodeo competitions and it is reckoned to be one of the most difficult. The saddle is of a standard type which must meet the specifications prescribed in the rules of the Professional Rodeo Cowboys Association and the horse wears a halter with a 6ft (1.80m) long 1½in (4cm) thick rope rein which the rider holds in one hand. The rider must have his spurred heels well forward, in line with the horse's shoulder as it leaves the chute at the start of the timed 'round' and, after the first buck, must 'spur' smoothly with both legs in a long arc from front to rear in rhythm with the horse's movement. He must stay on the bucking horse for 8 seconds, after which a bell is rung to signify the end of the round, and this is judged according to his ability to do this and also by two judges who each award marks out of 25 for both the rider and the horse. The rider scores for his style, control and the smoothness and fast regularity of his spurring stroke. The judges take account of how difficult the horse seems to be to ride, and register a score of zero if the rider uses his free hand or loses a stirrup, and they also each judge the horse out of 25 marks for the energy and vigour of his bucking.

Bareback riding is judged and scored as for saddle bronc riding, except that the rider is required to hold his right hand up in the air and is disqualified if he touches any part of the horse with it. With his left hand he grips a handhold attached to a stout leather 10in (25cm) wide surcingle and the strength with which he retains his grip of this attachment significantly affects his ability to stay on the otherwise bare back of the bucking horse for the requisite 8 seconds. Bareback riding is less highly regarded by rodeo purists than saddle bronc riding, presumably because of this grip with the rider's hand on which it largely depends.

Bull riding is done bareback with the rider holding on to a rope round the animal's brisket with one hand just behind his withers. Bulls of Brahma or similar breed, which must weigh at least 2,000lb (900kg), are used and, because they twist and spin more readily than horses, although they do not buck so high, riders seldom stay on them for the full 8 seconds so that the clock usually does the judges' job. Because the bulls normally attack fallen riders, bull riding is a dangerous contest which is invariably the last one of a rodeo programme. Mounted pick-up men rescue fallen riders and bold active 'rodeo clowns' distract bulls from them.

Bucking broncos or buckjumpers, which are all big horses and by no means ponies, as also bucking bulls, are highly valued and very well treated and looked after and frequently become star performers in their own rights. They have straps studded with prickles fitted round their stomachs to encourage them to buck, but these only irritate and do not injure them. Since bucking horses soon cotton on to what is required of them and, indeed, seem to appreciate the praise and admiration which they get, particularly from the cowboys who ride them and who stand to score highest marks by doing this successfully on the most active horses, the straps only serve to remind them to give their accustomed performances.

Today's buckjumpers need to be equine athletes and are beginning to be specially bred from good bucking stock for the job. High Tide, winner of the World Championship for Bucking Horses in 1976, was of distinguished ancestry. He was a grandson of the late Man O' War and some twenty years ago a buckjumper called Uncle Max changed jobs and became a successful showjumper of near international repute in the hands of Britain's Ted Edgar. He displayed admirably diplomatic discretion by limiting demonstrations of his former occupation to after his show jumping rounds, but the strength and agility which enabled him to jump big fences also enabled him to dump his rider whenever he wanted to.

The average hours of work to which a bucking horse travelling the rodeo circuits is committed amount to no more than sixty or so performances, each of 8 seconds, each year so that he is certainly never over-worked. Since he obviously cannot be ridden between engagements but must be kept keen and fresh for his work, the only deprivation which he is likely to suffer will be that of steady exercise and the pleasanter aspects of association with human beings whose amicable consequences would be unhelpful to him in his work. To such extent as simple creatures like horses ever suffer from boredom, the bucking horse is relieved of this by the travelling he does and the interest and excitement which he meets with in the surroundings of the arenas where he spends so much of his time.

The link in terms of horsemanship between broncos and the cowboys who ride them in rodeos is a tenuous one, the more so in that the horse is supposed to get rid of the rider as quickly as possible rather than submit to him and co-operate, which is his usual role. However, to the extent that the cowboy needs to study and understand the horses which he must try to ride, and since they must perform together, that link may just be said to exist.

Calf roping, steer roping and team roping contests are all decided on time. In calf roping a single cowboy ropes or lassos a single calf, which is really a half-grown steer. The calf enters the arena at the same time as the cowboy does so that it is running fast, and the cowboy must dismount and throw it on to its side and tie three of its legs together with a separate short rope while his horse backs sufficiently to keep the rope or lariat tight without dragging the calf. The best performers complete the whole process in less than 10 seconds and the calf must remain tied for at least 6 seconds for it to qualify.

In steer roping a single cowboy must rope a full-grown steer round the horns and throw it to the ground by stopping and manoeuvring his horse to the most effective angle with it with his rope secured to the horn of his saddle. He then jumps off and ties it as for a calf while his horse backs to keep the rope tight and prevent the steer from getting up. This feat has also been done in 10 seconds.

Team roping involves two mounted cowboys who must rope a steer simultaneously, one round the horns and the other round the hind legs. The steer is not thrown and the contestants do not dismount but are reckoned to have finished when they have the roped steer standing between their two horses which must face each other with both ropes tight. Winning times for team roping are seldom much more than 5 seconds from the two cowboys crossing the start line.

The part played by the horses is critical in all three roping competitions. Their co-operation with their riders must be instant and exact and the careful training which they need must result in their performing about half of the part which they play in all three roping competitions by instinctive reaction rather than in response to conventional aids. This consideration does not seem to detract from the high level of eminently practical horsemanship which their riders must demonstrate, in addition to their skills with the lariat and their general strength and agility. The partnership between a rodeo roper and his horse is closer than that between almost any other competitive rider and his mount, short of that established in top level dressage, show jumping or Three-Day Events.

Steer wrestling, or bulldogging as it was once called, requires a cowboy (the 'dogger') to gallop alongside a free running Longhorn steer, which must weigh 500lb (227kg) or more, and to grasp its horns, with the right one in the crook of his right elbow and the left one in his left hand, before jumping off, digging his heels in the ground in front of him, and throwing the steer on to its left side while transferring the grip of his left hand to its nose. The contest is completed as soon as the steer is on its side with its feet off the ground and the clock is often stopped within 5 seconds of the competitor crossing the start line. A second cowboy called the 'Hazer' plays an important part by riding on the other side of the steer to keep it running straight.

Though hardly a test of horsemanship, and not a demonstration of practical cattle handling since the risk of injury would be unacceptable to a working ranch hand, steer wrestling is one of the original and most exciting of all rodeo displays. It demands strength, great agility and critical timing on the part of the dogger who must overcome and subdue a semi-wild animal of up to three times his own weight in a remarkably short space of time.

British humanitarians who protest that rodeos involve cruelty to horses should perhaps also spare some sympathy for the steers and calves. They are obviously roughly handled and frightened to some extent – the horses are not – but they are always produced in very good condition and are not struck or beaten in any way or subjected to arduous travel so that they are arguably better off than many others of their species in European cattle markets. There is a difference between violence and cruelty and, although peaceful people may justifiably object to both or either, they should recognize the distinction between them and appreciate that, whereas cruelty can never be defensible in any form, some degree of controlled violence is necessarily permissible in many sports and games and cannot be excluded even from all those in which animals are essentially involved.

Misconceptions about rodeos gain currency as a consequence of feeble attempts to reproduce them in countries other than the USA and Canada, where the animal performers are never of the right type or strong or good enough. The spectacle of indeterminate numbers of youths emerging from the beer tent at a 'Bank Holiday Fayre' in Britain to entertain their girlfriends by clambering on to the backs of

Bulldogging or steer wrestling; a traditional rodeo competition. The 'dogger' jumps from his horse to grasp the horns of the 600 or 700lb (270 or 320kg) steer and throw it to a supine position on the ground, often in 5 seconds from starting, while the 'hazer' remains mounted to keep the steer straight as it emerges from the chute.

frightened Forest ponies or half-grown Friesian heifers at the behest of a facetious commentator, even to raise money for charity, is not edifying and not rodeo.

Cloverleaf barrel racing became a standard rodeo competition, especially for women, in 1948. Contestants race individually against the clock to circle very tightly round three barrels set out in a cloverleaf pattern; they must turn right-handed round the first barrel and left-handed round the second and third to complete a total course of about 100 yards (90 metres). There is a 5-second penalty for knocking over a barrel which effectively eliminates any rider who does this from this very fast tightly timed competition. Barrel racing at rodeos under the jurisdiction of the Professional Rodeo Cowboys Association is for women only and women cannot enter for other events at them but at many other rodeos of only slightly less importance women also compete in calf roping and men may compete in barrel racing, which also takes places at many horse shows.

Quarter Horses are the ideal mounts for barrel races and women seem to win them more often than men. They also bring great glamour to the scene with their deliberately theatrical 'dude' cowboy costumes. The competitions themselves are simple by comparison with British gymkhana events or the Pony Club Mounted Games because they are designed to suit multiple programmes offering great variety for spectators. The speed and agility demonstrated by the specialist horses and riders concerned, however, exceeds any seen in English show rings.

Cutting Contests (see Chapter 8) are not standard rodeo events but are included in many rodeos as well as being frequently staged as separate events in their own right under the rules of the National Cutting Horse Association. They also take place at general horse shows, and shows run by the breed societies and associations of the horses which are especially suitable for this work: Quarter Horses, Appaloosas and Palominos.

The calves, of which two or three must be 'cut out' from a herd of twenty and held clearly separate from it in turn during a timed period of 2½ minutes, are actually yearling or two-year-old steers or bullocks which must weigh at least 500lb (227kg) and the trained Cutting Horse must 'work' the calf indicated to him by his rider so as to separate it from its fellows and hold it separate until his rider orders him to drop it and allow it to return to the herd. Apart from indicating the calf to be cut and the moment for it to be dropped the rider must give no aids or indications to his horse and is awarded a penalty from each of the five or three judges each time he does so out of the maximum bonus marks of 80.

A good Cutting Horse is, in any case, so much quicker to react to the movements of the calf than the man on top of him that the latter would gain no advantage by interfering with him and is fully occupied in remaining upright in the saddle, holding on to the horn on its pommel for extra security, while his horse twists and turns beneath him. Experienced horsemen invited to sit on a Cutting Horse for the first time while he is doing his job have often fallen right off.

The rider does not figure in the marking but only selects the calf to be 'cut' and the moment for the horse to drop it, but he will usually have trained the horse and will have used a very thorough understanding of horsemanship, horse psychology and the knowledge required of a sheepdog trainer in doing so.

Cutting contests, whose original link with work on the range and the ranch is now tenuous, have become major competitive horse events in the USA since the 1930s and the National Cutting Horse Association now has over 15,000 members, not all of whom live in America, and regulates competitions for which prize money totalling well over one million dollars is offered. There are a number of professional trainers and riders of Cutting Horses but the sport is still mainly amateur and open to both sexes.

The training and working of Cutting Horses reveals, perhaps uniquely, a level of instinctive intelligence with which horses are not normally credited, even by the most experienced horsemen who use them for other purposes. Since they must be carefully trained for this work it is not pure instinct which enables them to do it so efficiently but the development of a normally dormant instinct which requires the application of significant intelligence on the horses' part for it to be related to the work concerned. The fact that, when trained, they work more quickly than their human partners can envisage is tribute to their naturally faster reactions, which are appreciated by all regular riders, but willingness on the part of a herbivore with no natural instinct for hunting or catching prey to make positive moves to oppose and head off any other animal is unusual and seldom encountered or expected.

There must surely be some element of anxiety on the part of the horse to please its rider, once it knows what he requires of it, in this achievement. It is detectable to a very limited extent in horses and ponies which are used for herding sheep and cattle, and to a barely discernible extent in polo ponies which follow the ball, but it is not in itself a natural instinct and the training which induces or develops it is what horsemanship is all about.

Reining contests are held at some rodeos and a great many Western American horse shows. They are not standard rodeo events and are nowadays far removed from the work requirements of practical cowboys in whose repertoire they have no place. They consist of a series of up to ten movements, comprising one of nine standard published patterns made up of offsets (quarter turns of 90deg), roll-backs (half turns of 180deg), pivots (full turns of 360deg) and spins (full turns continued for the prescribed number of times), as well as sudden sliding stops, backs, and occasionally sidepasses (equivalent to full rather than half-passes in European dressage terms) all linked by short bursts of speed at the run (gallop) in which a good Quarter Horse may reach a speed of 35mph (56kph) within the confines of the arena and the pattern. Reining contests must be ridden in Western style with Western saddlery, including a long-cheeked single rein curb bit, and the reins must be held only in the rider's left hand so that the horse must respond, as all Western horses do, to neck reining.

Reining contests have been likened to dressage tests; quite astonishingly and obviously by uninitiated observers who have not seen beyond their format and general layout and the presence of five or three judges. Their origin is in fact the Californian style of Western riding with its slender links back to the vaqueros and the mounted bullfighters or *rejoneadors* of Spain (see Chapter 9) and present day interest in them may owe something to the influence of cowboy films in which several of the movements prescribed for them are often dramatically featured. These movements are strictly for show, not utility, and their effectiveness depends largely on speed and sudden, almost violent, reactions to aids which are more obviously forcible than those appropriate to good school riding.

Reining contests are diametrically different to cutting contests in that Cutting Horses must work on their own initiative without any aids or cues from their riders, whereas horses competing in reining contests must act only on the orders given them by their riders and make no move which is not dictated by them.

Judges in reining contests do not look for regularity or smooth precision of paces so they bear no resemblance to dressage tests in this respect. Sliding stops, pivots and spins are executed with hurried suddenness which is out of place in dressage and liable to cause sprains and injuries to which working cowboys would not want to subject their horses and of which equestrian purists might tend to disapprove. The training of horses for reining contests is a skilful business which calls for the application of many fundamental principles of horsemanship, and Quarter Horses especially possess the conformation and temperament to respond to it effectively. The contests themselves, however, amount to an extension of the capabilities required of a working Western horse into a realm of fantasy which is not closely associated with practical requirements or conventional concepts of horsemanship.

The Chuck Wagon Race is the highlight of the Calgary Stampede in Canada, which started in 1912 and is one of the premier rodeos of the North American continent. It is reproduced at a few other rodeos – notably Cheyenne and Wyoming – and at shows and exhibitions whose arenas are big enough to contain it. It is a thrilling spectacle, being probably the only recognized event in the world which involves teams of four horses in harness being driven in a flat-out race against each other.

When the starting signal is given the chuck wagons with their four-horse teams are loaded up with specified stores and equipment (including a kitchen stove) by cowboys who then mount their own horses and race with them round a twisting course marked by barrels to finish with a complete circuit of the large arena. The winning wagon is the one which crosses the finishing line first with its mounted escort up with it and rules are kept to a minimum, in keeping with the original concept of flight from attacking Indians, so that collisions and even pile-ups are not infrequent.

Rodeo is now big business and arguably one of the greatest spectator attractions in the world. From the first one ever held in public, in 1886 at Prescott, Arizona, the sport has grown to account for some 750 events of recognized status, and many more unofficial ones, held in forty different states and offering about 10 million dollars in prize money to nearly 10 thousand contestants and performers.

The link between rodeo riding and horsemanship is obvious and basic and, if its popularity may owe rather more to the slightly spurious glamour which the Wild West has acquired from representations of it in the cinema than to public interest in demonstrations of equestrian excellence, it is none the less more recently and more directly connected with the practical use of horses by those who ride them than most other sports, games and activities in which horses are nowadays involved. As such it deserves the attention, respect, and indeed admiration, of all horsemen.

13

Horsemanship in Harness

Driving is a craft rather than an art and, although its exponents were highly regarded in the Ancient World, particularly in a gladiatorial setting as for chariot racing, it has ranked as a semi-skilled manual labour since about AD 500 and only been associated with horsemanship and equestrian status since the beginning of the twentieth century.

It is not very difficult to drive a single horse or a pair of horses along the road for a journey provided that the horses concerned are broken and trained to harness and before the days of motor transport everybody, regardless of sex or age, was prepared to do this with no misgivings and after little or no instruction if they could not afford to pay someone to do it for them. The breaking and training of horses to harness has always been a process requiring special technical skills and a high level of general horsemanship and this has always been a well paid professional task, and still should be, since any failure to carry it out properly may have dire consequences.

To drive four or more horses all together, or indeed one in front of another in tandem, is a much more difficult undertaking which was only attempted in the old days by professional coachmen of the highest grades and a relatively few keen amateurs who could afford to keep teams of well matched horses and took pride in being able to match the skills possessed by the servants they employed.

Only in Hungary, and more generally in Europe, east of the Rhine, was a vogue established, in the middle of the eighteenth century, for owners to drive their own four in hands. This seems to have resulted mainly from the pride which the owners concerned took in owning horses of high quality, many of which they bred themselves, and their desire to be more closely concerned with them than their use simply as a means of transport would envisage.

There was undoubtedly another more practical reason which emphasizes the difference in travel between Western and Eastern Europe prior to the twentieth century. In Britain and the more developed countries of Western Europe public transport between cities and towns were established in some form in the early years of the eighteenth century and with it the system by which post horses could be

166

hired in most towns and at a number of isolated inns to pull the private travelling chariots and hired post *chaises* in which wealthy travellers made their journeys. The horses concerned were hired to cover stages whose lengths were limited to distances over which the horses could maintain good speeds without having to be changed and post boys rode them as postillions and changed with their horses. In the more sparsely populated countries of Eastern Europe such posting facilities were very few and far between, where they existed at all, and travellers could not rely on them to provide fresh horses to maintain the speed of their journeys. Accordingly they used their own higher quality and better conditioned horses for the total distances of their journeys. They usually used four or five horses harnessed to a light phaeton type of carriage to obtain the best relative horsepower and enable their horses to cover long distances without getting too tired. They often drove them themselves to save the weight of an extra servant and because they felt as well, or better, able to nurse their horses over the routes of their journeys as anyone whom they could have employed to do this. The Magyar magnates (noblemen and land owners) of the Austro-Hungarian Empire customarily drove their own favourite teams of four or five horses all the way between Budapest and Vienna, a distance of about 160 miles (257km), in two days with only one overnight stop and paraded them in harness on the third day to the admiration of their friends; and they were still doing this until well into the twentieth century.

An interest in driving as one of the skills of modern horsemanship and the concept of its relationship to equestrian education undoubtedly originated in Hungary in the nineteenth century and this provenance seems to be substantiated by the notable success of Hungarian drivers in today's driving trials. The Corinthian conduct of the Prince Regent and his cronies engendered an interest in four-in-hand driving, particularly of public coaches which were not supposed to be driven by amateurs for fun, in the early years of the nineteenth century. This enthusiasm revealed a number of bold competent amateur English four-in-hand coachmen, of whom the Prince Regent was not one, but their concern seems to have been more to try to break records and impress people with their magnificent and generally 'macho' image than to demonstrate horsemanship.

At the very beginning of the twentieth century driving was elevated to a precise skill and something of an art by Edwin Howlett, an English professional coachman who followed his father into private service in Paris and established a great reputation which justified his setting up the first ever school for teaching driving. Howlett had rationalized his handling of the four reins of a four-in-hand into a standard technique by which he was able to steer a coach and four horses round the sharp corners in the narrow streets and courtyards of Paris with greater accuracy and certainty than the other coachmen of his day could contemplate with the less effective individual methods which they employed.

Howlett's teaching achieved instant popularity with amateur coachmen of social distinction all over Europe and in the USA and the many pupils who came to Paris to learn from him included the German artist, horseman and harness enthusiast Benno von Achenbach who improved and elaborated Howlett's system and promoted it throughout the whole of Europe so that it became known as the Achenbach style. Achenbach's chief disciple Max Pape maintained the teaching after his death in 1936 and lived himself until 1977 so that he was able to take an interest in driving trials, which became recognized internationally in 1969, and relate the teachings of Howlett and Achenbach to their requirements.

Three distinctly separate styles of driving are now recognized throughout the world: The English or Achenbach style, originated by Howlett, which is classically correct in all the countries of Western Europe and the Eastern States of the USA and is now favoured in many, if not most, of the other countries of the world. The Hungarian style which is of older origin and is used exclusively in Hungary and, with some variations, in Russia and many countries of Eastern Europe. The Western American style, which is workmanlike, if less precise than the other two, and particularly suitable for teams of six or more horses, and which was used by the early settlers in America and Australia and still prevails among the descendants of those pioneers.

The only aids which can be used to direct and control horses in harness are the reins, the voice and the whip, as an extension of the driver's arm. Since the only permanent contact which the driver has with his horse(s) is with their mouths through the reins, his handling of these must be positively precise so that his demands for turns and circles made through them will never be confusing and he will be able to maintain the appropriate tension to balance his horse(s) and encourage them to show their best paces as well as to be able to call for changes of pace and halts.

It is not always fully appreciated that, although a considerably greater length of rein is involved, a man who is sitting in a cart pulled by a horse is no better able physically to restrain or control the horse's forward motion by pulling on the reins than if he were sitting on the horse itself. The scientific principle involved is that which states, facetiously, that 'you cannot raise yourself from the ground by shortening your braces', and it can be more explicitly proved by anyone who cares to launch himself down an ice-covered hill on a toboggan and try to stop it by pulling on a rope attached to its front. It is as easy to be run away with by a horse which is being driven as by one which is being ridden, but the consequences of the former misadventure are usually more alarming.

The reins of horses in pair harness are always coupled together with coupling buckles well behind the pads which occupy the same positions as saddles on their backs. Both left reins and both right reins therefore join together well in front of the driver's hands, leaving him only two reins to manipulate to control both horses. For rein-handling purposes, a four-in-hand can be regarded as two pairs, one in front of the other, so that all four horses are controlled by four reins in the driver's hands. A tandem, being one horse harnessed in front of another, requires the driver to manipulate four reins.

When five horses are to be driven – normally three abreast in front of a pair, which is not unusual in Hungary and is a sensible formation in that the three leaders cannot pass through any gap or gateway

Mrs Araminta Barnard (née Winn) driving Mr Underwood's team of Welsh Mountain Ponies. A beautifully sporting lady's turnout with which its highly accomplished coachwoman once won a national driving trial and the championships at the Royal Show in the same week.

which may be too narrow for the wheelers and the carriage – the reins of the three leaders are coupled together as for a pair so that the driver still only holds four reins. To drive a six-in-hand the coachman must hold and manipulate six reins and in principle there must be an extra pair of reins for every extra pair of horses added to the team.

Since the total length of a four-in-hand driven to a normal coach or carriage will be between 30 and 40ft (about 10m) the driver must make a special hinge or joint between the leaders and the wheelers in order to make accurate right-angled turns so as to avoid cutting corners, as for negotiating narrow gateways off or on to roads.

This requirement makes it necessary for him to apply the opposite rein on the wheelers, to keep them going straight forward for a few yards, to the rein which he applies to the leaders to indicate the start of the turn. The need to apply this 'opposition rein' at precisely the right moment and to keep it applied for precisely the right amount of time in order to steer four horses accurately is what makes the driving of a tandem or a four-in-hand much more difficult than the driving of a single horse or a pair. The procedure is like that which would be required to steer an articulated lorry towing a trailer, from the rear rather than the front and it calls for a meticulous rein handling technique to which a coachman must become accustomed by intuition, or almost by instinct, if he wants to drive his team of horses through gateways and in narrow or crowded streets without constant risk of accident.

With six or more horses the complexity of the rein handling increases considerably, as does the weight or tension which the coachman must sustain to restrain and control his team, so that teams of six horses have seldom been driven from the box seat in Britain, except to demonstrate the skill of their owners or for economical exercising. Their use is of practical advantage only in open hilly country with no proper roads, such as the prairies of America, the bush of Australia and the veldt of South Africa, where tight accurate turns are not called for. English amateur coachmen at the turn of the last century, who did not fancy their chances of handling teams of six horses successfully, made a virtue of their inability to do this by declaring that 'No gentleman ever drove more than four horses' and an ancient statute restricts the use of a carriage drawn by six horses in the streets of London solely to the monarch.*

In the English or Achenbach method and style of driving, all four or more reins must be held in the driver's left hand with his fingers separating them as much as possible, although the right lead rein on

---

*Probably the last person to have been prosecuted under this statute was Mr Patrick Coke who worked for Bertram Mills' Circus in the 1930s. He defended himself successfully by claiming that he was driving mules, not horses.

top of the left wheel rein normally slot together between his first and second fingers with a four-in-hand and a similar grouping applies with a six-in-hand from left lead over the first finger to right wheel between third finger and little finger. The driver keeps his right hand relatively free to manipulate the individual reins, making loops between the left hand fingers which already hold them to maintain the extra tension required to apply opposition reins during turns, as also to shorten all or any reins by pulling them through from behind his left hand. He uses his right hand to help to support the strain on his left hand by using the fingers of his right hand in front of it, and to use his whip freely and instantly whenever this is required.

This method was originally devised by Edwin Howlett to enable coachmen to drive four-in-hands at a collected park pace with great accuracy and precision from the high box seats of coaches and park drags. They are expected to sit upright to do this and not to lean or reach forward, and thereby risk falling off their perches, so that this method, which enables them to alter the effective lengths of their reins by up to 3ft (90cm), and to do so instantly, without altering the positions of their own bodies, is ideally suitable for driving English carriages in English style with one, two or four horses.

In Hungarian driving style, which incorporates low, light carriages of phaeton design in which the driver sits no higher than he would if riding his horses, the reins are all coupled together just in front of his hands so that he can use either or both of them to hold all four, or more, reins and to take a good pull at them with all his fingers over them. The original Hungarian method actually involved the reins being buckled to a thick handpiece called a Brezel which was especially easy to hold, but this is no longer in use. The Hungarian coachman can take up any of the lead or wheel reins separately by reaching forward in front of the coupling buckles and, because his seat is much lower than that of his British or Western European counterpart, he is not prohibited from leaning well forward and straightening his arms to take a shorter hold of his reins whenever he needs to do so.

Hungarian rein handling seems at first sight to be easier and less complicated than that associated with the English or Achenbach style, particularly to riders who wish to take up driving, but the adjustment of the coupling buckles is critical and must take account of the position of the horses in relation to the carriage as well as their sizes and degree of keenness and general way of going in relation to each other, and the reins must be manipulated with equally instant precision for either technique.

The method developed by the pioneers of the American West for handling the reins of the teams pulling their big prairie schooners and, rather later, the public Concord coaches which were often pulled by six horses, involves the right hand reins being held in the driver's right hand and the left hand ones being held in his left hand with his fingers separating them, much as for riding. He has to be able to 'club' his reins by transferring those in his right hand temporarily to his left hand to use his whip and he cannot make very accurate turns with his reins held in this way, nor adjust the lengths or tensions of them very quickly or precisely, but this was seldom needed in the wide open spaces over which he travelled.

Six reins can obviously be held more easily in two hands than in one and the construction of the big heavy Concord coaches in particular, and the positioning of the driver's seat on them, imparted a continuous back-and-forth swinging motion to the driver's body so that he would hold his hands well down between his wide apart legs to counteract this as much as possible and try to keep some contact with his horses' mouths. This style of driving is rough and ready by comparison with that advocated by Achenbach and his disciples, by whom it was considered inelegant and imprecise, and it did not prevail in the more sophisticated Eastern States of the USA, but it was, and still is, practical for its purpose. It is usually demonstrated well in cowboy films and very well in the Chuck Waggon Race at the annual Calgary Stampede in Canada.

It is a mistake for self-professed experts on driving to be too dogmatic about rein handling. Except in Hungary it has only been standardized for rather less than 100 years and people have been holding and handling their reins according to their own individual instincts and inclinations for the past 5,000 years without getting into any serious permanent difficulty. Drivers who compete in modern driving trials are tending to adapt the classic Achenbach style to suit the special requirements of competition driving, usually by introducing some of the techniques practised by the Hungarians.

The most important requirement, which applies to any kind of driving of any combination of horses in any circumstances, is that a driver must be able to shorten both or all of his reins instantly, evenly, and by as much as 3ft (90cm). He needs to be able to do this so as to be able to 'get hold' of his horse(s) and re-establish firm steady contact with their mouths during the period of only 2 or 3 seconds in which fright or sudden excitement may prompt a determination to take off and run away. The effective length of the reins from the driver's hands to his horses' mouths will vary by two or three feet, depending on the size of the horse(s) and the type of vehicle being pulled, according to whether they are well into their collars with their traces tight on a fairly loose rein, or right back into their breechings under strong restraint.

If the driver has separated his reins and is holding them separately in his right and left hands respectively his instinctive reaction when trouble threatens will be to lean back and bring his hands back as far as possible to a position on each side of his chest. This action will seldom serve to shorten his reins enough for him to regain a firm hold on his horses' mouths and to increase its effect the only expedient left to him will be to slacken the rein(s) held in one hand so as to use it to take a fresh hold of both or all reins with both hands at a point further forward along them.

When the reins on one side are suddenly slackened or even dropped in this way the horse(s), which by this time may already be moving at a fast pace and almost running away, will be liable to turn or swerve sharply and risk turning the carriage over. This is the more liable to happen with a single horse driven to a two-wheeled cart and it is chiefly to avoid this situation that novice drivers, in particular, are advised never to separate their right and left reins entirely. They are to ensure that both reins are always ultimately secured in their left hand so that their right hands can be removed instantly from them to take a shorter grip on them in emergency.

The driver should hold his whip in his right hand at all times and never lodge it in the whip socket. When he needs to use it he will usually need to do so instantly. He should lay the thong on firmly but smoothly beween the horses' collars and pads. The stick of the whip must be long enough to enable him to do this easily, because flicking with it behind the pad or saddle may irritate a horse and cause him to kick, or swish his tail and get it over the reins. The whip should be regarded as an extension of the driver's arm in the case of a single horse or a pair and used as much to reassure and to attract attention, particularly away from alarming sights and sounds which may cause shying, as to induce acceleration.

The thong of a whip for use with a single horse or a pair must not be so long as to tickle the backs of the horses perpetually when it is not in use, or to need to be twisted round the stick to avoid this and thus take longer to bring into action. The art of using the point of the 12ft (3.6m) or so long thong of a team whip on the leaders of a team or tandem is a dying one which few coachmen now possess and it requires special study and hours of practice. It is a valuable skill which a fully competent coachman should be able to demonstrate, even if he may restrict its use to training sessions and be shy of the consequences of getting it wrong in public.

The driver's voice is an essential aid, especially with a team or tandem. His horses must know their own names and they learn them very quickly. Intelligent harness horses recognize up to twenty or more separate words of command and will listen for them and respond to them. They will often be seen to have one ear facing backwards for much of the time when they are being driven in circumstances requiring concentration. This is to listen for orders and the ear will go forward again when they have gotten the message. This reaction is usually particularly noticeable in a tandem leader being driven between the pairs of traffic cones which must be negotiated, with continual changes of direction, in the obstacle competition of a driving trial.

Horses recognize words by the intonation, emphasis and length with which they are pronounced rather than by the separate syllables which comprise them, so the names of horses in a team should be reasonably distinguishable from each other and the driver should give each different command in a distinctive tone of voice and always maintain the same distinctive tones.

Driving in Britain began to be recognized as a skill related to equitation and horsemanship as displayed in the *manège* rather than just a proficiency in controlling horse-drawn vehicles in 1897, when the 12th annual show of the Hackney Horse Society (held at the Agricultural Hall at Islington in London) included classes for Hackney horses to be shown in harness. The horses concerned were judged on their merits as good examples of the breed, but these essentially included their ability to move well at the trot, displaying straight progressive well-balanced and regular action such as would enable them to cover the ground well and present an impressive appearance as high quality carriage horses. The manner in which they were schooled and driven obviously had a significant bearing on the show which they gave in the ring and due credit was accorded to the drivers who handled them.

The art of preparing and exhibiting horses in harness for the show ring to catch the judge's eye and impress him with the quality and excellence of the whole turnout stemmed from these beginnings and has now progressed to being something of a specialist skill, particularly in the case of modern Hackneys which are judged primarily on their spectacularly extravagant action. This is induced mainly by careful schooling, in long reins from the ground and in harness, which results in great impulsion being precisely restrained and controlled by the horse's acceptance of firm contact from the bit with quite high head carriage and a pronounced bend at the poll. This causes his top line to slope slightly upwards in relation to the ground and encourages him to engage his hocks strongly and well underneath his body to

174

propel him forward vigorously while raising and lightening his fore-hand to free his forelegs to be lifted well up and stretched well forward into spectacular extension.

Hackneys have an inherited inclination to step high but, contrary to popular misapprehension, this is not developed or encouraged solely by gadgetry attached to their legs. Firm but sympathetic rein handling and careful attention to initial mouthing and subsequent bitting, together with natural keenness stemming from good health and a reasonably light vehicle to pull, are what encourages a horse of any breed to show his best paces in harness. High stepping with pro-nounced knee action is natural and desirable in Hackneys, Welsh Cobs and some other breeds such as Dutch Friesian horses but it must always be progressive and capable of displaying extension and it is inappropriate in most breeds and should not be attempted to be induced entirely by artificial means.

Good manners are of pre-eminent importance in horses which are to be driven rather than ridden because an upset in harness nearly always has more serious and more widespread consequences than one under

Mr A P Knight driving his Knight Errant to a gig in the show ring.
This Anglo-Arab is of unusual breeding for a harness horse but he is a
prolific winner of ride and drive classes and concours d'elégance as
well as in private driving classes.

saddle. A riderless horse will usually return to his stables or his companions, often at a fast pace but generally doing his best to avoid any collisions on the way, but a horse attached to an upturned cart or carriage will usually take fright and may bolt in blind panic from what, to his simple mind, has changed from the harmless vehicle which he was accustomed to pull quite happily into a menacing and vengeful pursuer. He will be liable to collide with obstructions in his path, including people and animals, and even if he avoids these himself they are likely to get a nasty swipe from the wreckage which he has in tow.

Harness racing, which makes considerable demands on horsemanship and the skills of the coachman allied with those of the jockey, can claim ancient origin in terms of its relationship to the chariot racing of Greece and Rome but this is tenuous and indirect.

People who wonder why the single horses which compete in present day harness races only trot and pace and never gallop, and suggest quite correctly that races at the gallop would be faster and more exciting, have obviously never sat in a two-wheeled cart pulled by a single horse between shafts. The motion which a gallop imparts to the vehicle through the shafts is distinctly violent, and far greater than that transferred through a less firmly held pole between a pair of horses, and it quickly builds up to a pitch which threatens to eject the driver and make it impossible for him to maintain steady contact with his horse's mouth through the reins.

The racing of trotters in harness has developed steadily as an organized horse sport in Russia and most European countries, notably France, since the middle of the nineteenth century. It is now the most popular and widely practised competitive activity for horses which are driven rather than ridden in the world, with as many participants and adherents as Thoroughbred racing in all countries except Britain. In Britain only semi-private matches took place until well into the twentieth century, since when harness racing has been well organized by a relatively small number of sporting enthusiasts on a few tracks, mainly in Wales and north-west England, without attracting much public notice.

In the USA the sport flourished as a mainly rural low-profile recreation organized by a number of separate associations until these were amalgamated in 1938 to form the United States Trotting Association. Harness racing quickly became a nationwide interest earning a very large revenue from *pari mutuel* betting so that it is now one of the top five spectator sports in America.

The American Standardbred, so-called because his immediate ancestors were obliged to prove their ability to reach the standard speed of 1 mile in 2 minutes 20 seconds to be eligible for the register, is the

176

harness racer *par excellence*. His forefathers are native American, with a predominance of Morgan blood, and that of the Throughbred Messenger (1788), through the prolific sire Hambletonian (1849). He is rather faster, though smaller and lighter, than his only pure-bred rival, the Russian Orlov Trotter, which, like him, has also been used extensively to develop and improve the nationally recognized Trotter breeds of France, Germany and many other countries.

The Standardbred can easily be taught to pace instead of trot and the former lateral rather than diagonal gait (which is actually artificial to the horse although some seem to be predisposed to it by heredity and can easily acquire it) is now fractionally faster in record breaking terms (1 minute 49.2 seconds for the mile as compared with 1 minute 53.4 seconds). There are now more races round the standard $^1/_2$-mile tracks for pacers than trotters in the USA, but trotting still predominates in all other countries of the world and distances are wider-ranging and often longer than the one mile which is the norm in America.

Driving a good trotter or pacer at speed to a racing sulky is an exhilarating experience, involving strong rein contact and as close bodily contact with the horse as can be envisaged without sitting on it. At only about 20 seconds slower over a mile distance than the speed of a galloping Thoroughbred racehorse, it is also as fast as anyone other than a flat race jockey can hope to travel with a horse over any appreciable distance.

Training and driving horses for harness racing demands many of the normal skills of horsemanship and an extra pre-eminent requirement to keep the horse balanced in its stride so that it does not break pace. Pacers have been fitted with hobbles (which strongly inhibit this) since 1885, but hobbles are far less effective on trotters. Horses which break pace in a race are required to be pulled to the outside of the track where they will not impede those behind them. This is critical, particularly in handicap races in which starts are staggered to achieve the same effect as weight differences in ridden races, but, although the rule also penalizes the horse which has broken, the break itself will so interrupt the horse's stride as to cause him to lose many lengths and have little chance of winning the race.

The possibility of breaks of pace affecting a harness horse's performance in a race and the impossibility of preventing them or determining blame for them with certainty is tacitly acknowledged to be one of the main and most regrettable reasons for the apparently restricted appeal of harness racing in Britain, where there is no Tote monopoly and the results of races could all too easily be predetermined at the instigation of bookmakers. The British Harness

Racing Club runs its activities in strict accordance with the most honourable traditions of sportsmanship and can only be sure of maintaining these if it can control betting on its races by being able to verify the integrity of the relatively few professional gamblers who lay the odds on them.

Driving in Britain was remarkably revived in the mid-1950s when the dozen or so members of the Coaching Club who had helped to horse and drive the carriages for The Queen's coronation procession (*see* Chapter 10) extended their initiative to found the British Driving Society (BDS). The BDS grew from 300 members in 1956 to 6,000 members in 1990 and has inspired the formation of similar associations in many countries of the world. A few of its older early members were just able to remember participating actively in carriage driving when this was at its peak just before World War I and their advice enabled the society to resuscitate and perpetuate the best traditions of coachmanship and turnout of the pre-motor age. Young members responded so well to this challenge that in the 1970s and 1980s many old members declared that horses and carriages were being turned out on public occasions in Britain to a higher standard of excellence than they ever remembered seeing in their lives.

Driving received a great boost and took on an extra dimension worldwide when in 1969, at the instigation of the Duke of Edinburgh who had just been elected to the presidency of the International Equestrian Federation, driving trails, modelled on the format of the ridden Three-Day Event, were instituted to be regulated by international rules under the jurisdiction of the FEI. This enterprise considerably extended interest in driving by establishing a sphere of competition for it dependent on the all-round performance of horses and their drivers as well as speed and stamina or impressive appearance.

Dressage, on the first day, tests the obedience of the horses and the regularity and flexibility of their paces as well as the rein handling and general control demonstrated by their drivers. The marathon, an incongruously misnamed test of speed, strength and stamina over a partly cross-country 15-mile (24km) course includes eight intricately designed obstacles or hazards. It also demands instant intelligent responses from horses to orders given to them, mainly through the reins, which must in themselves be instantly conceived and transmitted and accurately calculated to be within their capabilities. The obstacle competition, on the third day, which requires competitors to drive between narrowly-spaced traffic cones laid out to form a tortuous course, within a tight time limit, is intended to equate with show jumping. It is not an exciting spectator attraction to serve as the culmination of an impressive display of equestrian endeavour, but it is a crucial test of the precise skill of drivers and the agile obedience of their horses.

A small extra competition, added to the proceedings of the first day in the original rules and designated 'presentation', was simply an assessment of general appearance judged at the halt. It aroused controversy among competitors who claimed that it was out of place in trials of performance, but it is acknowledged to have encouraged and preserved an admirable standard of traditionally appropriate turnout and in 1987 it was reduced to just an extra, sixteenth impression to be assessed as part of the dressage test.

To the extent that horses do not need to possess special quality, or qualities, or exceptional physical abilities to do well in driving trials, it may be fairly reckoned that their human partners probably exert relatively more influence on successful results than in almost any other branch of competitive pure horsemanship. By the same token, drivers and coachmen do not need to be particularly athletic or agile, or trained to a high pitch of physical fitness to get the best out of their horses in driving trials. They need only quick reactions, good muscular co-ordination, and sound judgement, plus reasonable strength in their arms and shoulders if they drive teams of four horses, and may be well into middle age and even suffering from some physical disablement without disadvantage. They must practise an effective rein-handling technique to perfection and should be able to manipulate a whip with accuracy and precision, especially if they are to drive a team or a tandem, but beyond this the skills which they employ will be largely mental rather than physical and amount to horse sense and pure horsemanship.

Today's top four-in-hand coachmen regularly demonstrate feats of accurate precise driving in negotiating labyrinthine obstacles and surmounting intricate situations such as their predecessors would never have contemplated even approaching. The craft of driving has progressed remarkably during the past twenty years (up to the time of writing, early 1990) and has surely earned its elevation to the status of one of the premier arts of horsemanship. At the other end of the scale, it remains a pleasantly undemanding recreation for the quiet enjoyment of any owner of a small cart and single pony.

14

Horsemanship on the Polo Field

Polo is arguably the oldest game in the world, since records reveal that it descends from an early version played in Persia in 500 BC. It is the second fastest game in the world; ice hockey players move faster though for shorter distances. It is played on the largest pitch used for any team ball game in the world; 300 × 200yd (274 × 183m), but only 160yd (146m) wide if the sides are boarded on grounds which are not quite big enough.

Almost all polo players who have played other games seriously, and most of them have, claim that it is the best of all games and the most comprehensively sophisticated. It embraces the supreme satisfaction of hitting a ball well – both stationary as in golf and moving as in racquets – the mobility, strategy and tactics crucial to all team games, the boisterous body contact encountered in football, and the enjoyment of doing all this on the back of a horse.

Polo was brought to Europe from northern India by British army officers in 1870 when the first match was played in England, between the 9th Lancers and the 10th Hussars on Hounslow Heath. It was taken up quickly in America and the first international match was played between Britain and the USA in 1886 when the British Hurlingham club team beat the United States Meadowbrook team at Newport, Rhode Island. By the beginning of the twentieth century the game, which was still flourishing all over India, had spread to all countries of Western Europe, Australia, Canada, New Zealand and South America, and most notably to Argentina, which won the match played at the Olympic Games in Paris in 1924 and has produced the best players ever since.

The original rules, which varied slightly as between those of the Indian Polo Association, the British Hurlingham Polo Association and the United States Polo Association, were effectively the Hurlingham ones for international matches until, in 1983, they became those of the International Polo Federation whose headquarters were established in Buenos Aires. The game is played between four players on each side

180

and divided into chukkas each lasting for $7^1/_2$ minutes with 3-minute intervals between them. The interval at half time is of 5 minutes or rather longer. High goal matches consist of a total of 6 or 8 chukkas, medium and low goal matches usually last for 4 chukkas.

The handicapping system, which provides for matches to be played between teams of comparable ability, or for the team with the lower aggregate handicap to be given a predetermined advantage by being credited with goals or half goals to even up the difference, is unique to polo among team ball games. It depends on every one of almost ten thousand registered players in the world, of whom more than half are Argentinian, being given an annually reviewed personal rating or handicap ranging from minus 2 to 10. Minus 2 is the lowest handicap for beginners and is relevant only in Britain, and 10 is the highest which is credited to only eight or ten players in the world, of whom half are Argentinian. Players are referred to as 5, 6 or 7 etc., goal players according to their handicaps and games. Matches are rated and designated according to the bracket into which the total of the handicaps of either of the teams involved fits. Thus: low goal games are to be played between teams whose aggregate handicaps total from 0–6; medium goal are for those between 9 and 16; high goal matches are for teams rated above 16.

The handicap of any individual player is unrestricted in assessing the rating of a team so that an 8 goal player may be a member of a team whose other three players have handicaps of 0, minus 1 and minus 1 respectively, for the purpose of playing in a low goal game. Handicaps are assessed on a national basis in each of the sixty or more countries in which the game is played so that they are not internationally consistent at the lower levels, but players with handicaps of 5 or better have their ratings compared carefully with those of their equals in other countries. Those with handicaps of 0 or less are likely only normally to play club polo so that the actual worth of their handicaps is liable to vary considerably as between the 700 or so different polo clubs which are now established all over the world. Only one 40 goal match, between two teams of players of whom all eight each had a handicap of 10, has ever been played; between two Argentinian teams at Buenos Aires in 1975, but there are usually plenty of 5 and 6 goal players in high goal matches.

By way of brief explanation, a polo stick, or mallet, has a generally cigar-shaped head made of hard wood, fixed at an angle of $77^1/_2$deg to a bamboo, or occasionally malacca, stick of length to suit the rider and his pony. This length is usually between 49 and 53in (124cm and 1.5m), with a handle as for a tennis racket fitted with a soft webbing wrist loop. A polo ball is made traditionally of willow root, but is nowadays often made of plastic, and has a diameter of 3¼in (8.5cm) and a weight of 4–5oz (113–141g). The ball is struck with the side of the mallet head, not the end as in croquet. This is a popular misconception which would make the game extremely difficult to play.

A very good shot should send the ball through the air for a distance of 150yd (137m); a speed and length comparable with that achieved by a batsman's best strokes in cricket, and it hurts if it hits you. Polo players must hold their reins in their left hand and their sticks in their right hand. Players who may be left-handed are not permitted to wield their sticks in their left hand since this would obviously be confusing and highly dangerous.

Before 1912 polo ponies were not allowed to be more than 14.2hh., but in that year the height limit was abolished and the game speeded up considerably. The best modern polo ponies mostly come from Argentina and are usually between 15 and 15.2hh. and are three quarter or more Thoroughbred, but very tough and resilient. Since they do not play more than two chukkas on the same day, they never become tired to the point of fatigue and are always keen and willing to gallop at a speed of 35mph (56kph), but they are vulnerable to sprains and minor injuries in the course of play so a regular high goal player needs to have at least six at his disposal, and may have to ride all of them in a big match, and it is not possible to contemplate playing even in low goal friendly games without at least three.

Although this consideration is not relevant to the horsemanship involved, no polo player would wish the opportunity to be missed of paying tribute to the very generous patrons who pay most or all of the expenses of young players, including frequently the prices of their ponies, and who are thereby directly responsible for the present high standards which the game has attained. Many of these benefactors play themselves, as members of the teams which they sponsor and pay for. However, because sponsors are generally older and busier than their protégés, they can seldom aspire to such high handicaps and are often rather overwhelmed in play, with little chance of excelling themselves in the high goal matches which their philanthropy makes possible. Others, and most of the former when age relegates them to the sidelines, are content to promote the fortunes of promising young players and the best interests of the game by meeting costs which can amount to more than £500,000 a year.

The primary concern of a polo player is to get to the ball as quickly as possible and hit it hard and straight in the right direction. In doing this he will not be much influenced by consideration for the principles of equitation or elegant horsemanship. Comparatively few good polo players are also really good horsemen, and most of them are too honest to deny the evidence to this effect which photographs of them in action provide. Those who are good horsemen are invariably very good indeed and prove this by the excellence of their ponies, which they school themselves, but they put the dictates of the game before any anxiety to appear to be riding nicely or even any special regard for the sensitivity or immediate comfort of their ponies.

To hit a polo ball hard and well a player must stand in his stirrups so as to position his shoulders over his pony's withers with his left hand, holding the reins, supporting himself from a firm purchase on its neck. He must turn the upper part of his body well to his right for shots on the off-side of his pony and even further to the left for near-side shots, in particular near-side backhanders. He may have to twist himself even further round to hit a ball under the pony's tail, which is often a critical requirement in defending his own goal. A rider who must spend much of his time standing in his stirrups with his body twisted at right angles to his horse's direction of movement cannot maintain a classically correct seat by equitation standards or keep his horse on the bit or even his legs in conventionally accepted contact with its sides, particularly if he frequently needs to anchor himself by bracing his left hand on its neck.

Polo players on the Indian sub-continent, and particularly those of Rajput or Mahratta descent and Afghans and Pathans who come from Pakistan and the territories surrounding it, generally sit closer to their fairly small ponies. They look neater and more tidy in the saddle than their European and North and South American counterparts. They tend to use long whippy sticks and to hit the ball with strong effective wrist action while sitting down in their saddles (rather than with full swings from the shoulder while standing up in their stirrups), so that their style is more attractive to onlookers. However, the ball runs on much faster and farther on their hard sun-baked grounds than it does on the softer grass in damper climates and when 'Indian' players play on slower grass fields, and usually on bigger longer-striding ponies, than they are used to in their own countries, they begin to adapt their style and their stick work to make fuller, more vigorous-looking strokes to get extra length into their shots.

Polo ponies need to go foward very freely but not on the bit, or indeed taking hold of it very much. They must balance themselves and constantly alter their centre of balance to cope with sudden acceleration, deceleration and sharp turns under the burden of a rider whose weight will be constantly shifting on their backs and who will do little or nothing to help them to stay collected or balanced beneath him. They will be, in effect, almost always behind the bit, but not evading it, and ready to respond to spasmodic indications and signals rather than regular aids which will generally be communicated to them with intermittent urgency by their rider's hand and legs.

Pictures of polo ponies in action nearly always seem to portray them with their head up in a star-gazing position, apparently resisting the restraint of bits which often look fierce and complicated and are usually reinforced by tight standing martingales. It would be idle to pretend that during much, if any, of the duration of a game, polo ponies bend at the poll, accept even contact from the reins and display head carriages which are correct by school riding standards. Most of them get more than their fair share of jags in the mouth, often inadvertently from riders who lose their own balance temporarily while playing difficult shots, but not infrequently by way of urgent signals to stop or slow down which are sometimes too roughly applied. Since photographers obviously want to take pictures of players making shots, many of those published show ponies suffering temporary discomfort during this process.

Although very few polo ponies ever run away to the extent of being out of control – and they would probably run right off the field if they did so – most of them are very keen. They will gallop flat out in pursuit of the ball and, unless their riders are very confident of their ability to hit it while travelling at high speed, they are likely to receive urgent signals to slow down just before they reach it.

There is no doubt that polo ponies do learn to follow the ball after only a few games. They also turn automatically and immediately when their riders hit back hand shots and they would not be much good if they did not quickly acquire both these semi-instinctive reactions. Players, however, must often ride in other directions to that in which the ball may be travelling so as to receive passes or fall back in defence and, since their ponies cannot be credited with any understanding of the strategy or tactics of the game, their inclinations will frequently be at variance with the wishes of their riders. A contest of wills may ensue, which must be resolved by the urgent application of vigorous aids to ensure that the player's intentions prevail over those of his pony.

Most polo ponies, like all other horses, need to raise their head well up to move their centre of balance backwards so as to stop suddenly with their hocks underneath them. They need to do this constantly from a flat-out gallop during a fast game and are often photographed while doing it, although they have already received and responded to a signal from the reins which are no longer in tight tension with their mouths.

Most, though not all, polo players (including many of the elite few who play in high goal matches, but also school their own and other people's ponies) will opine that polo ponies enjoy playing the game. If this is true, it must depend on a carefully limited interpretation of the word 'enjoy'. It is undeniable that almost all polo ponies display excitement as soon as they are mounted and ridden onto the field to play a chukka. It is also certain that they follow the ball in play with an apparent enthusiasm far greater than that which could possibly be inspired in them by any impulsion induced by their riders or even by their instinctive inclination to gallop with other horses.

The undoubted fact that they turn up immediately to face the opposite way without prompting as soon as their riders play a back hand shot may be attributed to direct association of the one action with the other rather than to an appreciation of the new direction in which the ball is likely to go. However, it proves a rather intelligent general interest in the actions and movements which their riders are performing on their backs.

Some good players who are also educated horsemen have claimed that very experienced ponies which they have ridden have been able to determine whether or not shots which they have hit at goals will succeed or not and that the ponies concerned have proved this by slowing down before well-aimed ones have reached the goal mouth in

Riding off during a game of polo. The pony on the left is making good use of his own and his rider's weight to push his opponent off the line of the ball at the gallop. A legitimate tactic which is often used when both players are on the line of the ball.

anticipation of a resultant pause in play, but by speeding up to give their riders a second hit at misdirected ones. That a pony can very quickly recognize the direction which the ball is taking is not surprising, but that it can appreciate that this is about to fulfil its rider's intention and result in an interruption to the progress of the game seems hardly credible.

When a player wants to 'ride off' an opponent by pushing him sideways as they both gallop together – which is permissible, provided that they are both riding straight and on the line of the ball – both ponies will lean into each other and push with enthusiasm, seeming to enjoy the rather rough body contact which is involved. If a player falls off his pony it will invariably gallop off the field straight back to the pony lines.

When a pony falls and, as almost always, gets to its feet before its rider it may very occasionally wait to be remounted, but will normally gallop back to the lines. There is no record of a riderless pony ever having remained on the ground and attempted to continue to take part in the game without a human partner as horses in races will frequently do, as will horses whose riders fall off in set-piece exhibitions such as musical rides. Polo ponies, however keen in action, invariably stand placidly in the pony lines during chukkas in which they are not themselves engaged and seem to take no interest in the play in progress even when it is clearly in their view.

Fast ponies which are normally ridden by good players in high goal games and matches become very impatient and frustrated if they are ever required to carry novice players in slow chukkas. To over-mount themselves in this way is a mistake which beginners make all too often and it is one of the most usual reasons for unedifying spectacles of players seeming to be struggling roughly to control apparently unruly ponies, and for regrettable photographs of such scenes.

Suggestions sometimes advanced by carping critics, whose own riding is done mainly at slow paces in enclosed *manèges*, that polo ponies would benefit from dressage and training along strict riding school lines are nonsense. After and beyond basic training to teach a degree of submission and obedience to fundamental aids, and to accustom it to readjust its balance to carry a rider at all paces, a polo pony needs to be schooled more as if for gymkhanas or work with cattle than for dressage competitions. It must not be put on the bit but go rather behind it on a generally loose rein responding to neck reining. It will develop impulsion of its own accord if it is to be of any use for playing polo and must learn from the start to balance and collect itself for stopping and turning quickly and not come to rely on constant or continuously applied aids from its rider to induce this facility. Many of the best polo ponies, being from Argentina, have been broken and largely schooled by South American horsemen and top class grooms of gaucho extraction who are fine natural riders but have very limited experience of school riding and only an instinctive understanding of the requirements of dressage.

In general terms, horses which are destined to do their work at fast paces, carrying riders who must hold their reins in one hand, will not benefit greatly from being schooled at precisely regulated slow paces by riders who use both hands to maintain constant contact with their mouths. This procedure is likely to make them hard-mouthed by polo standards and a polo pony with a 'soft mouth' which will respond instantly to light rein aids is highly prized by good players.

It is generally held that as soon as a prospective polo pony can balance himself and turn quickly on his hocks at the canter, and has become accustomed to the ball being hit from his back on both sides, he will continue to learn more quickly and enjoyably by being played in cantering chukkas, in which galloping is prohibited, in company with other ponies than by being submitted to further intensive schooling on a tediously regular basis on his own. A few ponies never take to the game or develop an aversion to it, but these are a small minority of those which are started correctly and they can nearly always be relegated to other useful work.

A few very good players who are also good all-round horsemen find the time to school their own ponies. Such ponies nearly always get the best possible start to their life's work and the benefit of having faults and idosyncracies competently corrected as soon as they arise. A person who aims to school polo ponies must be able to play the game himself and, in almost every one of the 700 polo clubs in the world there are a few very valuable individuals who do not have high handicaps or aspire to play in important matches but are expert at schooling ponies and do this, often quite profitably, on a regular basis for their fellow club members.

Young potential polo players in Britain can now start at Pony Club level and absorb all the proper principles of horsemanship while enjoying an easy and relatively inexpensive introduction to the game.

Some high goal players who appreciate the contribution which the ponies they have ridden have made to their high ratings have generously conceded that this may amount to at least half of the success of a partnership. It is undeniable that high handicap players cannot play to the value of their ratings when they are less well mounted than they usually are and probable that some competent players would play better if they were better mounted, their ponies' speed being a crucial factor. However, it is equally certain that an inept player will be likely only to get into trouble on a good fast pony, particularly if he is also a bad horseman, and end up being run away with all over the field as a menace to other players.

Even very experienced ponies do not really seem to look after novice players to the extent of forgiving continual mis-hits and slowing down to a more steady pace so that their riders will have a better chance of hitting the ball. Although they certainly seem to know whether the ball has been hit or not, they do not turn of their own volition to go back to one which has been missed. No horse in fact ever goes more carefully because he has an incompetent rider on his back, except in the kindly imagination of sentimental novices who credit them with finer feelings than their intellects can conceive.

The best help that any player can expect from his pony is that it will go freely forward, straight and without bouncing, slow down, stop or turn in response to moderately applied aids from the reins only, and not resent these if they are occasionally stronger than usual, turn up instantly and automatically when he hits a backhand shot, through an arc of 180deg and in the direction corresponding to the side on which the shot was hit, and use its full weight to 'ride off' an opponent whenever this is called for. A pony will fulfil all these requirements more readily and more happily if it is ridden by a capable sensitive horseman, and will learn to do so quite quickly in the hands of a very good one, but the horsemanship involved is only remotely related to the equitation normally taught in riding schools and, inevitably, more rough and ready than that required for performing dressage tests.

The question which crops up constantly in conversations about horses and polo is 'Do polo ponies enjoy the game?' and the answer is almost certainly 'No!' What seems most probable is that they display the truly admirable mental characteristic possessed by nearly all horses; that of being anxious to do a simple task well and to their utmost ability as soon as they are completely accustomed to it and so long as their rider remain on their back to direct their efforts and preserve the main purpose of them.

Rudyard Kipling's famous story about a polo pony called the Maltese Cat deliberately misrepresents the thoughts of its hero to equate them romantically with human ones. However, in emphasizing the pony's determination to give of his best in adversity despite the painful knocks and bumps he receives, as well as his sensitive responses to the much reduced aids which he receives from his rider after the latter falls and breaks his collar bone, he makes a fair statement about the contribution which good horses make to all activities which they undertake and endure in partnership with man.

15

Horsemanship in the Riding School

There are still a number of old and famous riding schools in the world in which the tenets and traditions of classical High School are taught and preserved. Foremost and senior of these is the Spanish Riding School in Vienna, which has been in virtually continuous active existence with its own stud of Lipizzaner stallions since the late sixteenth century. Second in world renown is the French cavalry school at Saumur, which was founded by King Louis XVIII in 1814 and whose famous corps of *écuyers* and instructors, the Cadre Noir, have taught and practised the arts of *haute école*, along with all the skills of general equitation, ever since.

High School riding is also demonstrated today on a regular basis at riding schools in Spain, Portugal and Lipizza in Yugoslavia. The latter was originally in Austria and the home of the horses from Spain and Italy which first established a stud there in the middle of the sixteenth century. However, it does not form part of the normal curriculum of any of the other several hundred thousand riding schools of the modern world. These consist of a few in each of the countries which subscribe to the International Equestrian Federation that are able to teach and coach riders up to the highest standards of horsemanship, at least for the competitive activities or 'disciplines' recognized by the FEI, and a great many more at which paying pupils are taught to ride to varying standards, normally to enable them to pursue their private recreations.

The study and practice of High School or *haute école* riding has declined during the twentieth century and is now confined to the few riding schools which preserve classical traditions and a small number of individual specialists who demonstrate their skills as a form of pure art and sometimes more freely and less precisely in the circus (*see* Chapter 9). Although High School may reasonably be regarded as the ultimate extension of dressage, it has never been a competitive under-

189

taking or one with a practical purpose or outcome and always was, as it still is, for exhibition only.*

The movements incorporated in modern dressage tests overlap those recognized as pertaining to classical High School at the level of piaffe (*see* Chapter 6), which is demanded in advanced dressage tests and is also the basis for teaching all the movements above the ground. The passage (the highly elevated, strictly cadenced 'Spanish Trot') may be induced from the piaffe or developed from a well collected school trot, but the latter procedure is more usual for teaching it. Although both are recognized High School movements, it is reasonable and logical to consider piaffe as more advanced than passage and derived from it. Horses turned out loose into a field will sometimes perform a recognizable though unschooled and irregular passage from pure high spirits so that this may be regarded as a partly natural movement. No loose horse will ever execute a piaffe, so that this must be regarded as an artificial movement and, to this extent, more advanced.

The piaffe usually performed in the circus involves a rolling motion from side to side and little or no hock action so that, as it is also invariably less regular, it must be regarded as less correct than the piaffe of the classical school. Other and more complicated forms of the piaffe, such as the see-saw piaffe, much beloved of James Fillis, obviously count as less conventional High School movements, as do complicated forms of the canter, such as the canter on the spot, the canter to the rear and the canter on three legs, which Fillis also taught to some of his horses but which are nowadays seldom, if ever, practised.

The movements above the ground are taught to horses in the first instance without a rider. The trainer controls the horse from the ground with rather short long reins and also makes use of the pillars. The pillars consist of a pair of posts about 3.5 ft (1m) apart, between which the horse may be attached by short reins from a special head collar of cavesson type. The precise procedures for working a horse between the pillars are beyond the scope of this book, but the principle involves creating impulsion by discreet use of a whip or wand about 4ft (1.2m) in length (a hazel switch is often used for everyday work in Vienna). The horse – being restrained by the pillars or the dismounted trainer – expands the impulsion in piaffe and, being in a state of extreme collection, is ready to release it into a more explosive movement 'above the ground' as soon as it is slightly increased.

The prescribed movements or 'airs above the ground' are the Levade, in which the horse raises his forehand from the ground in an

---

* The widely promoted theory that the movements or 'airs above the ground' (*sauteurs* in French) were originally devised as battle tactics for war horses is nonsense. Destriers or war horses in the Middle Ages may sometimes have kicked or bitten their adversaries, but an armoured knight would have been quite unable to induce his horse to perform any High School movements on command in battle and would probably have fallen off it if it had executed any.

190

apparently crouching position with his hocks well underneath him so that they seem almost parallel to the ground and his forelegs held up so that his feet are close to his elbows. In Levade the horse's body inclines at an angle of less than 45 deg with the ground, but if the angle increases to more than 45 deg so that it is standing more upright, the movement, which is less conventional, is known as Pesade.

In the Mezair a series of Levades are executed by the horse taking short jumps forward when his forelegs touch the ground and his hind legs follow them to re-assume the position of Levade each time. This movement which has also been called Demi Courbette, is also relatively unusual.

The Courbette, which is a difficult movement imposing considerable strain on the horse's hocks and hind legs, consists in the horse making from three to eight jumps forward on his hind legs only, while retaining the position of the Levade or Pesade, and only bringing his forefeet to the ground after the last of up to eight jumps is completed. In the less classically correct Lancade the horse makes the same series of jumps as in Courbette but with his hind legs straighter so that the movement seems relatively stiff and less elastic.

The Croupade is like the Courbette, except that the horse brings his hind legs well up to his stomach at each jump and it is taught as a preliminary to the Ballotade, in which the hind legs must be similarly brought up under the horse's body but with the fetlock joints flexed so that the shoes are visible from behind.

The Capriole is regarded as the ultimate culmination of the Courbette, Croupade and Ballotade and it consists of the horse springing straight up from the ground and tucking his fore legs up as in the preliminary movements, but kicking out vigorously with both hind legs together, keeping his body horizontal to the ground before landing on the same ground from which he jumped up. In theory, this movement could be executed a number of times in succession, but in practice it is only performed in single jumps.

The Capriole is considered to be the most difficult of all the 'movements above the ground', and many initiated riders probably regard it as the most demanding of all the High School movements, so that it may arguably be rated as the highest achievement in all classical equitation. Such high level appreciation of it must depend on the perfection with which it is executed. To the casual onlooker who cannot recognize the finer points which it must demonstrate, the horse's body remaining always horizontal to the ground with his forelegs raised and tucked well up and an absence of any forward movement so that he returns to the same point on the ground from which he springs up, can look like a buck coupled with a vicious kick.

191

Indeed, honest *écuyers* will admit that it is most easily taught to horses which have an inclination to kick when touched with the whip. However, the measure of its difficulty in terms of correct execution may be gauged from the fact that only one or two mature specialist stallions at the Spanish Riding School are ever asked to perform it, while at Saumur, where twelve *écuyers* all perform Croupades and Courbettes in unison, and only slightly less perfectly than in Vienna, the Capriole is only demonstrated singly by a few individual horses. Discriminating spectators of the exhibitions concerned may discern that horses sometimes perform the Capriole without their forefeet ever leaving the ground and are accordingly 'cheating' by only really kicking to order.

Movements above the ground cannot be taught under saddle but must be demonstrated by riders if they are to look effective. The final stage, after they have been brought to near perfection between the pillars and in the hands of dismounted trainers, is for them to be performed at the instigation of their human partners sitting on their back.

To the problem of the less positive control of which a mounted presenter is capable in inducing the execution of these movements must be added the extra weight and strain which he imposes on his horse's hind legs. Lipizzaners, though phenomenally strong in their hind quarters, are quite small, many being little more than 15hh. Riders both in Vienna and Saumur sit in special saddles without stirrups to demonstrate the movements above the ground and these saddles are of white buckskin in both cases and of ancient origin, being modelled on the tournament saddles of the sixteenth century.

It may be argued that these stereotyped traditional 'airs above the ground' are pointless survivals from a bygone age which have never had any practical value, and that they are now no longer of any great interest to even the most dedicated modern horseman who can now witness far more dramatic feats of equestrianism within a few hours' journey of their own homes, or indeed watch them at second hand on television from the comfort of their armchairs.

Few of today's riding enthusiasts will have the time or patience to teach their horses to perform perfect Courbettes, and train their horses to demonstrate them, simply to show off to a few friends and neighbours without any hope of distinction in any competitive field from this achievement. Such demonstrations of spectacular horsemanship can also be counterfeited to the complete satisfaction of undiscerning spectators, and frequently have been to circus and cinema audiences for the past 150 years.

People who are influenced by such ignoble thoughts as these should reflect that these peculiar postures and jumps are important in that they represent the ultimate expression of the art of equitation in the sense of school riding on which much, though not all, of horsemanship is based. There can be no short-cuts to their achievement in the form in which they are so precisely and correctly demonstrated in Vienna and at Saumur where they are the result of dressage practised to Grand Prix standard by expert horsemen whose specialist skills have been developed through the whole range of school riding in the classical tradition.

Their exponents have not confined their experience just to the riding school since the riders in Vienna have all proved their ability in what they call 'campaign riding' and the members of the Cadre Noir at Saumur all compete regularly in tough cross-country riding competitions. If the system and training which is preserved at these two famous centres of equitation is now obsolete and of no practical value, then the current teaching of riding worldwide is a travesty, most of today's riding schools are obtaining money under false pretences, and dressage in its modern competitive concept is a delusion.

Few, if any, educated horsemen would support any such suggestion and the whole horse world acknowledges its admiration and respect for the few remaining establishments whose history is matched by their present achievements and which have stood the test of time.

Riding schools of comparatively recent foundation which are not concerned with High School fall generally into two categories: the relatively few which aspire to the highest standards of modern competitive horsemanship and can justifiably be called, in modern parlance, 'Centres of Excellence', and the remainder which offer sound teaching to varying lower standards from elementary cross-country riding, as required for a pupil to ride safely to hounds in Britain, upwards.

From the first category one in each of a few countries rank as National Equestrian Centres by virtue of their entitlement to train national teams and generally to set national standards. Four of these latter Centres, in France at Saumur, in Russia in Moscow, in Germany at Warendorf and in Sweden at Stromsholm are state-owned and one at Deurne in Holland is state-aided.

The recognized National Centres can be found in the USA at Gladstone, New Jersey, in Spain in Madrid, in Italy in Milan and in Switzerland at Elgg. They are private establishments which draw no official government funding but attract public support and some commercial sponsorship. There are state-owned studs in all the countries of Eastern Europe, some of which can teach and train their own promising young employees to high standards. These latter obviously have state-owned horses, whereas at the National Centres in the West except Saumur, international riders in training and most of the less advanced students usually ride their own horses.

Regrettably, the British Equestrian Centre, a department of the British Horse Society, does not rank with National Centres in other countries despite its designation because it has no director or instructors of international distinction and no land of its own for cross-country riding. Its two indoor riding schools and two all-weather outdoor arenas are used for competitions, for courses conducted by visiting instructors, and for examining potential national instructors. Lack of state, public or commercial funding to the level required continues to inhibit its expansion to a 'University of the Horse' with the status of a true national foundation.

An International Equestrian Institute with admirable if slightly unusual aims and establishment existed at Morven Park, Virginia, USA from 1968 until its sad dissolution in the mid-1980s. Funded by a charitable American trust which appointed two Englishmen in succession as its directors, and owning all its own horses, which numbered well over a hundred, its aim was to produce professional instructors rather than normally amateur top level competitors. Its programmes were based loosely on those of the British Cavalry School at Weedon, and its post-war successor at Melton Mowbray, and students from all countries of the world paid generously subsidized fees to attend a long nine-month course or a short two-month one held each year.

Morven Park found its own instructors from its own best graduates and well paid jobs worldwide for most of its alumni who survived its rigorous routines and passed out well at the end of them. It had ample land, good buildings and generous patrons who gave it some decent horses, as well as essential charitable funding, and it made good use of these benefits to produce capable riders who could teach other people at costs which were probably less in all respects than those of university education.

Most of the riding schools in the world are not financially supported by governments or charities and, since most of them do not enhance national prestige or increase national earnings, they do not expect to be. They have to be run on sensible commercial lines and pupil and clients generally get what they pay for in terms of the use of quite valuable horses, which are as expensive to keep as any used for any other purposes short of racing. They also get the use of land, buildings and equipment whose capital and maintenance costs are equivalent to those of farms and businesses covering similar areas of ground, plus the services of instructors who deserve the same pay as school teachers.

The success of a riding school depends on the progress made by its pupils and this probably depends rather more on the suitability of the horses with which they are provided than on the expertise of the instructor or the scope and scale of the facilities. A good school needs a selection of horses graded to suit beginners upwards. Beginners need quiet placid horses on which they can ride passively until they have learned to sit correctly and confidently, but not slugs which need to be constantly driven forward. Advanced pupils need to ride horses which will gallop and jump freely and they will benefit from experience of some with individual quirks and foibles, short of dangerous vices, which they can learn to cope with and overcome.

Being used for trekking or continual hacking by unsupervised inexperienced riders who are often clumsy and inept tends to spoil school horses for their primary work; the quiet ones are liable to become sluggish and the lively ones to develop resistances, evasions and bad habits. Since horses owned by a riding school need to be profitably employed for an average of at least four lessons a week throughout a whole year, or five a week for forty weeks each year, to earn their keep and their contributions to the overheads of their establishment at realistic charges, only the proprietors of popular busy schools can afford to keep them solely for fully supervised instruction and decline to hire them out for recreational riding. This is a dilemma which faces many riding school owners who may be philanthropically concerned to pass on their own knowledge and experience and promote the best interests of equitation but do not want to go broke in the process. To earn the money to keep their establishments in business, they must hire their horses to any respectable clients who want to ride them just for 'air and exercise' and cannot afford to keep them just for pupils who want lessons.

Riding instructors must be able to ride more capably than the pupils they instruct because they must give convincing demonstrations of the knowledge they impart. This is an essential requisite for teaching riding at all standards up to medium grade national competitive level at which valuable help from the ground can be given, by way of coaching, by a teacher whose own achievements may be, or have been, one stage lower than those of his pupil.

At standards up to medium grade national competitive level (e.g. Pony Club A Test) students usually learn more quickly and enjoyably in company with others as members of a small 'ride' but more intensive coaching after this is better done on an individual basis.

195

A frustration constantly suffered by enthusiastic instructors at commercial riding schools is the reluctance of some of their pupils to endure the physical strain and discomfort from which the preliminary stages of learning to ride are inseparable. Pupils must be 'stretched' to some extent in this respect if they are to make steady progress, and the more timid ones must be subjected to exercises and experiences of which they may be fearful. However, tolerances to both commitments vary widely as between pupils on the same 'ride' and paying customers must be cherished.

Good horsemen do not necessarily make good teachers and, although riding masters may often display a certain asperity in dealing with their pupils, they need patience and sensitivity, as well as the ability to communicate well, to be able to produce successful results.

Indoor and covered riding schools are a boon to riding instructors and their pupils and, to a lesser extent, to the horses on which both crucially depend. Few indoor riding schools existed, at least in Britain and other countries with temperate climates, before the middle of this century. Those of reasonable size – at least 40 × 20yd (36 × 18m) – are very expensive to build and maintain and can only be afforded by well endowed or generously sponsored establishments which do a high volume of business. An indoor school cannot by itself replace all the outdoor facilities which a riding establishment needs. These are at least one large outdoor *manège* as well as paddocks and land for cross-country riding and nearby routes for reasonably traffic-free hacking and exercising.

A modern trend for new riding schools in Britain to be located in densely populated suburban areas whose roads carry a high volume of traffic often results in undue dependence on one indoor riding school and this restricts the scope and experience of pupils and the horses which they ride. Riding is fundamentally an outdoor recreation which should include galloping and jumping natural fences on grass and riders and their horses become bored and frustrated if their activities are confined to receiving instruction or participating in low level competitions in small enclosures, whether outdoors or indoors.

Trekking centres and stables which hire horses out for hacking without professing to teach their customers more than the rudiments of riding serve a useful purpose in providing a pleasant and inexpensive introduction to horsemanship for people who want an active holiday outing in the open air. They do not deserve to be disparaged, as they sometimes are, by owners of more sophisticated riding schools who promise success in insignificant examinations and competitions to clients who generally pay higher charges for less enjoyable elementary equitation.

It makes sense to reflect that only a very few of the many people who nowadays ride horses will ever make a lucrative living from it, either as competitive riders or as teachers. Jobs for grooms in Britain are not scarce and British grooms, particularly girls, are in some demand abroad, but there is a thin dividing line between professional dedication and hippophilia, and horse-mad youngsters are all too often exploited in low-paid employment in stables on which they waste the years which they might better spend in learning more remunerative trades.

Riding today is a recreation, and a requirement for the pursuit of one sport, hunting, and one game, polo. A large range of competitive activities, variously and incongruously designated as sports or disciplines, are agreeable concomitants to riding in most of its recognized forms but only racing, show jumping, horse trials or the Three Day Event and, to a lesser extent, dressage offer participants opportunities to win significant money prizes such as may justify professional or full-time amateur commitment to them, and only a few competitors at the top of their respective leagues can ever earn a good living from their success at them.

It has been suggested that as many people, at least in Britain, ride horses regularly today as did so during the middle of the nineteenth century before the days of motor transport. If this is true it is certain that more people ride 'nicely' and correctly than ever before and since almost all of them now ride for pleasure rather than for travel, the extra enjoyment which they get from doing it well must amply justify the extra efforts they make to receive special instruction rather than just advice and guidance from relatives, friends and grooms.

Instruction is better in general and far more freely available than it was before recreational riding hit its present-day peak of popularity. However, a spirit of commercialism in recent years, particularly in Britain, has resulted in a rash of often ephemeral riding establishments many of which are below the standard to which a nation of professed horse enthusiasts would wish to entrust its equestrian traditions. Over 3,000 riding establishments are licensed by local government authorities in England, Scotland, Wales and Northern Ireland and over 2,000 claim to teach riding. Most of the latter are assumed, at least by implication, to have the sanction if not the positive recommendation of the British Horse Society or the Association of British Riding Schools, but neither of these organizations, nor any other, has legal jurisdiction over them or can control or regulate them except by bringing prosecutions in accordance with law.

Riders with a little learning but no great practical experience are keen to take examinations offered by the British Horse Society and some other associations and to get paid for teaching other people to ride if they pass them. The consequence is a constant escalation of largely assumed expertise which has resulted in Britain in too many would-be instructors trying to set up too many riding schools to try to earn money by passing on their limited and often rather irrelevant knowledge to other riders who do not need very much of this to be able to pursue their private recreations enjoyably, but need much more than is normally available to aspire to careers as professional horsemen.

Learning to ride and to cope with horses is mainly a physical rather than a mental undertaking and not an academic study. Its successful achievement depends primarily on hours spent actively in the saddle on suitable horses under strict supervision in an appropriate environment. For best results, the hours of learning involved should be logically consecutive and planned for a reasonably condensed time scale in which physical fitness may be developed progressively without interruption in a regular routine. Five hours of active riding a day on three or more appropriately selected horses, amounting to about 30 hours in the saddle each week, should produce a competent horseman in six months but 3 hours of inevitably less intensive riding a week, much of it on the same horse, will probably only produce a person who is able to ride comfortably even after five years.

Tack cleaning, mucking out, general stable work and listening to lectures and watching video films are all experiences which a student of horsemanship must undergo and when these activities regularly occupy about half as much time as he spends in the saddle, the progress of his learning will be well balanced and effective. If, however, the proportions of time spent in riding and ancillary activities are reversed, the course of instruction is likely to proceed more slowly and less successfully.

When the ancillary activities consist mainly of manual work which can be taught by one or two simple demonstrations – and this includes the basic procedures of grooming – and when this occupies more than one third of the total working hours of a paying pupil or more than three quarters of the time of a working pupil, some deception must surely be suspected. Exploitation of this order is regrettably not unknown in Britain today where the high cost of wages for full-time workers tempts proprietors of some riding schools to try to manage without regularly paid stable staff and rely on pupils to do all the work.

Paying pupils who sometimes prefer a warm tack room to a cold session in a *manège* have only themselves, or their parents, to blame if they do not get full value for the fees which they pay for a residential course at a riding school. However, working pupils who often cannot easily alter the planned arrangements on which their bed and board may depend may have a legitimate grievance if for a year or more's hard work they get only some occasional riding and the opportunity to take a rather insignificant examination which certifies their ability to ride whenever they get the chance to do so in future, and to continue to work in stables.

A tradition on the continent, which was always more apparent in Eastern than in Western Europe and which lasted until well into this century was that horse owners and their sons, and quite often their daughters as well, were expected to be more proficient at managing and looking after their horses in all respects than the servants whom they employed to do this for them. Their English acquaintances, most of whom just got onto their horses at their front door to go riding or hunting and left the management of the stables and their occupants to their normally very capable grooms, tacitly admired the horsemanship and general horse knowledge of their continental counterparts, although they probably appreciated on reflection that the fundamental reason for it was that the latter's grooms were much more rustic and less intelligent and capable than their own.

In the present age of egalitarianism and high wages, British horse owners mostly have to look after their horses themselves and often have to try to train and school them themselves with only a modicum of professional help and advice. Modern riding schools have mushroomed in Britain and most Western European countries to satisfy public demand for riding as an increasingly popular recreation and the need of a growing number of horse owners to learn to do all the work connected with them themselves.

The vast majority of today's riding schools are no longer temples dedicated to the preservation of the high ideals of classical equestrianism, but commercial workshops designed for the teaching of riding and horse management mainly on a self-help basis. The study of fundamental equitation is accordingly more widespread than it has ever been before and few people would dispute that horsemanship is enhanced rather than diminished by its current appeal to mass population.

16

Horsemanship in the Show Ring

The idea of submitting their horses to a critical comparative assessment of their relative merits and worth by just one, or occasionally two, individuals does not appeal to all owners. Those who choose to have their favourites commended or condemned by this procedure, which involves no investigation of their breeding or provenance and virtually no test of their performance, must seem to be reposing singular confidence in the judge, who must make decisive choices from as many as thirty animals after looking at each one for not more than 2 minutes and riding them for no longer when this is appropriate.

The concept is English in origin and is now a tradition which is over 100 years old and which also prevails, with some national variations, in the USA, Canada, Australia, New Zealand, Southern Africa among the European settlers, and Ireland. It obviously arose from a desire by breeders of good stock, hounds, dogs and farm animals as well as horses, to have their animals looked at and admired by their neighbours and it quickly developed into a good 'shop window' in which they could display them for potential buyers. The hunter classes at Ireland's premier show at Ballsbridge in Dublin still serve this primary purpose and nearly all the horses exhibited in them are sold, mainly to foreign buyers, by the end of the show.

The system has not in general extended to other countries in the world where British colonies have never existed and English horses have not had an early influence on the breeding of bloodstock. In countries where this peculiar British procedure has never been established or prevailed, the quality and value of horses is estimated, perhaps more logically, in terms of their performance rather than just of their appearance and, even when this cannot be positively tested as in the case of young stock offered for critical and comparative inspection prior to an important sale, the judging involved is undertaken by a panel whose members must observe specific criteria. Of the latter, movement has a much higher priority than it has in British show rings

200

and the colt or filly's parentage is carefully considered, even sometimes to the extent of its dam and sire being paraded for inspection.

Continental horse shows and those in countries other than the USA and former British colonies display less variety in their programmes than British shows since they normally consist only of show jumping and dressage competitions, with occasional tests or trials of horses in harness. British and American shows probably offer more variety for spectators to enjoy than any others in the world and the multiplicity of different breeds and types of horses exhibited at them, added to some show jumping competitions and non-competitive displays, can fill three rings for up to five days with no class or competition lasting much more than one hour.

At British shows hunters, hacks, cobs, 'riding horses' (horses which are pleasant to ride but cannot be classified as hunters or hacks) and often Arabs, as well as children's ponies, are shown under saddle, and horses and ponies are also shown being driven in harness. In addition, hunters and horses and ponies of up to a dozen different breeds are shown in hand and, as representatives of their breeds, may be judged in separate classes according to their age as: stallions, Brood mares, three-year-olds, two-year-olds, yearlings and foals.

Ridden hunters are judged in up to eight separate classes which are divided by weight-carrying capacity, height, novice status, age, suitability to carry a lady side-saddle and working hunters, with a height division, which must jump a course of fences as a preliminary to their being judged as the others. Weight limits are: lightweight – to carry up to 12 stone 7lb (79kg) – middleweight – up to 14 stone (89kg) – and heavyweight – above 14 stone. When there are only two weight classes, as is usual for working hunters, the division is normally at 13 stone (82kg).

The height limit which decides eligibility for small hunter classes is 15.2hh. Novice status is decided by prizes and prize money won prior to the close of the entries. Separate classes for four-year-old ridden hunters of any height or weight-carrying capacity are quite customary and all ridden hunters must be four years old or older. Classes for ladies' hunters to be ridden side-saddle are not normally divided by weight, height or age.

Working hunters in their two classes divided by height are normally required to jump a course of eight natural looking fences of a maximum height of 4ft (1.2m) and 60 per cent of the judge's assessment of them is awarded for this phase, in the ratio of 40 per cent for actual jumping and 20 per cent for style and presence while doing so, before they are judged as for the other classes.

The judge must ride all the horses in all hunter classes, or at least all those which may be remotely in contention, but inevitably only for a very short time in each case, which can seldom exceed 3 minutes. In working hunter classes only, he is required to award 20 marks for conformation and 20 marks for his assessment of the ride he gets from each horse and then to add these marks to those he has awarded for the jumping phase to arrive at a total out of a maximum of 100 marks for each horse which decides his placings.

This arithmetical procedure is not obligatory or normally employed in ordinary hunter classes, which are not for working hunters, and in them the judge is never required to give reasons for his final decisions. Two judges are sometimes employed in ordinary hunter classes and often used for working hunter classes. In the latter case they will often divide responsibility for the separate criteria between them. They may exceptionally be required by the conditions in the schedule to do so for ordinary non-working classes, normally as between conformation and ride. More usually, however, they each make their own complete assessments and then compare notes.

Judges do not ride working hunters over fences. A trial of an arrangement which required them to do so when working hunter classes were first introduced into Britain in the mid-1950s proved embarrassing for judges and nerve-racking for exhibitors.

Show classes for hacks, which are often in two divisions decided by height into small and large at 15hh., may sometimes be extended to provide for an extra class for novices and a special class for ladies riding side-saddle. They are judged generally as for hunter classes except that hacks are not required to gallop. Instead their riders are invariably asked to give a short individual show, and the judge does not always ride them.

Cobs are often divided by height at 15.1hh. and are judged generally as for hunter classes.

'Riding horses' have proved difficult to define for purposes of show judging. They are sometimes divided into small and large classes at 15.2hh. and are judged generally by the same criterion as hunters. However, they are usually not eligible for hunter, hack or cob classes at the same show, since the kindly intention of organizers who schedule classes for them is to cater for owners of worthy horses — horses which are pleasant to ride but do not fit into any of these three categories.

Arabs are often shown under saddle and judged generally as for show hunters. They may be judged in two separate classes as pure-bred and part-bred or Anglo-Arab, but with no height or weight-carrying divisions.

Show classes for any recognized breeds of horses or ponies to be shown under saddle are permissable and sometimes scheduled by British shows, particularly in regions native to the breeds concerned, but it is more usual for most of them to be shown in hand.

Children's ponies are shown under saddle in four height divisions related to the ages of their riders, which range from nine to sixteen, and there is usually an extra class for ponies not exceeding 12hh. on which children aged not more than seven must be on a leading rein. Unusually and quite recently some shows have scheduled classes for girls up to the age of eighteen to show ponies up to 15hh. under side-saddle.

Horses and ponies shown in harness are divided into singles and pairs and tandems, usually by height at 13.2hh., and sometimes into three divisions at 12.2hh., 14.2hh., and over 14.2hh., and normally also into Hackney and non-Hackney type. These classes, for which any breeds are eligible, are known in Britain as Private Driving Classes and there are also Light Trade Classes for horses and ponies pulling tradesmen's vehicles.

Hackney horses and Hackney ponies are shown in harness in Britain, as in a few other countries such as Holland where the breed is well established, driven to special light four-wheeled show wagons. Classes for Hackney horses are sometimes divided by height at 15hh. and ponies, a separate breed which must not exceed 14hh., may be judged in the two classes divided at 12.2hh. Hackneys are judged only at the trot and primarily on their action and excellence of movement.

Heavy horses are judged at British shows, and shows in many other countries, in harness in all combinations from single to six-in-hand.

Ridden classes for hunters, hacks, cobs, 'riding horses' and children's ponies at shows in Britain are confined to mares and geldings, though stallions may be shown in classes for ridden Arabs and for other specific breeds to be shown under saddle and are eligible for all driving and harness classes.

All breeds of horses and ponies, as well as hunters and riding ponies whose breeds are not specific, are shown regularly in hand in Britain and Ireland, and unusually in some other countries outside Europe, to be judged as breeding stock and young stock under four years of age. For the obvious reason, geldings are not normally exhibited in in-hand classes except as potential hunters and riding ponies at two and three years old and exceptionally in classes for Mountain and Moorland ponies at any age.

Procedures and conditions relating to show classes are virtually identical throughout the British Isles and similar in other countries in which they enhance the equestrian scene, but there are national variations, especially in the USA where they are markedly different in many particulars.

American horse shows cater for five divisions of showing in addition to show jumping, dressage and in-hand classes which are grouped under the halter division.

In the equitation division only the rider is judged, not the horse, and three separate classes are covered by it: hunt seat which may include some jumping, saddle seat, whose requirements, and actual saddle, are similar to those for English hack classes, and stock seat for which Western saddlery is used and turnout and suitability of all components are taken into consideration.

The Western division comprises three classes, one of which is subdivided, in all of which the horse, which must be over 14.1hh., is judged on performance and 'appointments' or turnout as well as conformation on a scale of percentages which varies between the different classes.

These are: the stock horse class in which the horse is required to demonstrate its obedience, flexibility and manoeuvrability, usually to a standard pattern of twists and turns but sometimes by working with cattle, and its novice equivalent the jaquima class for which horses must be no more than five years old and ridden with a snaffle bit or reins attached to a headcollar.

In the trail horse class, horses are shown at the walk, trot and lope or canter to demonstrate comfortable paces and may be required to help their riders in opening and shutting gates and to go through water.

In the pleasure horse class, horses are ridden on a loose rein in walk, trot and canter and are required to display extended paces.

The saddle horse division comprises two classes, for five-gaited and three-gaited horses which are ridden in straight-cut show saddles. Five-gaited horses are shown at the slow pace or foxtrot and the rack, which are artificially induced gaits, as well as the walk, trot and canter, at which three-gaited horses are shown. The American Saddlebred is a special breed, originally from Kentucky, whose representatives now present a distinctly unnatural appearance with very long feet and tails nicked and set up artificially. They are also shown in harness, driven to show wagons as used for Hackneys and are judged on movement and for their spectacular presence.

The harness division includes classes for horses driven in heavy harness style in the English manner and for roadsters which are driven to four-wheeled wagons of light or 'bike' construction or heavier 'road' build in separate classes. They are judged at the walk, jog, road

gait and fast trot and may be of any breed but are usually Standard-
breds. Specific breeds such as Morgans are also shown in harness in
America and Hackneys are exhibited in heavy harness classes as are
Hackney ponies crossed with Shetlands which, since the 1960s, have
been popular and are now registered as American ponies.

The hunter division is invariably the biggest at any American horse
show and, unlike their British counterparts, the horses exhibited are
unashamedly show hunters, as opposed to field hunters, and are
seldom if ever ridden to hounds. They are nearly all lightweights in
build and are often slow racehorses for whom a different use has been
found. The hunter division covers classes for breeding, conformation,
working and several miscellaneous requirements such as Corinthian in
which turnout is especially considered.

In all classes except breeding ones, horses must jump a course of six
or eight fences, varying in height from 3ft 6in (1m) to 4ft 6in (1.37m),
set out in an easy flowing pattern. They must do this with great
precision and fluency, jumping always from a regular stride without
any shortening or appearance of undue exertion and with their riders
seeming to sit easily with a fairly long rein. They are then judged for
conformation, for which only a few of the best performers are considered. Judging is by percentages, which vary according to the class
concerned, but performance always predominates, even in 'green'
hunter classes which are for those in their first two years of showing.

The showing of hunters in the USA is a specialist skill and much of it
is a professional undertaking and a full-time occupation for its
practitioners.

Uniquely in world equestrian circles, a full-time professional judge
is usually employed, sometimes with an amateur partner, to score each
jumping round with instant precision born of long experience and
reduce a total of often one hundred or more starters to a bare dozen or
so for final placing after an apparently cursory inspection for soundness and conformation.

Riders of American show hunters display rather stereotyped horsemanship of a high order in the ring as proof of the meticulously expert
schooling which they give their horses in preparation for it. The few
professional judges travel the horse show circuits to work full time at
their exacting employment and stand to lose it if they fail to satisfy
exhibitors. They make their decisions with incredible rapidity and an
unerring eye for the relatively simple assessments on which these must
depend and they see far too many horses to be able to rely on memory
of previous form.

American judges, whether amateur or professional, never ride any

Gill Oliver, wife of Britain's foremost show ring rider, Robert, turned out and sitting to perfection on her side-saddle.

of the horses which they judge and are not entitled to do so. They express astonishment at the British system which requires what they regard as a presumptuous and foolhardy undertaking.

The essence of showmanship is the need to emphasize the good points of a horse, mask any bad ones and persuade the judge that the partnership between the showman and his horse is creating enjoyment and elation, even when it is not. The principle holds good whether the horse or pony is being ridden, driven, or shown in hand on a leading rein and its demonstration is a matter of practised skill which requires more than a display of happy optimism and the employment of a few artifices.

In terms of fundamental horsemanship it is probably seen at its best in the hunter classes at the Dublin Show each year in which many of the horses exhibited make their first appearances in public. Often, they will have been ridden for the first time only a few months, and in some cases only a few weeks, before the occasion. The late and great Jack Gittins, who rode six supreme hunter champions and numerous other cup and prize winners at the Royal Dublin Society's annual show for the famous dealer Nat Galway-Greer between 1956 and 1966 and who died on the show ground in Dublin in 1977 never had more than three weeks to prepare the seven or eight horses concerned for the show – and most of them had barely been backed before he arrived from England each year to get on them for the first time before the show.

It is asking a great deal of a green four-year-old to put the undesirably traditional double bridle on him almost from the start and expect him to accept the two bits, be obedient and well mannered, and produce a strong balanced gallop round one of the biggest show rings in the world, all within a fortnight. Jack, however, did this year after year and in 1964 made a clean sweep of all three weight classes, plus the supreme championship with the high quality Galway-Greer horses which he had prepared in just this way.

The art required is that of the nagsman allied to that of the showman. The two crafts are complementary to each other and are still admirably exemplified in the skills of a select number of contemporary British and Irish professional horsemen who demonstrate them more obviously and profitably in the show ring than in the hunting field.

The old-fashioned nagsman of the years preceding World War II depended for his living on being able to ride a young horse quietly out with hounds within a very short time, usually about six weeks, of first backing and breaking him.

He usually started his career working for a big dealer who wanted to sell his horses quickly before the cost of their keep eroded the price he could charge for them and his main shop window was the hunting field. He needed to catch the eye of potential customers and a regular ploy was for him to make his way unobtrusively to the front of the field from time to time by anticipating the line of the fox and avoiding any difficult jumping and then to jump one or two impressive but innocuous fences. His employer, with the main body, could then pretend to be outraged by the 'reckless manner in which his man was riding his good young horse' and express his astonishmnent at its remarkable jumping ability in the hope of attracting a quick bid for it. Showmanship in fact in a rather different guise.

When the young nagsman could afford to set up his own yard to break horses for fees rather than wages, he was still expected to waste no time on the job and would often be willing to back his ability by charging only livery costs for any time over six weeks which he might need to complete the process to the satisfaction of his clients. Such clients would usually be satisfied with good manners and willingness to jump small fences as a preparation for having the horse hunted quietly by one of their own grooms so as to give it the better part of a season's experience before entrusting themselves to it.

Present day owners of potential show horses are generally equally reluctant to pay schooling and livery fees for any great length of time before anticipating tangible results in the ring so that time for professional showmen is also of the essence.

A slight digression from the subject of this chapter and a breach of the general intention that names of living horsemen shall not be mentioned in this book may be permissible and appropriate at this juncture to mention the remarkable work of Mr Monty Roberts in 'starting' young horses.

Monty Roberts is an American from California who speaks of 'starting' young horses rather than breaking them and does this to the effect that within 20 minutes of his first meeting them they can be mounted and ridden and after four half-hour sessions on consecutive days with him they can be ridden out in company with others. The only apparatus he needs to do this is enough high fencing to make a preferably circular enclosure about 50ft (15m) in diameter and a bridle, saddle and pair of long reins.

He has a young assistant who mounts each horse, by putting his foot in the stirrup iron in the normal manner after it has been in the enclosure for only about 20 minutes alone with Monty after first entering it. (Monty could do the mounting himself, and used to before he hurt his back.) His assistant only has to survive an average of two rather half-hearted bucks before riding the horse round the enclosure at a walk and trot and reckons that he has only been 'dumped' about five or six times in six years, or just once by about one in every 200 horses.

There is no deception or trickery about Monty Roberts's method and he acknowledges that any other sensible person with reasonable experience of horses can use it effectively by copying what he does; and he frequently proves this by supervising someone else doing it from a position outside the enclosure. He has been associated with horses all his life and started by helping his father to break horses by conventional methods. He proved his discerning judgement by buying and 'starting' the great racehorse Alleged as a yearling and subsequently selling him to Robert Sangster who syndicated him as a stallion for 16 million dollars.

Monty has now 'started' well over 6,000 young horses of all types and breeds, but mostly two- and three-year-old Thoroughbred racehorses, in America, Australia and, in 1989, in Britain, at the rate of about 300 a year with no apparent failures. He calls his method 'Advance and Retreat' and it consists in his being alone with his equine pupil in the enclosure and shooing and chasing it away from him, without any loud words or threatening gestures, until, in less than

5 minutes, it gets fed up with this and comes deliberately up to him in the centre and nuzzles him to seek his companionship. It usually leaves him again two or three times while he repeats the procedure but in less than 20 minutes it stays with him and follows him closely all round the enclosure so that he has achieved what he calls 'join up'.

His explanation of the horse's behaviour is that he arouses its curiosity and then its interest and finally, and very quickly, its wish for friendship with him, as the only other living being with whom it can make direct contact. As soon as this degree of trust and confidence has been established Monty can handle his horse all over, put a bridle and saddle straight on to it without alarming it, drive it rather perfunctorily for 2 or 3 minutes in long reins attached through the stirrup irons to the snaffle bit, and invite his assistant to come straight into the enclosure and mount it without assistance and ride it round the ring.

Three or four of such half-hour sessions on consecutive days are normally all that is needed to give the young horse confidence and a settled state of mind. He will then be able to be ridden out with others at all paces within his physical capacity by any competent rider who can then proceed with its schooling along conventional lines.

Monty Roberts's quick results are revolutionary, but his system really is not. It is the result of his rational study of horse and animal behaviour based on years of practical experience in handling, riding and dealing with young horses, and perhaps of his logical examination of some of the methods used much more haphazardly by all animal trainers for many centuries. If he has a secret, it is in the precisely contrived attitudes which he adopts to persuade his horses to 'join up' with him when he first meets them. These are essentially pacific, avoiding any semblance of aggression, and he admits that he takes much longer to cope with a horse which may have been mishandled or badly frightened; but then he does not expect to encounter many such among the two- and three-year-olds with which he deals, many of which are virtually unhandled when they are brought to him.*

Monty Roberts has reduced to two hours spread over three or four days the twenty or so hours spread over nearly two weeks which even the most capable of British nagsmen customarily take to produce the same result, which is a fairly calm contented horse with a degree of confidence in its rider. Done properly by either method the process provides the fundamental introduction to carrying a rider which enables a horse to display both its quality and its potential performance ability to a discerning judge or prospective purchaser.

* The author watched Mr Roberts give his first demonstration in England at Windsor Castle in April 1989 in the presence of H.M. The Queen who provided a three-year-old gelding and a two-year-old Thoroughbred filly for this purpose. He had flown the Atlantic only the day before and, under the eye of their royal owner, could not possibly have employed any deception in 'starting' the two horses, which he had obviously never seen before, with his usual successful results.

Mr Vin Toulson, a great show ring rider, on Mrs J Dewer's Seabrook winning the Hunter Championships at the Three Counties Show, Malvern, in 1987.

However, there is still a long way to go before the young hunter can make its critical debut in the show ring and the skill of the nagsman or showman largely determines the outcome of this venture and how soon it can be attempted. Sitting in an apparently relaxed manner with a length of rein which suggests the need for only minimal control, the good show rider will manage to keep his horse balanced at all paces, including several fast gallops along the stand side of the ring in the case of hunters, and will seem to be enjoying a comfortable easy ride which the judge may expect to experience with equal pleasure during his short session on the horse.

If the judge's expectations are confounded and he finds that he has been legged up on to a very green youngster which is reluctant to go forward and snatches intermittently at its bit in an apparent attempt to evade control and get its head down as a preliminary to an unsettling buck, the exhibitor may appreciate that preparations for his horse's first appearance in the ring may have been rather too hurried. However, there is always the possibility that the judge may attribute the difficulties he is having to his own failure to match the horsemanship displayed by the rider whose performance he has just admired and that he may make allowances accordingly.

A sympathetic thought should be spared for British horse show judges, particularly of hunter classes. Their decisions must always be made 'against the clock' on the basis of cursory inspections and very short rides on the horses presented to them and, although they are expected to ride quite passively so as to influence a horse's natural way of moving as little as possible, they will usually be blamed by the owners of horses which do not go well for them unless they seem to ignore this important aspect of their assessment on grounds of their own shortcomings in the saddle.

If they are too generous in this latter respect they will almost certainly be criticized by owners of any horse on which they seemed to be more comfortable but which they finally place below any whose manners may not quite match their quality. Although the contention that the judge can only satisfy the exhibitor to whom he awards the first prize is apocryphal, judges tend to do a thankless task for little reward except the pleasure of looking at and sitting momentarily on some very nice horses.

The British and Irish convention that hunters, in particular, generally only appear in the show ring in their youth and then go on to more practical employment does not prevail in other countries but has much to commend it in terms of its influence on the continuous breeding and production of high quality horses of the best riding type. The convention that horses which appear in British show rings must be well covered with fat, euphemistically called 'condition', and wear double bridles even if they are only four years old and barely accustomed to a single bit has nothing to commend it and only makes the tasks of those who exhibit them and judge them the more difficult.

These two regrettable requirements have come to be almost hallowed as traditions but the fat can conceal faults in conformation and put undue strain on the legs and wind of horses which must gallop carrying it. Premature use of a double bridle can impair the proper contact which a rider should have with his horse's mouth. It is greatly to the credit of the best British showmen, male and female, amateur and professional, that they continue to produce fat young horses which are not gross or pot-bellied and which seem to accept double bridles before they are ready for them without obvious resistances or evasions.

This latter skill is invariably attributed to the rider's possession of 'good hands' and it is undeniable that good showmen, as also good nagsmen, must have 'good hands' if their horses are to go well for them both under saddle and in harness and, to an extent, even when they are exhibited in hand on a leading rein.

There is, however, more to 'good hands' than the horsy colloquialism implies and it is not a matter solely of tenderness or even delicacy of touch. The contact through the reins must be exactly calculated with discretion as to the horse's willingness to endure it and precisely applied with varying strength appropriate to situations as they arise. It must be triggered by instant reaction and exerted with perfect muscular co-ordination from a firm seat maintained independently of the reins or any use of the rider's hands. The deceptively relaxed seat of the professional show ring rider, well down in the saddle and rather far back to display full length of rein, incorporates a strong driving force which can be imparted through the seat bones to set up impulsion and urge the horse to go freely forward without too obvious a use of the rider's legs.

Ring craft is learned mainly from experience and is concerned more with observance of conventional procedures than employment of tricks and stratagems. Despite regular protestations from 'collecting ring critics' it seldom involves deliberately upsetting the horses of rival exhibitors and does not envisage judges being deceived by distinguished showmen riding or handling unworthy horses. A judge may look twice rather than only once at an apparently indifferent horse being shown by a well known horseman, but if he ever seems to award a higher placing to one which has been temporarily transferred to the charge of a popular professional by its obscure amateur owner, this will undoubtedly be just because it has given a much better show in expert hands.

The craft of the showman incorporates all the fundamental principles of equitation, particularly in terms of the preparation and schooling which must precede a successful appearance in the ring. The time scale contemplated for the career of the average show horse in Britain is normally shorter than that considered for other competitive equestrian activities because, in most cases and very sensibly, showing is regarded as a preliminary to its participation in trials and recreations involving performance rather than mainly just appearance.

Good showmen, who must necessarily be able to produce and prepare their charges from the time that they are first backed and ridden are of great value to the whole horse world and nearly all of them can justifiably claim to be master horsemen.

Epilogue

Anyone who has plenty of time to spare and access to some big libraries can find most of the information contained in this book already in print. However, I believe that at least a quarter of it, and possibly a third of it, has not been previously recorded in writing. I cannot claim that much of this is solely the product of my own discerning observations, or even of my fertile imagination, because it is mostly hear say. This is my gleanings from the conversations and reminiscences of horsemen and equestrian enthusiasts which I have listened to with interest, often bordering on fascination, on racecourses and in the hunting field, in stable yards and tack rooms, the beer tents on show grounds, and in the few remaining mews and barracks where a rapidly passing generation of coachmen and cavalry soldiers still contrive to forgather.

As a self-confessed equestrian dilettante – and unashamedly so because it has always seemed to me to be preferable to diversify one's interests than to get stuck in a rut – I have contrived to practise most of the forms of horsemanship which I have sought to describe in this book. This is no proud boast, because I admit to having practised most of them very badly. However, I claim to have acquired a taste in some measure for nearly all of them and to have become involved in most of them to a practical enough extent to have gained an understanding of their whys and wherefores.

When I was asked to recommend the form which a book on horsemanship should take, my first thoughts were that each chapter should be written by a specialist expert. However, the few experts whom I approached about this project either wanted to write a whole book about their specialities or were too busy practising their expertise to be willing to write about it at all. It has been truly said that 'Those who can, do it, but those who can't, write about it' and although I had thought that this old adage referred mainly to teachers, it seems that it has wider implications. I eventually offered to write the whole book myself, on the understanding that it would cover horsemanship in its widest sense and not just that aspect of it which is concerned with learning to ride in conventional riding schools and demonstrating the skills so learned in competitive activities whose outcomes must depend largely on the physical ability of the horses concerned.

213

My opinion, which I hope is not too contentious because it is not intended to be, is that the word 'discipline', which is so widely used nowadays to refer to the equestrian contests regulated by the International Equestrian Federation, is a curiously misleading misnomer in all contexts – except perhaps that which relates to top class dressage competitions. In these, the culmination of several years of rigorous training, much of it resembling drill, is the demonstration of stereotyped movements performed precisely at the rider's command. In competitive dressage, the horse submits completely to the will of the rider but the submission must be willing and without resistance, so that a high degree of co-operation from the horse is involved and not just its total subjugation. Most other forms of horsemanship amount to a partnership which depends on mutual confidence and co-operation between mount and man, although the rider is usually the dominant partner and invariably makes the initial demands.

Nowhere is this partnership more evident than in the battlefield, the hunting field and the cattle ranching range and the often repeated excuse of jockeys 'I couldn't win without the horse' emphasizes its importance on the racecourse. In some equestrian endeavours (for example, work with cattle) the horse thinks and reacts by itself, and nearly always more quickly than the rider. I have only once sat on a Cutting Horse and then I fell off when it turned more quickly and sharply than I anticipated. In other forms of horsemanship, the rider dictates the requirements, but often only by way of general indications, and the horse must interpret these and react accordingly. After an initial struggle for supremacy, which a good horseman usually resolves in a surprisingly short time, the partnership nearly always becomes established and the horse thereafter seems mainly to be concerned to learn what is required of him and to please his rider by doing it well.

This co-operative partnership is the theme which I have sought to pursue throughout this book. For me, it has provided endless interest as a study both in practice and in observation and it accounts in great measure for my enduring fascination with horsemanship.

Select Bibliography

Benoist-Gironière, Y, *Conquête du Cheval*, Champs Elysées (Paris), 1952

Benoist-Gironière, Y, *Concours Hippique*, Champs Elysées (Paris), 1954

Benoist-Gironière, Y, *Epitre aux Amateurs d'Obstacles*, Champs Elysées (Paris), 1956

Brooke, G, *Horse Sense & Horsemanship of To-day*, Seeley Service & Co, 1928

Brooke, G, *The Way of a Man with a Horse*, (Lonsdale Library), Seeley Service & Co, 1930

Edwards, E H, *Horses and Ponies of the World*, Hamlyn, 1979

Felton, W S, *Masters of Equitation*, J A Allen & Co, 1962

Fillis, J, *Breaking and Riding*, 1902 (Reprinted by J A Allen & Co 1969–1986)

Hance, J E, *School for Horse and Rider*, Country Life Ltd, 1932

Howlett, E, *Driving Lessons*, R H Russell & Son (New York), 1894

Newcastle, Duke of, *La Méthode et Invention Nouvelle de Dresser les Chevaux*, Jacques van Meurs (Antwerp), 1658

Nolan, Captain L E, *The Training of Cavalry Remount Horses*, Edward Stanford, 1852

Pape, M, *Die Kunst des Fahrens*, 1966 (English translation: *The Art of Driving*, J A Allen & Co, 1982)

Pluvinel, Antoine de, *L'Exercice de Monter à Cheval*, 1624 (Griff, Paris, 1976)

Pluvinel, Antoine de, *Manège Royal*, 1624 (J A Allen & Co, 1970)

Rodzianko, P, *Modern Horsemanship*, Seeley Service & Co, 1936

Rodzianko, P, *Tattered Banners*, Seeley Service & Co, 1939

Rogers, F, *A Manual of Coaching*, J B Lippincott & Co (Philadelphia), 1899

Santini, P, *Riding Reflections*, Country Life Ltd, 1932

Santini, P, *The Forward Impulse*, Country Life Ltd, 1936

Santini, P, *The Riding Instructor*, J A Allen & Co, 1952

The Veterinary Department of the War Office, *Animal Management*, HM Stationery Office, 1933, 1956 and 1960

Wattjen, Richard L, *Dressage Riding*, 1902 (Translated from the German and published by J A Allen & Co 1958–1979)

Wright, G, *Horsemanship and Horsemastership*, (The official manual of the United States Cavalry School at Fort Riley), Wilshire Book Co of California, 1962

Wynmalen, H, *Equitation*, Country Life Ltd, 1938

Wynmalen, H, *Dressage*, J A Allen & Co, 1953

Wynmalen, H, *The Horse in Action*, J A Allen & Co, 1955

Young, J R, *The Schooling of the Western Horse*, University of Oklahoma Press, 1954

Xenophon, *Hippike*, 365 BC (English translation: *The Art of Horsemanship*, ed Maurice H Morgan, J A Allen & Co, 1962)

Other equestrian titles published by The Crowood Press:

The Arab Horse, Peter Upton
The Art of Western Riding, Bob Mayhew with John Birdsall
The Athletic Horse, Carol Foster
Breaking and Training Young Horses, Christopher and Victoria Coldrey
Carriage Driving, John Cowdery
Desert Orchid, John Dorman
Dressage, Kate Hamilton
The Equine Veterinary Manual, Tony Pavord and Rod Fisher
Eventing, Judy Bradwell
The Horse and the Bit, Susan McBane, ed.
Horse Breeding, Tony Pavord and Marcy Drummond
The Horse Care and Stable Manual, Marcy Drummond
Long Distance Riding, Marcy Drummond
Natural Riding, Audrey Townley
Racecourses on the Flat, John Tyrrell
Royal Ascot, Richard Onslow
Shetland Ponies, Anna Hodson
Shoeing for Performance, Haydn Price and Rod Fisher
Showjumping, John Smart
Successful Showing, Stuart Hollings
Thoroughbred Stallions, Tony Morris

Crowood Equestrian Guides

Basic Riding, Carol Foster
Basic Training, Barbara Ripman
Horse Management, Marcy Drummond
Your Horse's Health, Tony Pavord